PHILANTHROPY, PATRONAGE, AND CIVIL SOCIETY

Philanthropic and Nonprofit Studies

DWIGHT F. BURLINGAME AND DAVID C. HAMMACK, GENERAL EDITORS

PHILANTHROPY, PATRONAGE, AND CIVIL SOCIETY

Experiences from Germany, Great Britain, and North America

Edited by

Thomas Adam

INDIANA University Press

Publication of this book was assisted by the
Friends of Indiana University Press.

This book is a publication of

Indiana University Press
601 North Morton Street
Bloomington, IN 47404-3797 USA

http://iupress.indiana.edu

Telephone orders   800-842-6796
Fax orders   812-855-7931
Orders by e-mail   iuporder@indiana.edu

© 2004 by Indiana University Press

The paper used in this publication meets the minimum
requirements of American National Standard for Information
Sciences—Permanence of Paper for Printed Library Materials,
ANSI Z39.48-1984.

Manufactured in the United States of America

Library of Congress Cataloging-in-Publication Data

Philanthropy, patronage, and civil society : experiences from
Germany, Great Britain, and North America / edited by
Thomas Adam.
    p. cm. — (Philanthropic and nonprofit studies)
Reworked papers of a conference held at the University of
Toronto, May 2001. Includes index.
  ISBN 0-253-34313-5 (cloth : alk. paper)
  1. Charities—Germany—History—Congresses. 2.
Charities—Great Britain—History—Congresses. 3.
Charities—North America—History—Congresses. I. Adam,
Thomas. II. Series.
  HV274.P48 2004
  361.7'4—dc21
                                    2003012815

1 2 3 4 5 09 08 07 06 05 04

For Sarah

CONTENTS

Part 3. Jewish Philanthropy and Embourgeoisement

ACKNOWLEDGMENTS

This book is the result of the presentations and discussions at the conference Philanthropy, Patronage, and Urban Politics: Transatlantic Transfers between Europe and North America in the Nineteenth and Early Twentieth Centuries, which was held at the University of Toronto in May 2001. The idea for this conference was born at the German Studies Association conference in fall 1999 where I met Eckhardt Fuchs. He encouraged me to develop a concept for a conference and secured the necessary support of the German Historical Institute in Washington, D.C., for this project. After having experienced an extremely fruitful discussion at the meeting, David Hammack suggested the publication of the reworked papers of this conference and invited me to submit a proposal for the Indiana University Press series called Philanthropic and Nonprofit Studies. Neither this book nor this conference would have been possible without the generous support of the German Historical Institute, the University of Toronto, the Social Science and Humanities Research Council of Canada, and the Joint Initiative in German and European Studies at the University of Toronto.

I would like to thank James Retallack for his long-standing support and his invitation for a two-year research stay at the University of Toronto, which enabled me to carry out my research project on philanthropy and the bourgeoisie in nineteenth-century American, Canadian, and German cities. This research was generously funded by a Feodor Lynen Fellowship from the Alexander von Humboldt Foundation in Bonn, Germany. I am also indebted to James Retallack for the opportunity to teach and research at the University of Toronto and for rallying potential supporters for the necessary funds for the May 2001 conference.

All scholars involved in this project have invested much time in preparing, first, the papers for the conference, and second, in rewriting and reworking the chapters for this volume. I appreciate the efforts of every contributor to meet the deadlines and to provide the very best versions of their texts. Marilyn Grobschmidt and Kate Babbitt with Indiana University Press and Ronnie Hall of the University of Texas at Arlington helped give the manuscript its final shape.

I relied deeply on the help and support of my wife, Sarah Wobick, who translated the chapter by Simone Lässig and copyedited the English versions of the chapters by Tobias Brinkmann and Karsten Borgmann as well as my own chapter. To her I dedicate this book as a small token of my love and gratitude for her support and patience.

Thomas Adam
February 2003
Arlington, Texas

PHILANTHROPY, PATRONAGE, AND CIVIL SOCIETY

Introduction

THOMAS ADAM

THEMES

Throughout the nineteenth century, wealthy North Americans traveled to Europe to explore its lands, culture, and society. After Henry E. Dwight had visited the northern part of Germany in 1825 and 1826, he jealously reported in his letters about the famous royal library and the art gallery of Dresden, which displayed more than 1,400 paintings "of the most distinguished artists of every school and age, since the revival of painting in Italy."[1] George Ticknor, who traveled to Italy, France, Great Britain, and Germany between 1835 and 1838, spent a great deal of time in Dresden enjoying the advantages of the royal library, which possessed over 300,000 volumes, "among them the most complete collection of historical works in existence."[2] After his return to Boston, Ticknor took an interest in establishing a similar library in his home town. When the founding of the Boston Public Library became feasible in the 1850s, Ticknor could contribute his knowledge of the structure and functioning of the Dresden library.[3] Following Dwight and Ticknor, J. Bayard Taylor published his European travel notes in 1846, giving his fellow Americans an impressive description of the Grüne Gewölbe (Green Vault), a gallery in Dresden, which he admiringly described as "a collection of jewels and costly articles, unsurpassed in Europe."[4] Toronto mayor James Mavor brought knowledge of social housing projects from his native Glasgow to his adopted home; the Glasgow projects were, in fact, modeled on several important London foundations. During business trips to Europe, Mavor studied various social and cultural projects.[5]

This transatlantic version of the Grand Tour was very important for U.S. nouveaux riches after the Civil War. Insecure in their social status, they used the European experience to become more self-confident and to learn about European art and culture; their new knowledge gave them a basis for claiming "membership in a superior social class."[6] As William W. Stowe notes, "European travel was a way of affirming the respectability of one's race, class, or gender."[7] For Canadians, transatlantic travel began somewhat later, around the turn of the twentieth century. For example, after firmly establishing his career at the Canadian Bank of Commerce, Sir Edmund Walker started traveling abroad for business and pleasure—to Europe, Japan, the United States, and South America. Walker made a point of visiting churches, museums, private collections, commercial galleries, and artists' studios. It should come as no surprise that Walker was instrumental in the creation of the Art Gallery of Toronto, which opened in 1913.[8]

After their return, wealthy Americans and Canadians attempted to recreate what they had seen and experienced in Europe. When New York's upper class decided to create its own museums, John Fiske Comfort reminded his fellow citizens of the cultural treasures of Europe and recommended art galleries and museums in Leipzig, Amsterdam, Gotha, Berlin, and Nuremberg as models for the Metropolitan Museum of Art.[9] Museums, art galleries, and libraries in New York, Boston, and Toronto were the result of this transatlantic transfer. The transfer of social and cultural models has remained a generally unexplored historical topic. In his pathbreaking book *Atlantic Crossings,* Daniel Rodgers has reminded us that "the Atlantic functioned . . . less as a barrier than as a connective lifeline—a seaway for the movement of people, goods, ideas, and aspirations."[10] However, most of what now constitutes transatlantic history focuses on the premodern era—a time of exploration, migration, and the construction of the New World. Twice annually, Harvard University organizes a conference on Atlantic history but limits the historical survey to the time before 1800 (although it sometimes extends this date to 1825). Modern transatlantic history—the history of the interrelations and cultural exchanges between European and North American societies in the nineteenth and twentieth century—is an all-but-unknown field. As Rodgers points out, "Historical scholarship bends to the task of specifying each nation's distinctive culture, its peculiar history, its *Sonderweg,* its exceptionalism."[11] For example, while Germany is assumed to have taken a special path of modernization—industrialization without democratization—which led to an authoritarian model of industrialized society,[12] the United States is considered "special in starting from a revolutionary event" and has been described as the "most egalitarian nation in social relations and democratic in politics."[13]

The historical research presented in this volume explores the differences and similarities among nineteenth- and twentieth-century U.S., British, Canadian, and German societies. Several chapters investigate the transatlantic transfer of ideas and concepts and undermine previously held assumptions about the distinctness of the countries under study. As Sven

Beckert has recently demonstrated, late-nineteenth-century bourgeois who traveled from Hamburg to New York did not feel as though they were entering an alien or distinct culture; rather, they felt at home because of a shared transatlantic bourgeois culture.[14] In fact, German bourgeois life was imitated by New York's wealthy upper-class families, who copied the quasi-aristocratic behavior of the European bourgeoisie.[15] In this volume, the term "bourgeoisie" will be based on the German concept of *Bürgertum*, or wealth and the use of wealth. Berlin, London, Leipzig, and Dresden produced the blueprints for bourgeois philanthropic undertakings, which have been copied and implemented into North American urban society.

Nineteenth-century German society has been long described without reference to its philanthropic traditions.[16] Historians have argued that German cultural, educational, and social public institutions were established and funded by municipalities and the state. Despite extensive research about the German *Bürgertum* (bourgeoisie), the most bourgeois behavior—philanthropy—has not been considered.[17] Historians have assumed that the German bourgeoisie did not develop feelings of responsibility for German society; rather, they have argued, they expected the state to take responsibility for financing social and cultural public institutions. Philanthropy has thus been widely seen as an American invention and as a distinct American approach to modern life. This volume will show that nineteenth-century German society was organized along philanthropic lines—theaters, concert houses, art galleries, and even social housing projects depended on private financing schemes and the philanthropists who established and financed these institutions. Only after the turn of the twentieth century did German society shift from a philanthropic society toward a state-oriented society.

U.S. philanthropy has been a topic of research for decades, and a wide range of books has been written by historians, sociologists, and economists, including structural-historical investigations of philanthropic culture,[18] sociological analyses of present-day philanthropists,[19] biographical accounts of single benefactors,[20] and studies which focus on single institutions.[21] However, the limits of previous research on U.S. philanthropy are immediately obvious. First, historical research on philanthropy is still the exception. As Judith Sealander notes, most of the research conducted on U.S. philanthropy focuses on the time after 1930 and neglects the origins of philanthropic ideas. The emergence and development of philanthropy in the eighteenth and nineteenth century is not discussed.[22] Only a few works examine nineteenth-century U.S. philanthropy.[23] Moreover, research on philanthropy generally lacks not only a chronological but also a comparative context.[24] Only recently has the Johns Hopkins Comparative Nonprofit Sector Project conducted its cross-national research project.[25]

Furthermore, scholars have not combined research on philanthropy with research on the bourgeoisie, with the exception of Francie Ostrower.[26] Ostrower connects research on New York's upper classes with her studies of philanthropy.

On both sides of the Atlantic, scholars have failed to develop a united theoretical concept of philanthropy. This has resulted in a confusion of terms and in many misunderstandings. Having attended several conferences on the topic, I have come to realize that scholars from different backgrounds use terms such as "philanthropy," "charity," "benevolence," "giving," "donating," "voluntary sector," "independent sector," "nonprofit organization," and "NGO" interchangeably and without defining these terms. Nearly every paper presented at the conference Philanthropy, Patronage, and Urban Politics in Toronto (May 3–5, 2001) offered a different concept of philanthropy. Moreover, most of the authors were unaware of the variety of concepts and possible definitions of philanthropy before they attended the conference. For this reason, it is necessary to make clear what we mean when we use the term "philanthropy." Since all authors contributing to this volume use different approaches toward and concepts of philanthropy, the definition has to be broadly framed. Philanthropy has a long tradition stretching back to ancient times and has been defined as a religious duty in nearly every major religion. However, philanthropy has changed over time—the forms, concepts, and goals of nineteenth-century philanthropy differed tremendously from sixteenth-century and twentieth-century philanthropy. Philanthropy can be seen as a third sector between the state and the market.[27] This does not imply that philanthropy exists outside both and is not influenced or regulated by both—the state provides the legal framework, and some philanthropic enterprises produce a profit which is either distributed among the philanthropists or reinvested in the enterprise. Nineteenth-century philanthropy was an economic system that competed with other organizational models such as cooperation and the social welfare state. Philanthropy is part of a "mixed economy of welfare," and the dividing lines between cooperation and philanthropy are not always precise.[28]

The goal of philanthropy is to advance society by providing necessary social, cultural, and educational services which are not provided by the state or the market for political or economic reasons or which are provided by the state but not in a way that satisfies philanthropists. Philanthropy constitutes a relationship between donor/giver and receiver—or between collectives of donors and collectives of receivers. Both sides gain something in the process of giving—the receiver gains material and financial support; the donor financial or social advantages.[29] Philanthropy serves as a way to define social distinctions and social classes. The donor provides money, time, and ideas for a project, which he or she alone, or in connection with other donors, attempts to control. Philanthropy always has something to do with power and the shaping of the future of society.

STRUCTURE

The research collected in this volume explores philanthropy in a historical perspective and in a cross-national and transatlantic context. By using examples from Germany, the United States, Canada, and Great Britain, the authors display the emergence of philanthropy within a specific context, the transfer of philanthropic models between different places, and the change in philanthropy over time. Social scientists researching philanthropy agree that in order to understand the nature of the third sector it is necessary to investigate the emergence and development of philanthropy from the eighteenth and nineteenth century onward. The research in this volume challenges the current understanding of philanthropy and the third sector by looking at philanthropy not as a static social phenomenon but as a phenomenon which underwent changes because of a social-political environment that was changing. Philanthropy has changed a great deal over the last 200 years, both in vision and in interpretation.

The research presented here is part of the new field of transatlantic history because it explores the connections between communities and the transfer of ideas in the nineteenth-century Atlantic world and because it compares philanthropic cultures in several cities on both sides of the Atlantic. By focusing on the nineteenth and early twentieth centuries, these authors contribute to a significant expansion of the burgeoning field of transatlantic history, pushing the time period of that field into modern times.

This volume is divided into three parts, the first of which addresses philanthropy in a transatlantic community. The chapters in this section compare North American and German philanthropy, explore the transfer of philanthropic models among Germany, the United States, and Canada, and investigate the overlap between two social categories which are traditionally conceived as being antagonistic—philanthropy and cooperation. Thomas Adam investigates the travels of U.S. and Canadian philanthropists to Great Britain and Germany as part of their search for models of museums, art galleries, and social housing projects. He shows that philanthropy is a European, not an American invention. By comparing social housing projects in London, Leipzig, Boston, and New York, Adam shows how interconnected philanthropists from these different countries were and how U.S. philanthropists implemented European models in U.S. cities. Adam concludes that, despite different political systems, there were almost no differences between German and U.S. societies in the second half of the nineteenth century—both depended heavily on private support for social and cultural public institutions.

Karsten Borgmann's research on art museums in Germany and the United States after the turn of the twentieth century contradicts the view presented by Adam. Focusing on Berlin, Borgmann argues that there were fundamental differences between museum philanthropy in the United States and in Germany. While U.S. museums, for instance, were actually privately owned, German museums were state institutions which received financial support from museum associations. Building upon the Johns Hopkins study of civil society in different countries, Borgmann offers a new (cultural) version of Germany's special path. The differences between Adam's and Borgmann's conclusions are a result of the different time frames and the cities under study. Whether or not philanthropy or state support for social welfare and the arts existed in German cities depended on the absence or presence of royal courts and a nobility in these cities. Berlin's cultural life was dominated by the court of the Prussian king and, after 1871, by the court of the German emperor. The cultural life of Berlin centered on the Prussian/German nobility, which used both state sponsorship and private support. Leipzig, on the other hand, was a bourgeois city without a royal court or noble class to dominate its political and cultural life. There the support of cultural institutions became a local and purely bourgeois task.

Brett Fairbairn discusses the competitive concepts of cooperation and philanthropy and shows how intermingled these concepts initially were. Cooperatives first emerged in Great Britain, and the concept was transferred to continental Europe and North America. Fairbairn compares the emergence of the cooperative movement in Great Britain, Germany, the United States, and Canada, proving that the distinction between philanthropy and cooperation might be merely theoretical, given the social background of most leaders of the cooperative movement. The founders of the German cooperative movement were upper-class citizens who popularized the idea of self-help among the working class and encouraged the creation of consumer, production, credit, and building cooperatives. Fairbairn's investigation of the cooperative movement in four different countries leaves us with the impression that the cooperative movement was more a child of philanthropy than its aggressive adversary—at least in the nineteenth century.

David Hammack's chapter compares philanthropy and nonprofit organizations in seven major U.S. cities (Atlanta, Boston, Cleveland, Los Angeles, Minneapolis, Philadelphia, and St. Paul) over the last 200 years. Distinguishing between individual philanthropy and nonprofit organizations, Hammack asserts that the third sector has never adequately addressed the needs of society. According to his analysis, voluntary gifts to religious and nonprofit organizations equaled less than 2 percent of the national income over the course of the twentieth century. Philanthropists such as Astor, Vanderbilt, and Sage donated less than 1 percent of their fortunes for public purposes. Therefore, nonprofit organizations not only depended on large gifts from private donors but also to a large extent on direct and indirect subsidies from the state. In this view, the U.S. third sector does not appear to be substantially different from its European counterparts, which depend heavily on government subsidies. Hammack reminds us that U.S. nonprofit organizations have always been regulated, controlled, and subsidized by governments. Local, state, and federal governments in the United States have shaped, limited, controlled, and funded nonprofit organizations in key ways throughout the course of U.S. history.

The second part, entitled "Between Market and State: Philanthropy and Social Elites," elaborates on the arguments of Francie Ostrower and combines research on philanthropy with research on the nineteenth-century bourgeoisie. The chapters by Eckhardt Fuchs and Dieter Hoffmann and by Margaret Menninger disprove previous assumptions about the German bourgeoisie's orientation toward the state and the role of the state in financing schemes for cultural and scientific institutions. All three authors show that the new German bourgeois elite, not the state, financed concert halls and even research institutions. German research institutes and universities received financial support from wealthy industrialists who promoted and funded scientific projects. Werner von Siemens, for example, donated more than half a million reichsmark toward the new Imperial Institute of Physics and Technology. Fuchs and Hoffmann argue that new bourgeois elites became philanthropists in order to achieve social recognition and social distinction. Building on the interpretation of Manuel Frey, both authors argue that German philanthropy for scientific and academic purposes complemented governmental support. This complementary support was necessary because the German state did not possess the financial means for financing large-scale research institutes. However, German philanthropy was not limited to the advancement of academic and research institutions in Germany; it also reached beyond Germany. One of the most important results was the German-American academic exchange program between Berlin University, Columbia, and Harvard.

Margaret Eleanor Menninger discusses the structure and scope of nineteenth-century cultural philanthropy. Using the example of the Leipzig Gewandhaus Orchestra, Menninger shows how this institution was founded, financed, and run by Leipzig's upper class. While Fuchs and Hoffmann are concerned with new bourgeois elites in Berlin who were attempting to define their place in society, Menninger focuses on the old mercantile elites of Leipzig, who had dominated Leipzig's political and cultural life for centuries and attempted to hold on to its power during and after industrialization. The Gewandhaus symbolized the power of the old merchants and patricians and their cultural domination of urban society. Philanthropy was always connected with mechanisms of exclusion and inclusion. The seats in the Gewandhaus were reserved for the old mercantile elites, who financed the orchestra and, later on, the building. New elites were kept outside and only slowly integrated. In contrast to museums, which were as reliant on private financing as the Gewandhaus, the latter was closed to the lower classes, who received access to the music hall only after 1914.

Susannah Morris is less concerned with elites and more concerned with the ways in which the definition of philanthropy has changed over time. Morris's chapter uses the case study of social housing in nineteenth-century London to discuss traditional theories about philanthropy. She asserts that we are unable to capture the Victorian facets of philanthropy with our current understanding of philanthropy. Sir Sydney Waterlow, for instance, created a philanthropic housing enterprise in London in 1863. Nonetheless, he expected a return of 5 percent from his enterprise, arguing that only the connection of philanthropy with market economy could solve the housing problem. By the standards of many scholars, he would not be seen as a philanthropist. However, wealthy bourgeois who became involved in social housing projects argued that both sides would be best served if they both could expect to gain something from a philanthropic enterprise. Given this historical insight, Morris suggests that we need "a language and mode of analysis" which can identify and describe change in contemporary understandings "of the nature and role of voluntary activity and its position within the mixed economy of welfare."[30] Morris rejects existing economic and sociological concepts of philanthropy because they are ahistorical. The Johns Hopkins definition is, for instance, unable to cope with the institutional diversity of earlier periods.

The chapters in the last part of this volume focus on Jewish philanthropy in Germany and the United States. Maria Benjamin Baader explores Jewish women's voluntary societies in the late eighteenth and early nineteenth centuries, proving previous assumptions about the exclusion of women from the public sphere wrong. Voluntary societies played a prominent role in establishing the bourgeois public sphere. Jewish women founded mutual aid and charity organizations from the 1760s onward, occupying a space in the public sphere for women. However, the philanthropy provided by these female voluntary organizations was not the support of the poor by the rich. As Baader points out, German Jews did not distinguish sharply between mutual aid and philanthropy. She supports Fairbairn's argument that the dividing lines between cooperation and philanthropy were not as clear as we envision them today. Furthermore, Baader follows the concept of philanthropy developed by Frank Prochaska. In his approach, philanthropy is a social practice which characterizes the actions of not just one social class but of virtually all social groups in society.[31]

This all-encompassing view is rejected by Simone Lässig, who views philanthropy as a social and cultural practice of the Jewish and non-Jewish German bourgeoisie. Based on Pierre Bourdieu's concept of capital exchange, Lässig argues that philanthropy was part of the exchange of economic capital into cultural capital. By spending money for museums, art galleries, and charities, philanthropists converted newer money into social and cultural power. As such, philanthropy was a significant part of the integration of newer bourgeois groups into the urban bourgeoisie. With this discussion, Lässig continues the arguments put forward by Adam and by Fuchs and Hoffmann, who argue that philanthropy served to establish class divisions and to integrate individuals into social groups. The research of Lässig, Fuchs and Hoffmann, and Adam offers a concept of philanthropy which connects the establishment of class divisions and the inclusion or exclusion of peoples into social structures through the aid of philanthropy. Lässig and Fuchs and Hoffmann follow Bourdieu's concept of capital exchange. Lässig argues that economic capital was not sufficient grounds to be integrated into high society; only its exchange into cultural capital enabled wealthy citizens to be acknowledged by and integrated into the leading circles of their cities. Thus, Lässig defines philanthropy as one element of cultural capital.

Tobias Brinkmann's chapter continues the discussion started by Adam, Menninger, and Lässig about the potential of philanthropy to further integration and to support exclusion. Brinkmann compares the importance of philanthropy in the integration or exclusion of Jews in the nineteenth-century United States and Germany. Germany and the United States represent two quite different situations for Jews. While Jewish emancipation in Germany did not take place until the last quarter of the nineteenth century, emancipation was not an issue in the United States. Jews were one immigrant group among others there and enjoyed the same advantages and disadvantages as the other groups. Both German-Jewish communities and American-Jewish communities used philanthropy to support their poor coreligionists. However, although both German and American Jews employed the same strategies, they resulted in very different outcomes. While German Jews found philanthropy to be a stumbling block to full-fledged integration, American Jews successfully employed philanthropy to further their integration.

This volume provides a comparative historical perspective on philanthropy in Germany, Great Britain, Canada, and the United States and covers the eighteenth through the twentieth centuries. This research of the contributors will open new perspectives on the topics of philanthropy and transatlantic history and will contribute to the theoretical debate about the character of philanthropy. Each chapter in this volume offers a different definition of and perspective on philanthropy. Most of the authors contextualize philanthropy within a framework of social, cultural, and economic circumstances. This volume will make a significant contribution to the expanding field of comparative and modern transatlantic history.

NOTES

1. Henry E. Dwight, *Travels in the North of Germany, in the Years 1825 and 1826* (New York: G. & C. & H. Carvill, 1829), 369. See also Charles Carroll Fulton, *Europe Viewed through American Spectacles* (Philadelphia: J. B. Lippincott & Co., 1874), 23.

2. J. Bayard Taylor, *Views A-foot: Or, Europe Seen with Knapsack and Staff* (New York: George P. Putnam, 1852), 131.

3. *Life, Letters, and Journals of George Ticknor* (London: Sampson Low, Marston, Searle, & Rivington, 1876), 2: 299ff.

4. Taylor, *Views A-foot*, 131. See also Fulton, *Europe Viewed through American Spectacles*, 21.

5. Thomas Adam, "Philanthropic Landmarks: The Toronto Trail from a Comparative Perspective, 1870s to the 1930s," *Urban History Review* 30 (2001): 7–8.

6. William W. Stowe, *Going Abroad: European Travel in Nineteenth-Century American Culture* (Princeton, N.J.: Princeton University Press, 1994), 5.

7. Ibid.

8. Katherine Lochnan, "The Walker Journals: Reminiscences of John Lavery and William Holman Hunt," *Revue d'art canadienne* IX (1982): 58; Adam, "Philanthropic Landmarks," 7–9.

9. Quoted in Winifred E. Howe, *A History of the Metropolitan Museum of Art, with a Chapter on the Early Institutions of Art in New York* (New York: Columbia University Press, 1913), 119.

10. Ibid., 1.

11. Ibid., 2.

12. The classic account of the special-path theory is in Alan John Percivale Taylor, *The Course of German History: A Survey of the Development of Germany Since 1815* (New York: Coward-McCann, 1946). The most eminent German historian to propound the Sonderweg thesis is Hans-Ulrich Wehler. See Hans-Ulrich Wehler, *Das deutsche Kaiserreich* (Göttingen: Vandenhoeck und Ruprecht, 1973). For a short version, see Roderick Stackelberg, *Hitler's Germany: Origins, Interpretations, Legacies* (London and New York: Routledge, 1999), 24–25.

13. Seymor Martin Lipset, "American Society in European Perspective," in *Civic Engagement in the Atlantic Community*, ed. Josef Janning, Charles Kupchan, and Dirk Rumberg (Gütersloh: Bertelsmann Foundation Publishers, 1999), 23–24. For the notion of American exceptionalism in general, see Daniel T. Rodgers, "Exceptionalism," in *Imagined Histories: American Historians Interpret the Past*, ed. Anthony Molho and Gordon S. Wood (Princeton, N.J.: Princeton University Press, 1998), 21–40; Michael Kammen, "The Problem of American Exceptionalism: A Reconsideration," *American Quarterly* 45 (1993): 1–43; Ian Tyrrell, "American Exceptionalism in an Age of International History," *The*

American Historical Review 96 (1991): 1031–1055; and Byron E. Shafer, ed., *Is America Different? A New Look at American Exceptionalism* (Oxford: Clarendon Press, 1991).

14. Sven Beckert, "Die Kultur des Kapitals: Bürgerliche Kultur in New York und Hamburg im 19. Jahrhundert," in *Vorträge aus dem Warburg-Haus 4,* ed. Warburg Haus (Berlin: Akademie Verlag, 2000), 144.

15. Sven Beckert, *The Monied Metropolis: New York City and the Consolidation of the American Bourgeoisie, 1850–1896* (Cambridge: Cambridge University Press, 2001).

16. The first works on this topic are Jürgen Kocka and Manuel Frey, eds., *Bürgerkultur und Mäzenatentum im 19. Jahrhundert* (Zwickau: Fannei & Walz, 1998); Thomas W. Gaehtgens and Martin Schieder, eds., *Mäzenatisches Handeln: Studien zur Kultur des Bürgersinns in der Gesellschaft* (Zwickau: Fannei & Walz, 1998); and Manuel Frey, *Macht und Moral des Schenkens: Staat und bürgerliche Mäzene vom späten 18. Jahrhundert bis zur Gegenwart* (Zwickau: Fannei & Walz, 1999).

17. Jürgen Kocka, "Bürger als Mäzene. Ein historisches Forschungsproblem," in Gaehtgens and Schieder, *Mäzenatisches Handeln,* 31; Jürgen Kocka and Manuel Frey, "Einleitung und einige Ergebnisse," in Kocka and Frey, *Bürgerkultur und Mäzenatentum,* 8–10; Hans-Jürgen Puhle, *Bürger in der Gesellschaft der Neuzeit. Wirtschaft-Politik-Kultur* (Göttingen: Vandenhoeck und Ruprecht, 1991); Klaus Tenfelde and Hans-Ulrich Wehler, eds., *Wege zur Geschichte des Bürgertums* (Göttingen: Vandenhoeck und Ruprecht, 1994); Lothar Gall, ed., *Stadt und Bürgertum im Übergang von der traditionalen zur modernen Gesellschaft* (München: Oldenbourg, 1993).

18. Kathleen D. McCarthy, *Noblesse Oblige: Charity and Cultural Philanthropy in Chicago, 1849–1929* (Chicago and London: University of Chicago Press, 1982); Helen Lefkowitz Horowitz, *Culture and the City: Cultural Philanthropy in Chicago from the 1880s to 1917* (Chicago and London: University of Chicago Press, 1976); Paul Dimaggio, "Cultural Entrepreneurship in Nineteenth-Century Boston: The Creation of an Organizational Base for High Culture in America," *Media, Culture & Society* 4 (1982): 33–50; Paul Dimaggio, "Cultural Entrepreneurship in Nineteenth-Century Boston, Part II: The Classification and Framing of American Art," *Media, Culture & Society* 4 (1982): 303–322.

19. Francie Ostrower, *Why the Wealthy Give: The Culture of Elite Philanthropy* (Princeton, N.J.: Princeton University Press, 1995).

20. Franklin Parker, *George Peabody: A Biography* (Nashville and London: Vanderbilt University Press, 1995).

21. John Michael Kennedy, "Philanthropy and Science in New York City: The American Museum of Natural History, 1868–1968" (Ph.D. thesis, Yale University, 1968).

22. Judith Sealander, *Private Wealth & Public Life: Foundation Philanthropy and the Reshaping of American Social Policy from the Progressive Era to the New Deal* (Baltimore and London: Johns Hopkins University Press, 1997), 6–7.

23. See, for instance, McCarthy, *Noblesse Oblige*; and Dimaggio, "Cultural Entrepreneurship in Nineteenth-Century Boston."

24. Sealander, *Private Wealth & Public Life,* 6–7.

25. Lester M. Salamon and Helmut K. Anheier, eds., *Defining the Nonprofit Sector: A Cross-National Analysis* (Manchester and New York: Manchester University Press, 1997). In 1990, the Johns Hopkins Comparative Nonprofit Sector Project began to collect and analyze data about nonprofit organizations around the world in order to reach a common definition of the nonprofit sector. It involves over five hundred researchers in forty countries.

26. Ostrower, *Why the Wealthy Give.*

27. Lester M. Salamon and Helmut K. Anheier, "Introduction: In Search of the Nonprofit Sector," in Salamon and Anheier, *Defining the Nonprofit Sector,* 1.

28. Geoffrey Finlayson, *Citizen, State, and Social Welfare in Britain 1830–1990* (Oxford: Clarendon Press, 1994), 6.

29. Even Geoffrey Finlayson, who assumes that voluntary activity results from concern "with the advancement of others, rather than the self," contradicts this assertion by stating that "indulgence in paternalistic and philanthropic behaviour could also serve more self-interested motives. Noblesse oblige could merge into a way of quieting a conscience troubled by the possession of riches, or of justifying those riches by devoting a proportion of them to the benefit of others." See Finlayson, *Citizen, State, and Social Welfare in Britain,* 7 and 49.

30. Susannah Morris in her chapter in this volume.

31. For a discussion of Prochaska's theory, see Susannah Morris's chapter in this volume.

PART ONE

*Philanthropy in a
Transatlantic World*

ONE

Philanthropy and the Shaping of Social Distinctions in Nineteenth-Century U.S., Canadian, and German Cities

THOMAS ADAM

Because of the establishment of the United States and Canada as independent countries, the development of nation-states in Europe, and the existence of competing political forms on both sides of the Atlantic, it is commonly accepted that the modern era is best characterized by exceptionalism and separatism. This notion of exceptionalism, however, does not reflect a reality perceived or experienced by all members of North American or European society in the late nineteenth century. Wealthy North Americans traveled to Europe not only for pleasure but also with the specific intention of finding solutions to common social and cultural problems.

This chapter seeks to illuminate the similarities and differences in the philanthropic cultures of German, Canadian, and U.S. cities during the late nineteenth and early twentieth centuries. The Johns Hopkins Comparative Nonprofit Sector Project has broached the topics of the third sector and civil society from an international perspective.[1] The study on Germany concluded that "the German nonprofit sector did not develop in antithesis to the State, but in interaction with it."[2] Focusing on post–World War Two West German society and the associational system, and excluding Germany's long philanthropic tradition, Helmut K. Anheier and Wolfgang Seibel reiterate the idea that Germany took a special path toward modernity.[3] They wrongly conclude that the German nonprofit sector, in contrast to the U.S. version, was far more state-dominated.[4] The results of the Johns Hopkins Comparative Nonprofit Sector Project, or at least those of the group studying German society, follow a tradition of academic writing on Germany which asserts that financial support for cultural institutions and social welfare came almost exclusively from the state or under its auspices. The title of Milton Cummings Jr. and Richard Katz's book, *The Patron State,* is congruent with the belief that the state was always the most important philanthropist in German society.[5]

Germany did, in fact, have a long and fruitful tradition of philanthropic activity which was no more or less regulated by state involvement than parallel activities in the United States or Canada. My research has shown that public cultural and social institutions of Leipzig, Boston, New York, and Toronto were, despite their geographical separation, more similar than disparate. This similarity is due to the fact that the same philanthropic models were applied to both sides of the Atlantic. These models were transmitted from Europe to North America via wealthy citizens who traveled between both worlds. Though certain details of the philanthropic blueprints were altered during this transfer process, the basic philanthropic culture underlying these institutions remained the same. Upper-class citizens on both sides of the Atlantic felt responsible for their community and organized, financed, and supported the social, cultural, and educational public institutions of their municipalities.

It must be noted that several terms used in this discussion are potentially confusing or misleading. The term "bourgeoisie" is used in this chapter interchangeably with the term "upper class." I define "bourgeoisie" not as the middle class, but as the highest stratum of non-noble citizens. My understanding of the bourgeoisie as a class is not based on Karl Marx but on E. P. Thompson's approach. As he reminds us, class is not simply a "structure" or a "category," but something "which in fact happens (and can be shown to have happened) in human relationships."[6] Elaborating upon this idea, I define class not only or primarily as an economic category but as the product of a set of behavioral patterns of a given group of individuals. The bourgeoisie is not defined solely by its wealth but also by the use of this wealth. Individuals in Leipzig and New York, for instance, became philanthropists because they were interested in confirming their status within the bourgeoisie.

The phenomenon of philanthropy has been researched by historians, sociologists, economics, and political scientists. Thus, a multitude of often conflicting definitions has emerged.[7] I have chosen to define philanthropy as the process of providing financial, material, and intellectual resources for cultural, social, and educational institutions by upper-class citizens. Like Francie Ostrower, I see philanthropy as an upper-class phenomenon, not simply as a charitable act. Philanthropy includes the establishment of foundations and limited-dividend companies, the creation of membership organizations for museums and art galleries, and the donation of money through bequests and gifts. While many scholars, such as Prochaska, have chosen to study the support of social institutions (which they call charity) or the support of cultural institutions (which they call philanthropy), my concept of philanthropy includes both cultural and social elements. When the cultural and social dimensions of philanthropy are both examined, philanthropy can be seen as an organizational system similar to the social welfare state.

In the nineteenth and early twentieth centuries, philanthropy was the modus vivendi for German and North American societies. Communities existed only because of the active involvement of upper-class citizens who felt responsible for the good of the community. Leipzig philanthropist Willmar Schwabe, for instance, felt a duty to give back to the people who had made his wealth possible in the beginning.[8] The city was a network of active people who defined, financed, and represented not only the economic but also the cultural and social development of their community. For this reason it is appropriate to speak of philanthropic culture. This concept places the philanthropic act in the context in which it happens, thus encompassing economic, social-psychological, and cultural aspects, and changes the focus from positivistic descriptions of single philanthropists and their philanthropies to social-structural descriptions of a philanthropically based urban society. In this interpretation, the philanthropist is not a single benefactor independent from society but a member of a specific social group who acts according to this group's behavioral patterns. The philanthropist's actions are constrained by several factors, including the problems of the time and the available resources to resolve said problems. Social housing was seen as a key issue in the late nineteenth century, to a large extent because of the perceived links between adequate housing and social stability. Having set their sights on a problem, philanthropists sought solutions which corresponded best with their own worldviews. Finally, philanthropists had to contend with competition from outside actors (social democracy, trade unions, the state, cooperatives) as well as competition from other philanthropists who had competing visions about society and how best to resolve social and cultural questions. Therefore, philanthropic culture involves not only the act of giving but also the decision to give for a chosen cause in a specific way to engineer society according to the philanthropist's wishes. And most important, philanthropists had the resources to execute their plans.

The actions of philanthropists were determined by a latent desire to integrate themselves into social structures. Philanthropy is a behavioral pattern which was used by old and new social elites during the nineteenth century to secure social status or to gain social recognition from the established elites. It served to integrate (or exclude) new elites, women, and religious and ethnic minorities into (or from) the leading circles of urban society. Wealth was a necessary precondition for acceptance into the bourgeoisie, but it was not sufficient to ensure social recognition, as the example of the Vanderbilts demonstrates: Though they had lived on American soil since 1650, their wealth was relatively new and derived from building railways. As "new money," the Vanderbilts were not accorded social recognition from the Knickerbocker elite until they could link their wealth to cultural prestige through their financial involvement in the establishment of the Metropolitan Museum of Art and the Metropolitan Opera House.[9]

THE TRANSFER OF PHILANTHROPIC BLUEPRINTS

Philanthropy was a system designed in Europe to deal with the effects of industrialization on society. German and English municipalities developed philanthropic blueprints and became the testing grounds for philanthropic models which were subsequently transferred to the United States and Canada. During the nineteenth and early twentieth centuries, wealthy North American citizens traveled to Europe to see the sights and to find solutions to the social problems caused by industrialization. They saw the absence of hygienic and affordable housing for working-class families as the greatest threat to social stability and order.

Attempts to resolve deficiencies in the housing of the poorer classes had been made prior to the birth of the modern era. With industrialization, however, the question of developing adequate housing for the emergent working classes became more pressing and more universal. In this field, England became the source of three very influential models: the philanthropic housing enterprises of Sir Sydney Waterlow (investment philanthropy), George Peabody (pure philanthropy), and Octavia Hill (a system of social housing management).[10] In 1862, wealthy U.S. banker George Peabody decided to donate £500,000 for the creation of a social housing enterprise in London. This enterprise was self-perpetuating and the profits were used to expand the trust. Peabody did not desire any personal profit from this enterprise and was motivated by his conviction that capitalism could not solve the housing problem. In contrast to this purely philanthropic project, Sir Sydney Waterlow employed capitalist methods and started a commercial housing company in 1863 but limited the profit to approximately 5 percent. Together with his colleague and friend Mathew Allen, he built a small block of dwellings on Mark Street in London. Their intention was "to produce a housing unit which could be easily built and let at a suitable rent to artisans, while at the same time showing a profit of five-per-cent for the owner."[11] Philanthropy and capitalism were linked for the first time, and the idea of "philanthropy and five percent" was born. Philanthropic endeavors that followed the Waterlow blueprint chose as their legal form the limited-dividend company. Octavia Hill, in contrast to Peabody and Waterlow, did not build new houses; instead, she developed a system of "friendly rent-collecting." In this system, women of higher social standing collected rents from tenants while providing moral instruction and encouraging hygienic conditions. Starting in 1864 with the purchase of three buildings, Hill was responsible for administering over 5,000 apartment buildings within a year. All three social housing systems were successfully implemented in Europe and North America.

German philanthropists involved in the social housing question acquired information about the London philanthropists through travel and books. Princess Alice of Hesse-Darmstadt, the third child of Queen Victoria, was an avid supporter of the Hill method. Dissatisfied with life in a provincial German town, Princess Alice became involved in social welfare. In 1872, she organized a series of meetings, the "Parliament of Women," to discuss the nursing, education, and employment of the poor.[12] Princess Alice's involvement in social causes led her to return to England, where she met Octavia Hill and visited the houses under Hill's direction. Two years later, Princess Alice requested Hill's permission to translate her book, *The Homes of the London Poor,* into German. This translation found its way into the hands of Gustav de Liagre, a Leipzig merchant who also visited London. In 1883, inspired by the success of Hill, de Liagre and twelve friends decided to purchase two buildings with 240 rooms in Leipzig. De Liagre's implementation of the Hill method proved influential in Germany. Other philanthropists adopted Hill's methods and those of George Peabody—the most notable example being the housing foundation of Herrmann Julius Meyer (discussed below).[13]

In the 1870s, U.S. philanthropists began traveling to London to collect information about the three social housing models. Among them was wealthy Bostonian physician Henry Ingersoll Bowditch, who was instrumental in the establishment of the Massachusetts State Board of Health in 1869 and served as its first chairman. In late 1870, Bowditch toured Boston's slums and was shocked by the conditions of the dreadful tenements. This prompted him to call for a housing reform under the guidance of philanthropically minded Bostonians. Later the same year, Bowditch traveled to London and spent six months in the British capital, where he viewed firsthand the model tenements of Peabody, Waterlow, and Hill. He compiled his observations in his "Letter from the Chairman of the State Board of Health Concerning Houses for the People, Convalescent Homes, and the Sewage Question," which was published in the *Second Annual Report of the State Board of Health of Massachusetts* in 1871. Bowditch included an essay by Hill, thereby providing U.S. philanthropists with an account of her "organized work among the poor."[14]

Though Bowditch admired the Peabody Foundation, he doubted that this particular system could solve the housing problem because it was "almost purely philanthropic."[15] He was sure that Peabody's philanthropic undertaking would not induce imitation—one of Bowditch's goals. Waterlow's limited-dividend company, on the other hand, attracted Bowditch's attention, and he subsequently brought a written description of this endeavor back to Boston and used it to establish a similar housing company. When he returned from London, Bowditch immediately convinced a number of wealthy Bostonians to form the Boston Co-operative Building Company, which was capitalized at $200,000 and limited to 7 percent dividends.[16] Other philanthropists, such as Alfred Treadway White of New York City, followed Bowditch's example and visited London in order to get firsthand information about philanthropic undertakings. Like Bowditch, White was very impressed by the Waterlow enterprise. When he returned to New York City in 1872, he began the construction of the "Home and Tower Buildings." This housing enterprise was not only inspired by Waterlow's model, as was Bowditch's enterprise in Boston; it was a literal copy of the Waterlow model, both financially and architecturally.[17]

These philanthropic housing models also made their way to Canada. Toronto's mayor, James Mavor, who came to Toronto via Glasgow, was involved with the Glasgow Working Man's Dwelling Company (which was modeled along the Waterlow model) and the Kyrle Society (which had adopted the methods of Octavia Hill). In Toronto, Mavor made strong connections with Goldwin Smith, who was the first person to attempt to create a housing foundation in Toronto using Waterlow's blueprint. Smith complemented his discussions with Mavor with his own research on the housing enterprises in London. Though Smith's enterprise failed, Toronto merchant Frank Beer chose to pursue a social housing enterprise which linked the Waterlow model with the more recent notion of cooperative housing projects. The Canadian social housing experience was different from that of the United States and Germany in that British housing reformers traveled to Canada to propound new and improved methods of advancing working-class housing.[18]

Wealthy North American tourists also made sure to spend much time in Europe's excellent art galleries and museums. While they enjoyed the collections and exhibitions thoroughly, North American bourgeois were constantly reminded of the absence of equivalent institutions at home. In 1869, John Jay, an eminent lawyer and a grandson of the first chief justice of the United States, proposed the creation of an American art museum during his speech to a group of Americans who were celebrating Independence Day while in Paris. At the meeting in November 1869 that led to the founding of the Metropolitan Museum of Art, writer William Cullen Bryant reminded his fellow citizens that

Beyond the sea there is the little kingdom of Saxony, which, with an area less than that of Massachusetts, and a population but little larger, possesses a Museum of the Fine Arts marvelously rich, which no man, who visits the continent of Europe is willing to own that he has not seen. There is Spain, a third-rate power of Europe and poor besides, with a Museum of Fine Arts at her capital, the opulence and extent of which absolutely bewilder the visitor.[19]

The well-known museums of Leipzig and Dresden attracted wealthy and influential Americans and Canadians, who observed how the museums and art galleries of the city were organized and run.[20] During a business trip to Europe in 1899,[21] James Mavor studied art collections and galleries in Dresden, Leipzig, Munich, Nuremberg, Prague, and Stockholm. Mavor ordered photographs made of the museum buildings and the works displayed, and he collected catalogues of the collections. A small red notebook from his voyage confirms his deep interest in all organizational aspects of these institutions. Mavor made detailed notes about the entrance fees and the degree to which the art galleries were accessible to the public. This information became useful one year later, when Mavor, together with Sir Edmund Walker, an eminent Toronto philanthropist, started to organize the Toronto Art Gallery.[22]

One of the most influential people responsible for organizing the Metropolitan Museum of Art, George Fiske Comfort, traveled for six years through Europe, where he studied the workings of most of the major European art museums.[23] Upon returning to the United States and his professorship at Princeton, Comfort began an intensive campaign to create art museums in the United States. His hopes were congruent with those of several wealthy New Yorkers. As an obvious expert in the topic of art museums, Comfort was invited to the first meeting, held on November 23, 1869, by the Union League Club to discuss the creation of an art museum in New York.[24] Later, on December 13, 1869, Comfort wrote a letter to George P. Putnam, the chairman of the provisional committee concerned with the creation of the art museum, to remind Putnam of model museums: "I hope that the committee, in their deliberations, will not overlook the Leipsic [Leipzig] Museum—opened in 1858;—the Amsterdam Museum . . . the Gotha Museum . . . the 'National-Museum' . . . in Berlin . . . the 'Deutsches Museum' . . . in Nuremberg."[25]

PRIVATE PUBLIC MUSEUMS

Contrary to generally held (mis)conceptions about the financing schemes of public institutions in the nineteenth-century United States and Germany,[26] museums and art galleries in both countries were predominantly privately organized and financed, but they did receive some support from municipalities. Nevertheless, private initiative was responsible for the inception of such institutions. John Jay's proposition in 1869 that an art museum be created in New York met with general enthusiasm from the old Knickerbocker elite (Rhinelanders, Stuyvesants, Winthrops, and Phelpses) and nouveau riche families (Vanderbilts, Stuarts, and Kennedys). Both groups were interested in confirming and defining their place in New York and in increasing the reputation of the city as a cultural metropolis. When the Metropolitan Museum opened in 1870, the museum possessed its own collections but not a building. Not until ten years later was the Metropolitan Museum able to occupy its final location on the east side of Central Park. Despite the large number of private donations and subscriptions amounting to $200,000, the museum makers were convinced that the museum would be unable to operate without governmental subsidies. For this reason, Comfort drafted a petition asking the municipal government of New York City for financial assistance in erecting the museum building. Comfort took the petition to William M. Tweed, who approved it without long deliberation because the "names on the petition represented more than half the real estate of New York City, and a great many prominent businesses as well."[27] Even before the building of the Metropolitan Museum of Art was finished, the New York City government agreed to provide $15,000 a year to the Metropolitan Museum to help pay the rent and cover other expenses.

The governmental assistance that helped finance the building of the Metropolitan Museum became the blueprint for nearly all major museums in the United States. The only prominent exception in the United States was the Boston Museum of Fine Arts, "where the trustees neither solicited nor received any public funds at all" for the financing of the museum building.[28] This pattern of combining private and public funds also prevailed in Europe. The building of the Leipziger Kunstmuseum was also financed privately, although that is not to say that the municipality did not support the efforts of the Kunstverein (Art Association). When the Kunstmuseum was founded, there was no building available to house and show the collections. In 1848, the Kunstverein requested exhibition rooms from the city government, which approved the Kunstverein's petition and offered small rooms in one of the city schools, but this was not a permanent solution. Though the city offered the rooms without rent, the agreement was not without conditions: The Kunstverein agreed that the collections would become the property of the city. Later, in 1854, Leipzig merchant Heinrich Adolf Schletter left the Kunstverein sufficient financial resources to erect the first museum building at the Augustusplatz, which opened in 1858. In contrast to the Metropolitan Museum, the Leipziger Kunstmuseum's collections and building were both financed with private money.[29] It was only in the 1880s that the Leipziger Kunstmuseum received governmental support for the first time. While governmental and private assistance supplemented one another during the next decades, governmental support for the Leipziger Kunstmuseum led to the cessation of private donations to the museum and the city acquired the museum in 1909. This led to the absolute exclusion of any complementary private assistance by membership organizations.[30]

While wealthy citizens were expected in both Leipzig and New York to provide the necessary funds to purchase collections, philanthropy did not guarantee the bourgeoisie ownership of the collections or of the museums in general. New York philanthropists accepted Tweed's demand that the building of the Metropolitan Museum become the property of the city government, although the collections remained private property. In 1848, the Kunstverein of Leipzig announced that all paintings and sculptures bought by the association or donated and bequeathed to the association would become the property of the city government with the stipulation that these objects would never be used for purposes other than exhibition in a public art museum. Leipzig's bourgeois transferred their private property to the municipality without hesitation. Traditional historiography would interpret this apparent transfer of responsibility as a sign of the German bourgeoisie's weakness as a class and its desire to defer to the state. However, the transfer can just as easily be interpreted as an example of the bourgeoisie's sense of general ownership of the community. Leipzig's bourgeoisie was willing to transfer the ownership of the collections and the building to the municipality because they felt that they were the owners of the municipality. In fact, the bourgeoisie most likely did not see this as a transfer of private property to public property in which they lost control over the collections and museums, but as a conversion of one form of communal private property to another. They saw the German municipality as a network of wealthy individuals like themselves who organized, financed, and administered the community; they were de facto owners of it. This attitude is also demonstrated in the bourgeoisie's political will to exclude the working classes from political power through the suffrage restriction of 1894.[31] In New York, the bourgeoisie chose not to transfer the museum collections to the municipality because they had a different relationship to the municipality. Instead of considering the municipality as an extension of bourgeois culture, they viewed the corrupt city government as an opponent with which New York's bourgeoisie had neither the desire nor intention to identify itself. This is an irony in light of the fact that the city government had donated the property and financed the construction of the museum.

PRIVATE SOCIAL WELFARE

In nineteenth-century urban society, museums, art galleries, hospitals, and social housing projects depended on philanthropic aid. In May 1871, Henry Bowditch formed the Boston Co-operative Building Company with the goal of producing inexpensive apartments for working-class families. Following Waterlow's idea of investment philanthropy, Bowditch stipulated that the annual profits of the Boston enterprise be limited to 7 percent. The Boston Co-operative Building Company provided houses for working-class families in three ways: by building new houses in the city, by leasing and re-modeling old ones, and by building small houses in the countryside, which were to be sold to the tenants. The years that followed proved that the latter method had only limited success, and the company decided to abandon this plan. In 1888, the Boston endeavor rented out 209 apartments at $34 to $58 annually. While the number of apartments may seem very small, Bowditch and his colleagues chose to produce a small number of model dwellings to establish a blueprint for a limited-dividend company. They hoped that fellow businessmen who were not inclined toward philanthropic undertakings might be induced to participate in housing reform when they saw the blueprint. And indeed, many people from New York, Philadelphia, Baltimore, and several European cities visited the Bowditch project.[32]

The Boston Co-operative Building Company was a stockholder company, and its members expected the 7 percent return on their investment that Bowditch promised (the impetus for further imitation). Given its capitalistic nature, can this enterprise really be considered philanthropy? On one hand, the returns rarely reached their stated goal: Between 1876 and 1889, "dividends were stopped or reduced to three percent and earnings were invested [back into the enterprise]." In the 1890s, dividends reached between 5 and 6 percent.[33] Despite these lower returns, the investors maintained their involvement in the enterprise. We can only assume that making money was not their sole concern; the stockholders never sold their stocks, as they would have done in a truly capitalist and free-market company. The stocks were transferable but were not available for purchase or sale after the initial purchase.[34] There is evidence that many of the stocks (44 percent) were passed on from the original stockholder to trustees through last wills and testaments.[35] There was a tacit agreement that the stockholder would never withdraw his or her support, regardless of the financial success of the venture. In the end, maybe the question is not whether "philanthropy and five percent" was philanthropy but whether it was capitalism. And in fact, several German philanthropists rejected Waterlow's model because of its perceived connections with capitalism.

In 1884, Leipzig publisher Herrmann Julius Meyer decided to spend money on model tenements for working-class families. This philanthropic endeavor started as an association and became a foundation in 1900. By 1938 it had become the largest housing foundation in Germany; it had about 2,700 apartments. Like Bowditch, Meyer found the blueprint for his housing enterprise in London. However, Meyer did not adopt Waterlow's "philanthropy and five percent"; rather, he copied the model of Peabody's pure philanthropy, rejecting the possibility of making profit from his venture. Originally, Meyer established the Association for the Creation of Affordable Housing, which he alone owned and ran.[36] He saw making the charitable project into an association as the first step in ensuring the future of the housing complex. Meyer then had three options: He could keep it as a privately run association, create a foundation, or create a stock company. Max Pommer, Meyer's architect and friend, favored the idea of transforming the association into a stock company and in 1891 suggested the formation of a limited-dividend company (3 percent) by selling stocks to wealthy Leipzig merchants and industrialists.[37] In Pommer's opinion, such a company would have the added bonus of compelling other wealthy Leipzigers to create similar enterprises. Meyer rejected this Waterlow-inspired model for several reasons: 1) he would have had to share control over the company; 2) he did not have faith in capitalism's ability to solve social questions; and 3) he was not interested in creating an institution that would induce imitation.[38] In 1900, he decided to transform the Association for the Creation of Affordable Housing into the Foundation for the Creation of Affordable Housing in Leipzig.

As these examples of art museums and social housing projects suggest, upper-class citizens in German and U.S. cities felt responsible for the good of their community in addition to having less altruistic motivations. However, the question of inducing imitation highlights the most important difference between German and U.S. philanthropic cultures. While Bowditch envisioned a project that would induce imitation, Meyer was satisfied with the creation of a single philanthropic undertaking which provided a solution within a limited space and for a limited number of people.[39] Nevertheless, in both countries, civic activity occurred within a network of social relations. Wealthy citizens responded to the needs of their time and tried to realize their visions of the ideal urban society. Meyer's philanthropic endeavors were inspired by the long tradition of foundations created for the purpose of addressing nearly every social cause in Leipzig. In 1849, banker Christian Gottlob Frege created the first housing foundation in Leipzig, which was followed by the erection of similar institutions by various members of Leipzig's bourgeoisie over the following two decades.[40] And between

1891 and 1900, Hedwig von Holstein financed the creation of a housing foundation for hundreds of working-class families.[41]

Meyer's motivations for his involvement in the social housing question were linked to his activities as a social worker (*Fürsorgepfleger*). He volunteered his time to visit Leipzig's working-class districts and met with working-class families and observed their living conditions.[42] This experience convinced him that the housing question was one of the most pressing issues of his time, the key to social reform. The emergence of a very strong branch of the Social Democratic Party in Leipzig confirmed Meyer's belief that social reform was necessary.[43] Meyer accepted reforms in capitalist society to preserve it and to prevent massive social upheaval. It is not surprising that such preventative ideas found a large number of followers among the U.S. bourgeoisie during the 1870s. The wealthy New Yorkers and Bostonians—the Knickerbockers and Brahmins—were horrified by the Paris Commune; to them, the Commune proved the importance and necessity of social reforms. Inevitably, social unrest and revolution would result from unbridled free-market capitalism unless social welfare was provided for the lower classes. The (to them) horrific scenario in Paris and the economic recession of the 1870s increased their perception that limited social reform within the capitalist system was necessary in order to prevent social upheaval.[44] To this extent, one can speak of them as social engineers.

It is clear in the manner by which the Meyer Foundation was established and organized that philanthropic undertakings reflect both the views of the philanthropists involved and the social structures into which they were integrated. Meyer chose to produce small, hygienic, and inexpensive dwellings which were not concentrated in one part of the city. He wanted to avoid social segregation by class, which was thought to cause class conflict.[45] Meyer ruled that the political, religious, and social backgrounds of the prospective tenants should not be a consideration; however, he felt that civil servants, although they were not excluded, should not be given priority. Prospective tenants were expected to have a yearly income of at least 800 and no more than 1,800 marks. The rent was supposed to be one-seventh of the income of the tenant. People who depended on public relief were excluded from renting these dwellings, as were families with more than five children.

Meyer's ideas and the practical application of them did not differ from those of other philanthropists in London and Boston. Waterlow, Bowditch, and Meyer, for instance, not only created specific visions of society with their ideas and the architecture they chose; they realized them. Philanthropists did not create these housing projects for every kind of working-class family. Their goal was to house an upper stratum in the working class—families with exactly defined incomes and a limited number of children. The model housing projects provided private dwellings for this type of working-class family, securing privacy for each. These philanthropists rejected the corridor system that could be found in most private buildings and commonly used kitchens, sculleries, and lavatories. All three men believed that the family was the basic element of society. For this reason, they favored an architecture which encouraged nucleated housing for families.[46]

A "HAPPENING" CLASS

Philanthropy was one behavioral pattern which defined the upper class. Wealth was a necessary precondition for entrance into the bourgeoisie, but as the example of the Vanderbilts suggests, it was not sufficient. Philanthropists founded museums, art galleries, and social housing projects not only to improve the general welfare but also to claim leadership positions in urban society. The Metropolitan Museum of Art and the American Museum of Natural History in New York City were founded not because of an overwhelming demand for museums or because the university needed them but because the Knickerbocker elite and the nouveaux riches required these institutions to demonstrate their wealth and to gain leadership. While the Metropolitan Museum was financed by the old Dutch and English landowning families, such as the Rhinelanders, the Livingstons, and the Stuyvesants, the American Museum of Natural History was established by the new families of James Brown, Adrian Iselin, and William T. Blodgett. The latter were architects of their own fortunes and represented the industrialists and entrepreneurs who were wealthy but lacked social recognition from the older elites. They tried to copy the behavior of the old elites in order to gain entry into high society.

On both sides of the Atlantic, the nineteenth-century city was characterized by the chaos of the changing social order. Industrialization had produced the working class and a new social stratum of entrepreneurs and industrialists who are best described as self-made men and women. These individuals came mostly from the lower classes and had won their fortunes through the new industrial methods, but they lacked cultural education. The members of the old elites did not accept this emerging group as their equals and did not allow them to participate in elite social clubs, institutions, and gatherings. In 1876, 104 patrons, 119 fellows in perpetuity, and 92 fellows for life supported the Metropolitan Museum. Sixty-six percent of all philanthropists belonged to the old Knickerbocker families, while only 34 percent belonged to the families of the nouveaux riches.[47]

Only slowly, and after proving themselves as people of culture and social responsibility, did the *homo novae* find inroads into the highest circles of society. Philanthropy for social and cultural purposes was one, if not the most important, tool with which to integrate oneself and one's family into the bourgeoisie. Another useful method was to publish biographical data. The Knickerbocker families were particularly proud of their illustrious backgrounds and set the benchmark for ancestral claims. These families came to America from the Netherlands and Britain and settled in Massachusetts, New Jersey, and New York. Their ancestors had been of "good old colonial stock" (i.e., those who had arrived with the *Mayflower* and *Ann* in the 1620s). Levi Parsons Morton, for example, one of the philanthropists involved in the Metropolitan Museum of Art, was a descendant of George Morton of York (England). The latter was the financial agent for the *Mayflower* Puritans in London and came over on the *Ann;* he arrived at Plymouth, Massachusetts, in 1623 and settled in Middleboro, Plymouth County.[48] The biographies of most of these philanthropists were collected in two voluminous books: *Famous Families of New York* and *Prominent Families of New York.*

New York was famous for historians and genealogists who made their living by providing individuals, the new elites in particular, with invented family trees or family histories, which often stretched back to the Norman times, as well as coats of arms.[49] New and old elites shared the desire to possess elaborate and glorious family histories and an impressive coat of arms. Handbooks about heraldry became the basis for developing these coats of arms. It had been tradition for older families, such as the Livingstons, Schuylers, and Schermerhorns, to have very colorful and impressive family crests. Families of the nouveaux riches could not resist the temptation to copy this behavioral pattern.[50] These constructed identities found their way into several biographical dictionaries and became accepted by contemporaries. The Carletons, for instance, could boast that their family "dates from the time of the Norman Conquest in 1066. The name was originally a title of nobility, and its first bearer was a Carleton—Baldwin de Carleton."[51] The invention of family trees that included famous heroes and kings, the creation of crests, and the desire to publish these invented identities were not at all unique to New York's bourgeoisie. The same bourgeois behavioral pattern can be found in Boston, Toronto, and Leipzig.[52] The central office for German personal and family history under the direction of Johannes Hohlfeld in Leipzig collected genealogical information about wealthy Leipzig families and published illustrated family trees of new-money and old-money families. The most important publication was the three-volume *Leipziger Geschlechter,* which included photographs, family trees, and short histories of the important Leipzig families. Interestingly, Leipzig's wealthy and influential families were not only the subjects of this research and these publications, they were also the financiers of the project.[53]

This pattern of exclusion and dominance is further illustrated by the example of the Vanderbilts. "Newer" families such as the Vanderbilts were not permitted to acquire a box at the Academy of Music—the ultimate status symbol in New York. The eighteen boxes in the Academy of Music "were as exclusive as seats on the stock exchange and were completely controlled by old-guard Knickerbocker society."[54] When, in spring 1880, one such box became vacant, William H. Vanderbilt offered $30,000 for it. His offer was quickly rebuffed. Discouraged but not defeated, Cornelius Vanderbilt, Jay Gould, J. P. Morgan, and William Whitney suggested adding twenty-six boxes to the existing eighteen boxes. After the Academy's board of directors rejected this plan, the same group formed a corporation to build its own opera house—the Metropolitan Opera House. This new building, which the old Knickerbockers contemptuously called "the new yellow brewery on Broadway," contained 122 boxes—enough space for the new and old elites. The closing of the Academy of Music in 1885 and the integration of the old Knickerbocker families into the Metropolitan Opera House marked the defeat of the old elites and the social recognition of the new elites by the old elites.[55]

Philanthropy became an instrument with which to reconstruct the social order of nineteenth-century cities. Industrialization had caused an earthquake in the structure of society, producing not only the working class but also a new social stratum of industrialists and entrepreneurs. These new elites recognized that philanthropy was one of the behavioral patterns which would enable them to participate in high society. Spending enormous amounts of money for social and cultural institutions was not a problem for people who amassed millions of dollars in new industries. The example of the Metropolitan Opera House demonstrates that philanthropic behavior had the power to effect changes in high society. Philanthropy served to delineate the borders of the bourgeoisie.

NOTES

This chapter is part of an ongoing research project about philanthropy and the establishment of the bourgeoisie in Canada, Germany, and the United States during the second half of the nineteenth century. The research has been generously supported by a Feodor Lynen Fellowship from the Alexander von Humboldt Foundation in Germany and a George C. Metcalf Postdoctoral Research Grant from Victoria College, University of Toronto.

1. Lester M. Salamon and Helmut K. Anheier, eds., *Defining the Nonprofit Sector: A Cross-National Analysis* (Manchester and New York: Manchester University Press, 1997).

2. Helmut K. Anheier and Wolfgang Seibel, "Germany," in Salamon and Anheier, *Defining the Nonprofit Sector,* 131ff.

3. Until recently, philanthropy has not been a topic of research in Germany. For emerging historical work on this topic, see Manuel Frey, *Macht und Moral des Schenkens: Staat und bürgerliche Mäzene vom späten 18. Jahrhundert bis zur Gegenwart* (Zwickau: Fannei & Walz, 1999); and Jürgen Kocka and Manuel Frey, eds., *Bürgerkultur und Mäzenatentum im 19. Jahrhundert* (Zwickau: Fannei & Walz, 1998).

4. Anheier and Seibel, "Germany," 162. See also Helmut K. Anheier and Frank P. Romo, "Foundations in Germany and the United States: A Comparative Analysis," in *Private Funds, Public Purpose: Philanthropic Foundations in International Perspective*, ed. Helmut K. Anheier and Stefan Toepler (New York: Kluwer Academic and Plenum Publishers, 1999), 79–118.

5. Wolfgang Ismayr, "Cultural Federalism and Public Support for the Arts in the Federal Republic of Germany," in *The Patron State: Government and the Arts in Europe, North America, and Japan,* ed. Milton C. Cummings Jr. and Richard S. Katz (New York and Oxford: Oxford University Press, 1987), 45–67; Fry, *Macht und Moral des Schenkens*, 18–19.

6. E. P. Thompson, *The Making of the English Working Class* (London: V. Gollancz, 1963), 9.

7. For an excellent discussion of this, see Susannah Morris's chapter in this volume.

8. Willmar Schwabe is quoted in *Jahresbericht der Ortskrankenkasse Leipzig für die Jahre 1884–1889* (Leipzig, 1889), 94.

9. William Augustus Croffut, *The Vanderbilts and the Story of Their Fortune* (Chicago and New York: Belford, Clarke & Company, 1886); Edwin P. Hoyt, *The Vanderbilts and Their Fortunes* (Garden City and New York: Doubleday & Company, 1962); Allen Churchill, *The Upper Crust* (Englewood Cliffs, N.J.: Prentice Hall, 1970), 119–136.

10. For the philanthropic housing models of Waterlow, Peabody, and Hill, see John Nelson Tarn, *Five Per Cent Philanthropy: An Account of Housing in Urban Areas between 1840 and 1914* (London: Cambridge University Press, 1973); E. R. L. Gould, *The Housing of the Working People* (Washington, D.C.: Government Printing Office, 1895), 214–246; Susannah Morris, "Private Profit and Public Interest: Model Dwellings Companies and the Housing of the Working Classes in London, 1840–1914" (D.Phil., University of Oxford, 1998).

11. Tarn, *Five Per Cent Philanthropy,* 51.

12. Margaret J. Shaen, ed., *Memorials of Two Sisters: Susanna and Catherine Winkworth* (London and New York: Longmans and Green, 1908), 288–292.

13. For this transfer of philanthropic blueprints, see Thomas Adam, "Transatlantic Trading: The Transfer of Philanthropic Models between European and North American Cities during the Nineteenth and Early Twentieth Centuries," *Journal of Urban History* 28 (2002): 328–351.

14. (Henry I. Bowditch), "Letter from the Chairman of the State Board of Health, Concerning Houses for the People, Convalescent Homes, and the Sewage Question," in *Second Annual Report of the State Board of Health of Massachusetts* (Boston, 1871), 182–243.

15. Ibid., 198.

16. David M. Culver, "Tenement House Reform in Boston, 1846–1898" (Ph.D. diss., Boston University, 1972), 144–145; *The First Annual Report of the Boston Co-operative Building Co. with the Act of Incorporation and By-laws* (Boston, 1872); *Twenty-Fifth Annual Report of the Boston Co-operative Building Company 1896,* 8–13; Robert Treat Paine, "The Housing Conditions in Boston," in *The Annals of the American Academy of Political and Social Science* XX (July–December 1902), 123–136.

17. Richard Plunz, *A History of Housing in New York City: Dwelling Type and Social Change in the American Metropolis* (New York: Columbia University Press, 1990), 92.

18. Adam, "Transatlantic Trading," 343–347.

19. Winifred E. Howe, *A History of the Metropolitan Museum of Art with a Chapter on the Early Institutions of Art in New York* (New York: Columbia University Press, 1913), 108. See also Calvin Tomkins, *Merchants and Masterpieces: The Story of the Metropolitan Museum of Art* (New York: Henry Holt and Company, 1989), 28.

20. Eberhard Brüning, "'It is a glorious collection': Amerikanische Bildungsbürger des 19. Jahrhunderts auf 'Pilgerfahrt' zur Dresdner Gemäldegalerie," in *Jahrbuch der Staatlichen Kunstsammlungen Dresden 1996/1997,* 99–105; Eberhard Brüning, "Sachsen mit amerikanischen Augen gesehen: Das Sachsenbild amerikanischer Globetrotter im 19. Jahrhundert," *Neues Archiv für sächsische Geschichte* 67 (1996): 109–131.

21. Incidentally, this business trip was of a transatlantic nature. Mavor went to examine the possibilities of promoting emigration to Canada as well as to study the successes of the German and Austrian workmen's insurance systems.

22. Thomas Adam, "Philanthropic Landmarks: The Toronto Trail from a Comparative Perspective, 1870s to the 1930s," *Urban History Review* 30 (2001): 3–21; James Mavor Papers MS 119, Box 56A:22, Fisher Rare Book Library, University of Toronto; James Mavor, *My Windows on the Street of the World,* 2 vols. (London, Toronto, and New York: E. P. Dutton & Co., 1923), 1: 377–381.

23. Howe, *A History of the Metropolitan Museum of Art,* 112.

24. See George Fisk Comfort, *Art Museums in America* (Boston: H. O. Houghton and Company, 1870).

25. Quoted in Howe, *A History of the Metropolitan Museum of Art,* 119.

26. Seymor Martin Lipset, "American Society in European Perspective," in *Civic Engagement in the Atlantic Community,* ed. Josef Janning, Charles Kupchan, and Dirk Rumberg (Gütersloh: Bertelsmann Foundation Publishers, 1999), 42ff.

27. Tomkins, *Merchants and Masterpieces,* 40; Howe, *A History of the Metropolitan Museum of Art,* 138.

28. Tomkins, *Merchants and Masterpieces,* 41. For Boston, see Walter Muir Whitehill, *Museum of Fine Arts Boston: A Centennial History,* vol. I (Cambridge: The Belknap Press of Harvard University Press, 1970).

29. For Leipzig, see Thomas Adam, "Die Kommunalisierung von Kunst und Kultur als Grundkonsens der deutschen Gesellschaft ab dem ausgehenden 19. Jahrhundert," *Die Alte Stadt* 26 (February 1999): 91; J. Vogel, *Das Städtische Museum zu Leipzig* (Leipzig, 1892), 36; and Anett Müller, *Der Leipziger Kunstverein und das Museum der bildenden Künste—Materialien einer Geschichte (1836–1886/87)* (Leipzig: Nouvelle Alliance, 1995).

30. Tomkins, *Merchants and Masterpieces,* 45. For a good account of the current financing scheme of the Metropolitan Museum of Art, see Judith Huggins Balfe and Thomas A. Cassilly, "'Friends of . . .': Individual Patronage through Arts Institutions," in *Paying the Piper: Causes and Consequences of Art Patronage,* ed. Judith Huggins Balfe (Urbana and Chicago: University of Illinois Press, 1993), 119–133.

31. James Retallack and Thomas Adam, "Philanthropy und politische Macht in deutschen Kommunen," in *Zwischen Markt und Staat: Stifter und Stiftungen im transatlantischen Vergleich,* ed. Thomas Adam and James Retallack (*Comparativ* Heft 5/6 [2001]), 106–138.

32. *Annual Report of the Boston Co-Operative Building Company, 1872–1896,* 1–25.

33. Paine, "The Housing Conditions in Boston," 125.

34. *Sixteenth Annual Report of the Boston Co-operative Building Company* (Boston, 1887), 22.

35. *Forty-First Annual Report of the Boston Co-operative Building Company* (Boston, 1912), 8.

36. Herrmann Julius Meyer to Max Pommer, September 22, 1886, and February 12, 1887, Archive of the Meyer Foundation, Leipzig; Diary of Max Pommer, 15, private ar-

chive of the Pommer family, Leipzig; Verein für Erbauung billiger Wohnungen in Leipzig-Lindenau, Generalbericht April 1891 bis Juli 1895, 5, Archive of the Meyer Foundation; Max Pommer, "Gemeinnützige Bauthätigkeit und Bau von Arbeiterwohnungen," in *Leipzig und seine Bauten* (Leipzig: J. M. Gebhardt's Verlag, 1892), 450ff.; Thomas Adam, "Das soziale Engagement Leipziger Unternehmer—die Tradition der Wohnstiftungen," in *Unternehmer in Sachsen: Aufstieg—Krise—Untergang—Neubeginn,* ed. Ulrich Hess and Michael Schäfer (Leipzig: Leipziger Universitätsverlag, 1998), 110.

37. "Die Meyer'schen Arbeiterhäuser in Leipzig-Lindenau," *Leipziger Zeitung* (October 1, 1895): 39–40.

38. Herrmann Julius Meyer to Max Pommer, March 3, 1891, Archive of the Meyer Foundation.

39. Thomas Adam, *Die Anfänge industriellen Bauens in Sachsen* (Leipzig: Quadrat Verlag, 1998), 26; Tarn, *Five Per Cent Philanthropy,* 44–50.

40. Kap. 36 F Nr. 6, Stadtarchiv Leipzig; Kap. 36 S Nr. 181; Kap. 36 A Nr 39, Bl. 8; H. Geffcken and H. Tykorinski, *Stiftungsbuch der Stadt Leipzig* (Leipzig: Bär & Hermann, 1905), xxxviii.

41. For Leipzig's tradition of housing foundations, see Max Pommer, "Gemeinnützige Bauthätigkeit und Bau von Arbeiterwohnung"; and Ernst Hasse, "Die gemeinnützige Bauthätigkeit und die Herstellung kleiner Wohnungen," in *Leipzig in hygienischer Beziehung* (Leipzig: Duncker & Humblot, 1891), 102–108. For an overview of Leipzig's housing foundations, see Adam, "Das soziale Engagement Leipziger Unternehmer."

42. Adam, *Die Anfänge industriellen Bauens in Sachsen,* 19.

43. For the emergence of the social democratic movement in Leipzig, see Michel Rudloff, Thomas Adam, and Jürgen Schlimper, *Leipzig—Wiege der deutschen Sozialdemokratie* (Berlin: Metropol Verlag, 1996); and Thomas Adam, *Arbeitermilieu und Arbeiterbewegung in Leipzig 1871–1933* (Cologne, Weimar, and Vienna: Böhlau, 1999).

44. Edwin G. Burrows and Mike Wallace, *Gotham: A History of New York City to 1898* (New York and Oxford: Oxford University Press, 1999), 1002.

45. Joseph Stübben argued that social segregation in big cities (i.e., the emergence of separate districts for the working class, the middle class, and the upper class) would further class conflict. Michael John, *Wohnverhältnisse sozialer Unterschichten im Wien Kaiser Franz Josephs* (Vienna: Europaverlag, 1984), 203–205.

46. Adam, "Transatlantic Trading."

47. The analysis of the membership of the Metropolitan Museum of Art Association is based on my biographical database of New York philanthropists. The membership lists are taken from the annual reports of the Metropolitan Museum of Art for 1876 and 1895. The biographical information is drawn from L. R. Hamersly, ed., *Who's Who in New York City and State* (New York: L. R. Hamersly Company, 1905); *The National Cyclopaedia of American Biography* (New York: J. T. White, 1898–1984); George Austin Morrison Jr., *History of Saint Andrew's Society of the State of New York, 1756–1906* (New York, 1906); *Social Register, New York 1898* (New York: Social Register Association, 1898); *Club Men of New York* (New York: The Republic Press, 1893); Margherita Arlina Hamm, *Famous Families of New York: Historical and Biographical Sketches of Families Which in Successive Generations Have Been Identified with the Development of the Nation,* 2 vols. (New York, London: G. P. Putnam's Sons, n.d.); and Lyman Horace Weeks, ed., *Prominent Families of New York: Being an Account in Biographical Form of Individuals and Families Distinguished As Representatives of the Social, Professional and Civic Life of New York City* (New York: The Historical Company, 1897).

48. Weeks, *Prominent Families of New York,* 416.

49. Junius Henri Browne, *The Great Metropolis: A Mirror of New York* (1869; reprint, New York: Arno Press, 1975), 596–602.

50. C. W. Gwilt Mapleson, *A Hand-Book of Heraldry* (New York: John Wiley, 1852).

51. Weeks, *Prominent Families of New York*, 99.

52. For Boston: Mary Caroline Crawford, *Famous Families of Massachusetts in Two Volumes* (Boston: Little, Brown and Co., 1930). For Toronto: *Leading Financial and Business Men in Toronto: A Work of Artistic Color Plates Designed to Portray One Hundred Leading Men of Toronto, Both Financially And Socially* (Toronto, 1912); and Edward Marion Chadwick, *Ontarian Families: Genealogies of United Empire Loyalist and Other Pioneer Families of Upper Canada* (Lambertville, N.J.: Hunterdon House, 1894). For Leipzig: Johannes Hohlfeld, *Leipziger Geschlechter*, 3 vols. (Leipzig, 1933–1939).

53. Volkmar Weiss, "Johannes Hohlfeld, von 1924 bis 1950 Geschäftsführer der Zentralstelle für Deutsche Personen- und Familiengeschichte in Leipzig, zum 50. Todestag," *Genealogie* 49 (2000): 65–83.

54. John Warren Frick Jr., "The Rialto: A Study of Union Square, the Center of New York's First Theatre District, 1870–1900" (Ph.D. diss., New York University, 1983), 57.

55. Jack W. Rudolph, "Launching the MET," *American History Illustrated* (1983), 21–25; Frick, "The Rialto," 57--58.

TWO

"The Glue of Civil Society": A Comparative Approach to Art Museum Philanthropy at the Turn of the Twentieth Century

KARSTEN BORGMANN

THE HISTORIOGRAPHY
OF THE NONPROFIT SECTOR

R ecent comparative research on the nonprofit sectors of thirty-two countries has created new attempts to discuss a comparative history of a "global civil society."[1] Although the data collected by the Johns Hopkins Comparative Nonprofit Sector Project[2] has been used to underline common processes on a global level, especially the "future of welfare states" and the "global associational revolution,"[3] the results of this research could also be read as an impressive demonstration of international diversity. The voluntary or nonprofit sector, which frequently has been seen as an American invention is, thanks to the country studies of the national Johns Hopkins research teams, now seen as a variety of structures rather than one monolithic entity. This change in perception raises a question: Should not the search for new "sectors" also prompt a new pluralist understanding of "global civil *societies*"?

Comparative research on the international nonprofit sectors has focused mainly on the social economy of nonprofit organizations. These organizations have been called the glue that holds communities together because of their potential to balance diverse partisan group interests and a larger national understanding of the common good.[4] They are institutions where the accommodation of diverging public and private interests takes place and where private and public identities are communicated.[5] Therefore, they could serve as both a source of trust and identity in the socially heterogeneous environment of the nation-state and a source of social capital in a distinctive community.[6] As country studies in the Johns Hopkins Project become more and more elaborate, historiography may be charged with the task of interpreting these functions of nonprofit organizations and institutions and relating them to larger questions of comparative historiography.

Lester Salamon and Helmut Anheier have both argued for a more historiographical approach that could serve "as a bridge between the elegant simplicity of the economic models . . . and the dense detail of traditional historical accounts."[7] Calling for a search for the "social origins of civil society," they suggest a typology that takes into account both Gøsta Esping Andersen's "welfare state regimes" and Barrington Moore's routes to democracy and dictatorship.[8] They develop a mix of indicators of the tradition of the national welfare state and social segmentation in order to explore the historical circumstances that encouraged private activity for the public good. This approach has led them to identify four models of the development of the nonprofit sector. I will introduce here the two models that apply to Germany and the United States, which might serve as ideal types for further historiographical discussion.

In Anheier and Salamon's "social origins" approach, the United States represents the liberal model of a welfare state, which is based on a particular pattern of public/private arrangements in the nonprofit sector. Effective cooperation of both partners in the nonprofit sector is supported by limited welfare spending from the government, an ascending middle class, and a lack of opposition by both traditional landed elites and a very organized workers' movement. This situation has, according to Salamon and Anheier, resulted in "significant ideological and political hostility to the extension of government social welfare protections and a decided preference for voluntary approaches."[9] Thus, one may conclude, the nonprofit sector in the United States grew out of a distinct private-sector identity based on "private networks of reciprocity and civic solidarity," which Robert D. Putnam has described as the main source of social capital in the United States.[10]

The authors classify Germany, which contrasts with this "liberal" type, as the site of a "corporatist model," where arrangements between private-sector identities and national welfare policies had a more collaborative character.[11] Germany, with its history of high welfare spending, a once-powerful aristocracy, and a well-organized workers' movement, is a clear counterexample to the preconditions for the emergence of a strong nonprofit sector that we see in liberal states. Nevertheless, despite these unfavorable circumstances from a liberal point of view, Germany has developed a comparatively large nonprofit sector that ranks in the middle field of the world average.[12] As Helmut Anheier and Wolfgang Seibel have pointed out in their country study on the nonprofit sector in Germany,[13] a pronounced tradition of associational life, a commonly accepted principle of "subsidiarity,"[14] and a widespread belief in a noncompetitive communal economics (*Gemeinwirtschaft*) have historically shaped a "corporatist" non-profit sector, which still plays a crucial role in influencing economic, social, and cultural policy.[15]

Both the liberal and the corporatist models emphasize the role nonprofit institutions played in the process of transforming the fragmented structure of a premodern society into the national community of the modern welfare state. In the sphere between the state and the market, a process of accommodation took place whereby many existing traditional understandings of the common good were replaced with the new national definitions of the common good. Nation-building led to democratization and the representation of various geographical and political interests. In continental Europe as well as in the English-speaking world, the traditional power of local and religious elites and their organizations was challenged by increased social and regional mobility following industrialization in the nineteenth century. This mobility engendered new nontraditional communities in search of representation and participation in the national realm —notably the labor movement, the middle classes, and the industrial bourgeoisie. All these social formations were furthermore subdivided ethnically or religiously. The popular movements in Sweden, the component cultures (Versäulung) in the Netherlands, the political *Lager* (camps) in Austria, and the Catholic political party in Italy are all examples of nontraditional social formations which appropriated nonprofit institutions to represent the needs of their particular communities in official public policy-making.[16]

Most of these institutions were nonprofit organizations—foundations, associations, federations—and they created what has been called the emerging nonprofit sector. They were manifestations of civil society, but their basic function depended on their ability to accommodate both traditional local and emerging national identities. This ability, in fact, has been the "glue" that transforms a diverse civil society into a national community with adequate standards of living for all residents within a state territory. Nonprofit organizations had the potential to mobilize public participation and to protect societies from collapsing into civil war. In German history, one of the central questions of comparative historiography remains, Why did the "glue of civil society" not suffice to protect a considerable segment of the German population and culture from extinction when the society turned totalitarian in the first half of the twentieth century? A look back at the processes of cultural accommodation surrounding art museums as nonprofit institutions in the formative years of the German and U.S. welfare systems may help us understand why some particularities of the corporatist arrangement weakened the forces of civil societies that kept the liberal example on a much more stable course.

ART MUSEUM PHILANTHROPY
IN THE UNITED STATES AND GERMANY

Art museum philanthropy in Germany and the United States shares some common features which were also observed by contemporaries. In 1913, Woldemar von Seidlitz, advisor to the Royal Art Museum administration in Dresden, published an international listing of associations of museum friends (*Museumsvereine*) in the German journal for museology, *Museums-kunde*.[17] Von Seidlitz emphasized that the leading example of this "particular contemporary creation" (*eigentümliche Bildung der Neuzeit*) was to be found in New York. Von Seidlitz opened his article by stating that at the Metropolitan Museum, a "holders cooperative" (*Teilnehmergenossenschaft*) had been created which had developed into an increasingly popular and effective method of museum financing. The strategy to involve citizens in the public art collections, he concluded, had found many successful followers, especially in Berlin, Frankfurt, Munich, Paris, and London. Although von Seidlitz described the organizations as an international phenomenon, he informed the reader about the leading role the German Empire had already taken in this development.[18]

What von Seidlitz observed in 1913 was the international rise of art museum philanthropy: a succession of private initiatives to support national institutions with the goal of instructing the public about aesthetics. These initiatives could be observed in various forms in many countries around the western hemisphere, but they took on a very significant role for the industrial upper classes of Germany and the United States. While the art museums which benefited from private funding were a new type of institution, the nineteenth century had already seen public art collections for the appreciation of the arts as well as educational institutions to enhance the skills of industrial producers. The Louvre in Paris and the South Kensington Museum in London were the paradigmatic institutions which had influenced the creation of art museums and collections of industrial crafts all over Europe.[19] These public art institutions were able to raise both money and the interest of a large number of citizens in Germany and the United States by the end of the nineteenth century. Two things were new about them: The museums were reorganized to convey both the civilizing spirit of art and aesthetic knowledge as indispensable forms of capital for the emerging consumer society.[20]

Citizens in the German Empire and the United States wanted art museums to become useful not only for a select group of art enthusiasts but for the entire nation. They wanted their museums to meet international standards and to overcome regional and local limitations. In this regard, the main task of the institutions was to enhance public cultural policies and to put forward the idea of a national civilization and identity. But what was also evident with regard to art museum philanthropy in Germany and the United States was its relation to values and intellectual convictions of the highest and most influential upper strata of both societies. Reverence for art became a common element in the new industrial upper class, a social group distinguished by particular aesthetic attitudes and aristocratic aspirations.[21] Traditional and newer parts of society—aristocracies and arrivistes—developed new patterns of aesthetic self-expression through art collecting. The growing popularity of private art collections added coherence and continuity to upper-class identities and became an important element in the establishment of a new elite.

Both motives—the more utilitarian concerning public policies and the more private related to the individual appreciation of art—helped art museums enter their golden era as symbols of national cultural achievement. The increased number of treasures brought together through private collecting in Germany and the United States led to a significant expansion of national "treasure houses." Professional strategies were developed to secure a future stream of funding for artworks and to demonstrate the public use of the collections. The professionalization of art museum personnel began around the turn of the century. The museum as an institution had to make use of experts with educational as well as curatorial skills. Serving art and serving the community at the same time, the museum had to deal with multiple constituencies and had to integrate educational and curatorial functions. By serving two distinct objectives, the museums as nonprofit organizations helped to accommodate frictions within the upper classes as well as class differences on a national level.

Collaboration of the public and private sectors, the search for culture as an elite value, and the professionalization of curators and museum educators were common features of art museum philanthropy in Germany and the United States before the First World War. Both countries followed their own routes of nonprofit-sector development such that very different results emerged regarding the ability of art museums to serve as the national "glue."

THE GREAT COLLECTORS
OF THE UNITED STATES

William R. Valentiner, a German art historian who moved to the United States in 1904 to work for the Metropolitan Museum, was hardly impressed by what he remembered of German art collectors. These Berlin *Kommerzienräte* (commercial councillors) had been "poorly interesting personalities." Valentiner recollected that he frequently mixed them up because they all looked alike. Although their art collections were extraordinarily valuable as historical works of art, they were only remarkable as extensions (*Ergänzungen*) of the Berlin Kaiser-Friedrich-Museum, accumulated under the skillful guidance of its director, Wilhelm von Bode.[22]

In contrast, Valentiner's reminiscences on the U.S. art world are filled with sketches of remarkable American personalities who were involved in the conspicuous business of art acquisition and art collecting. One of the most prominent among them was the Metropolitan Museum's president, John Pierpont Morgan. According to Valentiner, this "great collector," although he had some typical American "collector's idiosyncrasies," left to the City of New York "grandiose monuments of his personal taste."[23] Morgan's legendary buying on the art markets of Europe spurred the imagination of U.S. and German observers. Morgan's successes in art acquisition achieved a prominent place in contemporary U.S. accounts.[24] "Privately owned art revealed national supremacy as clearly as steel production and coal production did," wrote Neil Harris of the impact of Morgan and a new generation of great collectors on the American national conscience.[25] Another form of public fascination with leading figures of the contemporary art world developed around women's art collecting and aesthetic consumption. In Boston, Isabella Stewart Gardner purposefully arranged her private art collection in her home, Fenway Court, to emphasize her own artistic taste and personality. Her conspicuous and tasteful art display challenged the conventions of Boston society. She nevertheless became the leading society hostess as well as a role model for the modern consumer.[26] "Queen Isabella," as the celebrated interior decorator Elsie de Wolfe used to call her, symbolized individual capacities for tasteful interior design, which became a widely published topic of female self-expression around that time.[27]

Gardner and Morgan were by far the most well-known proponents of this "status revolution" which played out in the U.S. upper classes on the East Coast at the peak of industrialization.[28] With their art purchases, they defined a new style of cultivated acquisition which distinguished them from the conformity of the older Victorian high society of Boston and New York.[29] Both Gardner and Morgan used the market not only to purchase the best works of art available but also to underline their leading positions in society. They used the same principles to acquire art that other members of this emerging industrial upper class used to achieve control over the national economy. The organizational skills of industrialists allowed them to delegate authority to experts and specialists in their corporations and to concentrate on the strategic policy of their enterprises.[30]

Morgan was notorious for buying entire collections that others had compiled over years. He did not seek to work with particular art dealers. Instead, he was surrounded by numbers of them competing for access to the
great purchaser. Morgan developed the habit of paying for his yearly acquisitions only at the end of each year, returning pieces that had been declared
to be of minor value by the critical eye of experts and the envy of other
dealers.[31] Gardner did no different when, instead of traveling to Europe
and buying art herself, she worked with an international group of art connoisseurs to secure the extraordinary quality of her art collection. U.S. ex-
patriates and aesthetes such as Bernard Berenson, who had exiled himself to
Florence, might have nursed a critical attitude toward wealthy art-seeking
Americans.[32] Yet where Berenson's villa, I Tatti, rose to a very exclusive symbol of art appreciation for a selected circle of cultivated insiders, wealthy
Americans such as Gardner and Morgan established "grandiose monuments of personal taste" for the American public. Although Berenson
claimed that the Gardner collection in Boston had been brought together
according to his taste and expertise, the museum Fenway Court remained
Gardner's unique and very personal creation.[33] Following her own credo—
"c'est mon plaisir"—she managed to establish a monument of exemplary
quality that set standards for public attitudes toward art and demonstrated
the power of a sophisticated consumer in an era of mass consumption.[34]

Morgan and Gardner paved the way for other industrialists to join
them in this kind of conspicuous and yet sophisticated style of collecting.
They could play this pioneering role because both were anything else but
parvenus. Morgan's father was an international financier who had already
collected art. Gardner married from the high society of New York into the
cultivated circles of Boston. Her efforts to create an exceptional art collection underscore her ambition to surpass existing conventions of "aristocratic" cultivation.

Morgan and Gardner were able to bridge the traditional esteem of art
and culture among the "genteel" U.S. upper classes and the new commercial skills of industrial society. They took advantage of the inspiration provided by a cosmopolitan community of aesthetes to expand, but not to
leave, the value system of established Bostonian and New York high society.
Authors such as John Ruskin and "apostles of culture" such as Charles Eliot
Norton presented the art history of Europe as a utopian moral alternative
to the industrial realities of U.S. society.[35] In this cultural utopia, the freedom to consume aesthetic products was accorded the highest moral value.
Gardner and Morgan exercised this freedom in a socially acceptable way
that confirmed the basic values of the urban upper classes. The conspicuous consumption of the "great collectors" of art affected the formation of a
new exclusive identity for a new national upper class.

WILHELM VON BODE AND
THE BERLIN ART COLLECTORS

To Germans, the competition between U.S. collectors willing to pay any price for the most important artworks was the "American peril."[36] They used caricature to distinguish the "serious" German art lovers from U.S. competitors for works by the Old Masters. German art collectors, as Valentiner pointed out, relied on the expertise and guidance of one independent authority: the museum director. They refrained from the suspicious advice of commercial dealers or agents and turned to the scholarly authority and credibility of a public servant.

Wilhelm von Bode's rise to one of the leading positions in the German *Kaiserreich* resulted, on the one hand, from his antiphilosophical approach to art history by which he applied a methodology of "scientific connoisseurship" to the study of art that emphasized his disinterest in any particular content or meaning of art.[37] This freed him from any partisan position in the daily struggles of the art world. On the other hand, he was able to develop a trusting relationship with the most influential, powerful, and wealthy members of German society through his rather single-minded professional mission: Bode was a tireless art collector, but the works he collected invariably went to the public art collections in Berlin. The beginning of his professional activity coincided with the rise of Berlin to the center stage of the new empire after 1870. From then on, he worked as a broker for both private and public collectors with the goal of making imperial Germany's art collections a leader in the international world of art collecting.

His intimate knowledge of the art market opened the doors of rich private collectors to him. Bode was a well-known and distinguished expert because of his breadth and depth of knowledge about historical artistic objects. The diversity of his expertise ranged from Renaissance painting to oriental rugs to ancient Asian porcelains. From the 1880s onward, German art collectors compiled internationally renowned collections that contained pieces from the same artistic eras and geographical regions Bode had favored while working for the museums in Berlin. In this regard, private acquisition contributed to the common cultural property of the German nation, an argument Bode and his colleagues never tired of repeating.[38]

Bode's leadership had an opportunistic flavor to it. In his writing for the very exclusive art magazine *PAN*, he gave scholarly credibility to fairly modern attitudes of art appreciation.[39] He dined with the heads of the "Berlin secession" and advised the emperor on "tasteful" and "serious" art acquisitions. Bode never tired of propounding the idea that public collections were "schools of taste." He also helped to promote the manifesto of Julius Langbehn's *Rembrandt als Erzieher*[40] which, although "unsatisfying in its scholarship," was recommended reading for anyone with a serious interest in the rebirth of German art.[41] He was also able to convince a distinguished Jewish merchant that buying art was a great service that would benefit German national culture. Yet he also recommended that a German aristocrat take care of his fine ancient carpets, which were endangered by too many "Jewish flatfeet." He was also a "naive monarchist," as Valentiner characterized him, who, in the days of the revolution of 1918, had no difficulties in obtaining special protection for the public museums from socialist leader Rosa Luxemburg. The latter, according to Bode, "was not equaled by any other German socialist in her love and understanding for art."[42]

Bode embodied the ideal of an unbiased expert for all these different factions. To understand his influence, one must take the authoritarian structure of German society into account. Public life in the *Kaiserreich* developed slowly and only in industrialized centers. Within this context, individuals were not the main players on the art market; rather, different social groups competed for cultural supremacy. A common "genteel tradition"—upon which continuity between the old and new elements of the industrial upper classes could be established—did not exist. Instead, the aristocracy, the monarchy, educated elites, and the industrial bourgeoisie each had their own modern concepts of what aesthetic culture for the contemporary German nation should be. Bode's use of his expert authority allowed him to associate with the many social factions on a purely business basis, thereby avoiding possible controversies. He confirmed the importance of each group's ideas regarding national cultural policy and thus increased cultural segmentation in Wilhelmine society.[43]

THE MUSEUM AND THE PUBLIC

Not only did the methodology of art acquisition vary between Germany and the United States; group conventions of philanthropy also developed quite differently. When von Seidlitz compiled his list of museum friends' organizations, he overlooked a crucial difference between the U.S. and the German manifestations of collective art museum philanthropy: In the United States, the museums were actually privately owned, whereas in Germany, museum friends' associations and individuals supported institutions that for the most part were incorporated into municipal or federal agencies. In the United States, board members, patrons, and trustees were loyal to and were personally involved with their own institutions. In Germany, individuals supported a public collection independently governed by administrative experts, who did not serve a particular community or official cultural policy. Instead, they served in the name of art and were not limited by the demands of collective organizational governance.

Let me elaborate by focusing on the interactions between philanthropists and the increasingly professionalized institutions in both countries. Most of the art museums founded in the 1870s in Boston, New York, and Philadelphia started as group endeavors by members of urban upper strata.[44] The first trustees were men who "had, for the most part, grown, studied and worked together."[45] These first museum foundations were structured in keeping with established patterns of private patronage for charitable institutions—which had been established in Boston, for example, from the beginning of the nineteenth century.[46] Despite their far-reaching goals, these early museum initiatives primarily addressed their immediate social environment, reflecting the values of genteel art appreciation prevalent in the Victorian upper classes. Nevertheless, the museums were in a position to join forces with a new generation of financial contributors and supporters over the following three decades.[47] These private institutions that were open to the public were capable of integrating these new groups into the upper classes while passing on traditional conservative value systems.[48] The influence of protagonists of the new industrial elite, such as Gardner and Morgan, worked toward a professionalization of charity, in whose name the museums were originally founded. Like the large foundations of the time, effective museum administration merged the concept of noblesse oblige with scientific methodology.[49]

Morgan's plans for the Metropolitan Museum in New York were ambitious. According to Francis Taylor, Metropolitan Museum director from 1940 to 1954, Morgan began in 1904 "to create in New York a greater museum than anyone deemed it was possible to realize."[50] The boards of U.S. art museums had always included very skilled and cultivated art amateurs, but the growing collections lacked quality standards as well as a systematic method of display. In the collections, reproductions were mixed with original artworks, which came from occasional bequests. But with the rise of the great U.S. collectors such as Gardner and Morgan in the 1880s and 1890s, the need for expertise in art history became obvious. Collectors at the turn of the twentieth century applied their sophisticated knowledge of the art market to museum governance. They were the first to use their influence to hire experienced curators to work on the collections policies and visual arrangements of the museum.[51] One can see the same principles of delegated authority that had previously facilitated Morgan's and Gardner's successful acquisitions.

When Morgan resumed the presidency of the Metropolitan's board of trustees in 1904, he searched for experts who stood for the internationally most advanced standards of art history. One such expert was the young

Valentiner, who came to New York as the "Bodisatwa," the missionary of Bode's Berlin museum regime.[52] Another was Roger Fry, a representative of the British aesthetic branch of connoisseurship. Fry had a falling out with the Metropolitan board of trustees, namely with Morgan. The disagreement centered not on scholarly issues but on disagreements concerning acquisitions. Fry detested the rich banker because his unilateral buying clashed with his own intellectual method of art acquisition.[53]

"Personal taste"—as propounded by the personal sensibility of the connoisseur—was not an acceptable justification for the museum boards which had to make strategic decisions about the shape of their institutions. They relied on expert knowledge to find the most effective solution possible. Though statements in favor of a more personal selection of artwork were used in one of the best-known early discussions of U.S. museology, the "battle of the casts," which was provoked by the plans for a new building for the Museum of Fine Art in Boston to house the collections in 1904, the museum never became the center of aestheticism and connoisseurship.[54] The debate among factions of trustees and personnel has been understood as an explicit statement against the "public use" of the institution and as an aesthetic manifesto.[55] Certain members of the museum staff argued that the art museum should be committed to the ideal of individual "art appreciation" that corresponded with the private cult of personal aesthetic sensibility exemplified by Isabella Stewart Gardner and her network of cosmopolitan aesthetes.[56]

However, in Boston, as with other U.S. public art collections, the private aestheticism of the cosmopolitan elites never became the dominant strategy for art display. Despite the united efforts of connoisseurs and the behind-the-scenes intrigues of Gardner, the actual outcome of the museum was quite different from her personal installations at Fenway Court. When the second building of the museum opened in 1909, it did not convey the individuality and personality of any particular collector.[57] The museological solution for the presentation of the collection avoided all the associations with private taste that made a visit to Fenway Court such a lively encounter. Instead, the Museum of Fine Arts displayed state-of-the-art museum techniques drawn from all over Europe. Experimental studies with lighting and architecture resulted in one of the most advanced gallery arrangements of the time, and the entire building was designed to facilitate the public display of art.[58]

The rationalization of museum work through the employment of specialized curators set the stage for the further process of museological professionalization. Museums became centers of a progressive culture of experts which employed trained intellectual leaders who were beginning to form the backbone of the progressive movement.[59] Focused on promoting the educational value of their institutions, museum experts collaborated with individual philanthropists to fight the tendency of donors to attach restrictions to gifts.[60] The American Association of Museums (AAM), established in 1906, became the place where the call for a more democratic use of institutions could develop. The AAM provided a home for the museum worker and demanded a much more active role for museums in U.S. public life. Progressive museum educators, such as the Newark Museum director John C. Dana or the Metropolitan's Henry W. Kent, began to actively seek municipal and foundation funding.[61] Most art museums in the United States used the additional funding to establish departments of education and industrial design after the First World War.

Nevertheless, the scholarly and curatorial orientation of art museums did not cease to exist. The rationalization of museum work and the reconsideration of the educational mission of the institutions opened up new constituencies for the museums. Just as educators such as Kent or Dana had envisioned, public art became increasingly important for various segments of the U.S. population.[62] Professionalization turned the U.S. art museum into a multifunctional institution able to serve multiple constituencies but one which still played an important part as the center of particular elite identities.

THE AESTHETIC MISSION OF
THE ART MUSEUM IN GERMANY

For German high society, art museum philanthropy never achieved this character of social obligation and identity confirmation beyond the factions already mentioned in the realm of art acquisition and collecting. Private philanthropy in Germany worked to bring about public ownership of art treasures, which had previously been housed at aristocratic courts or owned by local art associations in commercial centers of the country. By 1920, nearly all of these art collections had been reorganized for public display and had come under state or municipal ownership. Governance was handed over to specialized experts with considerable qualifications in public administration, most of whom had obtained a degree in art history.[63]

These expert directors of the modern art galleries of Germany (*fachmännische Direktoren der modernen Galerien Deutschlands*) pursued the goal of providing impartial service in the name of art, following the administrative example of Wilhelm von Bode in the Royal Collections in Berlin.[64]

In 1897, Bode had created one of the most influential philanthropic associations of the new German Empire, the Kaiser-Friedrich-Museumsverein in Berlin. This organization was built on an organizational principle that reduced the internal contacts between its members to a minimum. Exclusively created for the purpose of raising acquisition funds for the new museum in the national capital, the internal communication among its members was limited to annual reports listing the yearly acquisitions, the names of members, and the names of donors. This internal structure shows how group competition and functions of collective governance for art museums in the United States were replaced by bilateral interactions between the museum director and the individual philanthropists in Germany. The German art philanthropist could assume that others shared Bode's motives. But a mutual understanding was not necessary for participation in organized art museum philanthropy. By preventing royal highnesses, urban patricians, court nobility, wealthy aristocrats, bourgeois industrialists, and Jewish merchants from personally interacting with each other, this form of organized philanthropy allowed for many coordinated activities in support of the art museums in the German Empire. It crafted a model for the wave of organized philanthropic initiatives.[65]

Building on this experience, German museum directors developed a very particular professional conscience. They saw themselves as protectors of an independent realm of art and very often acted in opposition to the organized interests of artists and struggled with their superiors in state administrations. This feeling was expressed in 1936 by the longtime director of the National Gallery in Berlin, Ludwig Justi. Recalling nearly twenty-five years of service for the National Art Collections, he remembered that he always felt he had worked exclusively for "the service of art."[66] Bode had developed a successful model for organizing unanimous philanthropic support for the national art collections by neutralizing antagonisms between the different factions of the imperial elite.

Diverging from this effective method of bridging group differences in the simple name of national "acquisition," the generation of German museum directors that followed Bode felt a need for more aesthetic guidance than the method of collecting based solely on business principles that characterized Bode's era. In their installations of contemporary art in the modern public galleries, Hugo von Tschudi and Ludwig Justi were informed by very elitist visions of aristocracy. It was the cultivated educated aristocrat, a "harmonic personality, who adds to the bourgeois virtues aspects of formal culture," that inspired their professional strategies of art exhibition.[67] However, this sought-after aristocratic ideal did not correspond to the lifestyles of any faction of the cultured elite or high society, not even those of Crown Prince Frederick and Crown Princess Victoria, who were renowned for their serious interest in art.[68] In fact, the aristocratic ideal was an abstraction of a higher individual with many resemblances to the type of *Übermensch* present in the popular writings of Julius Langbehn and Friedrich Nietzsche.[69]

As early as the opening of the Kaiser-Friedrich-Museum in 1904, Bode had made an attempt to illustrate the advantages of a more personal "tasteful" selection through a superior individual. The private art collection of Jewish textile merchant James Simon, donated on the occasion of the museum's opening, was prominently installed in a "collector's cabinet"—arranged the way it had been in Simon's home. This display was not presented as a reference to the personality of an extraordinarily cultivated Jewish merchant, because that would have been considered an affront toward the emperor, who was still officially in charge of his royal collections. Bode instead promoted Simon's personal cabinet as the latest achievement in art museum technology.[70] Bode's installations in the Kaiser-Friedrich-Museum were well received in the feature pages in the daily press. Highlighting Bode's achievements in the context of reactionary manifestations of autocratic *Kunstpolitik*, symbolized by Emperor Wilhelm, even the Social Democratic *Vorwärts* praised the new and harmonious presentation of national treasures that had been brought together through private initiative and opened to the broader public.[71]

Bode's program worked as long as the climate of imperial national art acquisition helped to accommodate the diverging positions of cultural politics in German society. However, the neutralization of the cultural and political conflicts in Wilhelmine society in the context of nation-building was brought into question in 1896, when Hugo von Tschudi became the director of the National Gallery. Tschudi promoted French Impressionism as the exemplary model for all future German art.[72] When Tschudi took over a public institution with the explicit goal of catering to the tastes of only a faction of the Wilhelmine cultural elite—namely the rich bourgeoisie in the industrial centers of Germany—a neutral collective agreement became impossible. Different visions of an "aristocratic" ideal clashed.

Tschudi's successor, Ludwig Justi, pursued a policy of avoiding all direct confrontation with the emperor, the Ministry of Culture, artists' associations, and the modernistic press and established once again the principle of an expert-led cultural policy. Unlike Bode, Justi was unable to find the same breadth of philanthropic support. His time as director was characterized by constant conflicts with every group that had supported the museum during Bode's time. Justi heroically defended his conviction that the museum had an independent leading role in the aesthetic education of society. His hopes, and those of many of his colleagues, were based on a belief that the expressionist avant-garde could help to reconcile the German cultural tradition with the industrial realities of the time.[73] Even after Justi's removal from office in 1933 by the National Socialists, he still hoped for a rational orientation of the National Socialist cultural policy that would be based on professional criteria. Only in 1937, when the confiscation and destruction of contemporary art in preparation for the exhibition "Degenerate Art" (*Entartete Kunst*) began, did the complete defeat of any professional standards for the governance of art museums in Germany become clear.[74]

CONCLUSION

The private collection and support of art in Germany and the United States demonstrate how public art institutions contributed to individual and national identities in an industrial society. The collecting and funding of art supported a common system of values within the upper class. It also allowed philanthropists to pursue an aesthetic ideal and to develop bonds with like-minded individuals. The museum as a public institution provided social cohesion between old and new elite groups, helping to establish a class identity. These developments in Germany highlight how different concepts of aesthetic education could be synthesized into a single vision. The authority of the museum director confirmed, on the one hand, the antagonistic group identities and aesthetic attitudes of various factions of the Wilhelmine upper classes. On the other hand, it permitted cooperation among these groups while preventing confrontations between them and obviating the need for boards of directors. This mechanism became the "glue" that held civil society together.

My investigation of the institutional and professional practice of museums shows that there were differences in the goals and the functions of elite groups in the United States and Germany. If one follows the model of Putnam, one has to acknowledge that the social interaction in boards of trustees increased trust and cooperation in these very heterogeneous bodies. Museums that were founded and financed by a single individual, such as Isabella Stewart Gardner's Fenway Court, remained exceptions and were considered part of the private sphere; they did not claim an educational role as the Museum of Fine Arts in Boston did. Museums and private art collections in the United States provided an opportunity for the new industrial elites to gain control over culture as they had acquired power over the economy.

In Germany, art collecting was less entrepreneurial and more reliant on the state, paralleling the reliance of German industry on state coordination and support. Wealthy individuals were willing to cooperate with one another in financing museums but did not accept responsibility for managing these institutions. The state control of museums that this upper-class abdication necessitated helped to create a progressive cultural atmosphere in which modernist art appeared in German museums earlier than it did in the United States. The social function of museums in the United States contrasted with their purely administrative function in Germany. After the majority of museum directors in Germany included modernist art in their collections, they lost the support of the former philanthropists, who had more conservative artistic preferences. Ludwig Justi personifies the defeat of civil society in Germany in 1933. The reason for this defeat lies, in part, in the structural changes in the support of public institutions. After Justi and his predecessors had alienated the philanthropists through their decisions to acquire modern art, the upper class did not come to the defense of the museums when they were needed. In the United States, by contrast, these institutions were still dominated by the elite groups, who might have defended them had they been threatened.

NOTES

1. Lester M. Salamon, *Global Civil Society: Dimensions of the Nonprofit Sector* (Baltimore: Johns Hopkins Center for Civil Society Studies, 1999).

2. Lester M. Salamon and Helmut K. Anheier, eds., *Defining the Nonprofit Sector: A Cross-National Analysis* (Manchester and New York: Manchester University Press, 1997). For a German overview, see Lester M. Salamon and Helmut K. Anheier, *Der Dritte Sektor: Aktuelle internationale Trends, Eine Zusammenfassung,* The Johns Hopkins Comparative Nonprofit Sector Project, Phase II (Gütersloh: Verlag Bertelsmann Stiftung, 1999).

3. Lester M. Salamon, *Partners in Public Service: Government-Nonprofit Relations in the Modern Welfare State* (Baltimore: Johns Hopkins University Press, 1995), 203–270.

4. Elizabeth T. Boris, "Organizations in a Democracy: Varied Roles and Responsibilities," in *Nonprofits and Government: Collaboration and Conflict,* ed. Elizabeth Boris and C. Eugene Steuerle (Washington, D.C.: Urban Institute Press, 1999), 3.

5. The term "accommodation" is used by Daniel M. Fox in "Introduction to the Transaction Edition" of *Engines of Culture: Philanthropy and Art Museums* (New Brunswick, N.J.: Transaction Publishers, 1995), 8. Arend Lijphard discusses accommodation prominently in the sense of "settlement of divisive issues and conflicts where only a minimal consensus exists," using the example of the subdivided society of the Netherlands. See Arend Lijphard, *The Politics of Accommodation: Pluralism and Democracy in the Netherlands* (Berkeley: University of California Press, 1968), 103.

6. Robert D. Putnam and Kristin A. Gross, "Einleitung," in *Gesellschaft und Gemeinsinn: Sozialkapital im internationalen Vergleich,* ed. Robert D. Putnam (Gütersloh: Verlag Bertelsmann Stiftung, 2001), 15–43; Robert D. Putnam, "Bowling Alone: America's Declining Social Capital," *Journal of Democracy* 6 (1995): 66. See James Coleman, *Grundlagen der Sozialtheorie,* vol. 1, *Handlungen und Handlungssysteme* (München: Oldenbourg, 1990).

7. Lester M. Salamon and Helmut K. Anheier, "Social Origins of Civil Society: Explaining the Nonprofit Sector Cross-Nationally," *Voluntas: International Journal of Voluntary and Nonprofit Organizations* 9 (1998): 213–248.

8. Gøsta Esping-Andersen, *The Three Worlds of Welfare Capitalism* (Princeton, N.J.: Princeton University Press, 1990); Barrington Moore Jr., *Social Origins of Dictatorship and Democracy: Lord and Peasant in the Making of the Modern World* (London: Allen Lane, 1966).

9. Salamon and Anheier, "Social Origins of Civil Society," 229.

10. Putnam, "Bowling Alone," 66.

11. See Gøsta Esping-Andersen, "Die drei Welten des Wohlfahrtskapitalismus: Zur Politischen Ökonomie des Wohlfahrtstaates," in *Welten des Wohlfahrtskapitalismus: Der Sozialstaat in vergleichender Perspektive,* ed. Stephan Lessenich and Illona Ostner (Frankfurt am Main and New York: Campus Verlag, 1998), 19–56; Helmut K. Anheier, "Der Dritte Sektor und der Staat," in *Dritter Sektor—Dritte Kraft: Versuch einer Standortbestimmung,* ed. Rupert Graf Strachwitz (Stuttgart: Raabe, 1998), 351–368.

12. Measured by the nonprofit share of total paid employment; Lester M. Salamon and Helmut K. Anheier, "Civil Society in Comparative Perspective," in Salamon, *Global Civil Society,* 3–40, 14, Fig. 1.5.

13. Helmut K. Anheier and Wolfgang Seibel, "Germany," in Salamon and Anheier, *Defining the Nonprofit Sector,* 128–167.

14. Ibid., 134–136. "Subsidiarity" means the general principle of public policy that delegates public authority to lower units of social organization; for example, industrial interest-group associations or religious welfare associations. See Christoph Sachsse, "Entwicklung und Perspektiven des Subsidiaritätsprinzips," in Strachwitz, ed., *Dritter Sektor—Dritte Kraft,* 369–381.

15. Ibid., 163.

16. See Karsten Borgmann and James A. Smith, "Foundations in Europe: The Historical Context," in *Foundations in Europe: Society, Management and Law—An International Reference Guide,* ed. Andreas Schlüter et al. (London: Directory of Social Change, 2001). For example, the transition from private associations and private enterprises to cooperatives, which is investigated by Brett Fairbairn in his contribution to this volume, can be seen as elements of the process through which the industrial and agricultural workers aligned their interests in order to fit the workings of the liberal market economy. This mass movement, which competed with social democracy, articulated a middle-class ideology with its own separate identity which was compatible with industrialized society.

17. W. v. Seidlitz, "Museumsvereine," *Museumskunde* 9 (1913): 36–43.

18. Examples in Manuel Frey, *Macht und die Moral des Schenkens: Staat und bürgerliche Mäzene vom späten 18. Jahrhundert bis zur Gegenwart* (Zwickau: Fannei & Walz, 1999), 112ff.; Robin Lenman, *Die Kunst, die Macht und das Geld: Zur Kulturgeschichte des kaiserlichen Deutschlands 1871–1918* (Frankfurt am Main: Campus Verlag, 1994), 78ff.; Peter Gay, *Bürger und Boheme: Kunstkriege des 19. Jahrhunderts* (München: Beck, 1999), 251ff.; Andreas Hansert, *Geschichte des Städelschen Museums-Vereins Frankfurt am Main* (Frankfurt am Main: Umschau, 1994).

19. Kenneth Hudson, *Museums of Influence* (Cambridge: Cambridge University Press, 1987), 39–64.

20. Traditional and changing missions of the art museum are discussed in Alexis Joachimides, *Die Museumsreformbewegung in Deutschland und die Entstehung des modernen Museums 1880–1940* (Dresden: Verlag der Kunst, 2000), 110–113; Neil Harris, "Museums, Merchandising and Popular Taste: The Struggle for Influence," in *Cultural Excursions: Marketing Appetites and Cultural Tastes in Modern America,* ed. Neil Harris (Chicago: University of Chicago Press, 1990), 56–81; Fox, "Introduction to the Transaction Edition," 31–41.

21. See Frederic Cople Jaher, *The Urban Establishment: Upper Strata in Boston, New York, Charleston, Chicago, and Los Angeles* (Urbana: University of Illinois Press, 1982); and Dolores L. Augustine, *Patricians and Parvenus: Wealth and High Society in Wilhelmine Germany* (Oxford and Providence: Berg Publishers, 1994).

22. W. R. Valentiner, "Reminiscences," W. R. Valentiner Papers, Manuscripts, AAA R #214, Archives of American Art, Smithsonian Institution, Washington, D.C.

23. Margaret Sterne, *The Passionate Eye: The Life of William R. Valentiner* (Detroit: Wayne State University Press, 1980), 94 and 92. See Wilhelm von Bode, *Mein Leben,* ed. Thomas W. Gaehtgens and Barbara Paul, 2 vols. (Berlin: Nicolai, 1997), 1: 296.

24. Neil Harris, "Collective Possession: J. Pierpoint Morgan and the American Imagination," in Harris, *Cultural Excursions,* 250–276; Rémy G. Saisselin, *The Bourgeois and the Bibelot* (New Brunswick, N.J.: Rutgers University Press, 1984), 77–115.

25. Harris, "Collective Possession," 260.

26. Martin Green, *The Problem of Boston: Some Readings in Cultural History* (New York: W. W. Norton, 1966), 111.

27. Address cited from a letter from Elsie de Wolfe to Isabella Stewart Gardner, January 29, 1923, Isabella Stewart Gardner Papers, Microfilm Roll no. 397, Archives of American Art, Smithsonian Institution, Washington, D.C. See also Elsie de Wolfe, *The House in Good Taste* (New York: The Century, 1914); Priscilla Leonard, "Mrs. Gardner's Venetian Palace," *Harper's Bazaar* 37 (1903): 660–662; Mary Augusta Millikin, "The Art Treasures of Fenway Court," *New England Magazine* 33 (1905): 240–250.

28. Richard Hofstadter, *The Age of Reform: From Bryan to F.D.R.* (New York: Knopf, 1955), 131–163.

29. Nathaniel Burt, *Palaces for the People: A Social History of the American Art Museum* (Boston: Little, Brown, 1977), 235–312; William G. Constable, *Art Collecting in the United States of America: An Outline of a History* (London and New York: T. Nelson, 1964), 96–140.

30. See Alfred D. Chandler Jr. and Takashi Hikino, *Scale and Scope: The Dynamics of Industrial Capitalism* (Cambridge: Belknap Press, 1990), 85–89.

31. Bode, *Mein Leben,* 1: 296–298.

32. Ernest Samuels, *Bernard Berenson: The Making of a Legend* (Cambridge, Mass.: The Belknap Press, 1979).

33. Kathleen D. McCarthy, *Women's Culture: American Philanthropy and Art, 1830–1930* (Chicago: University of Chicago Press, 1991), 149–176.

34. Rollin van N. Hadley, ed., *The Letters of Bernard Berenson and Isabella Stewart Gardner 1887–1924: With Correspondence by Mary Berenson* (Boston: Northeastern University Press, 1987); Constable, *Art Collecting in the United States,* 104.

35. Roger B. Stein, *John Ruskin and Aesthetic Thought in America, 1840–1900* (Cambridge Mass.: Harvard University Press, 1967); Kermit Vanderbilt, *Charles Eliot Norton: Apostle of Culture in a Democracy* (Cambridge, Mass: The Belknap Press, 1959).

36. Wilhelm v. Bode, "Die amerikanische Gefahr im Kunsthandel," *Kunst und Künstler* 5 (1906): 3–6.

37. Bode, *Mein Leben;* Edward P. Alexander, "Wilhelm Bode and Berlin's Museum Island," in *Museum Masters: Their Museums and Their Influence* (Nashville: American Association for State and Local History, 1983), 207–233.

38. For an overview of Berlin art collectors before World War I, see Sven Kuhrau, "Ein Hauch ererbter Kultur. Kunstsammeln also soziale Praxis im kaiserzeitlichen Berlin" (Ph.D. thesis, Free University Berlin, 2002).

39. For the role of German museum directors in the promotion of modernist art, see Robert Jensen, *Marketing Modernism in Fin-de-Siècle Europe* (Princeton, N.J.: Princeton University Press, 1996), 227–234.

40. Julius Langbehn, *Rembrandt als Erzieher: Von einem Deutschen* (Leipzig: Hirschfeld, 1890).

41. Hilmar Frank, "Übereilte Annäherung: Bode und der 'Rembrandtdeutsche,'" in *Wilhelm v. Bode als Zeitgenosse der Kunst: Zum 150. Geburtstag,* ed. Angelika Wesenberg (Berlin: Nationalgalerie, 1995), 77–82.

42. Bode, *Mein Leben,* 1: 416; cf. 2: 363 for Bode's anti-Semitic remark. The letter is mentioned in Werner Weisbach, *"Und alles ist zerstoben": Erinnerungen aus der Jahrhundertwende* (Wien: Reichner, 1937), 103ff.

43. The different factions of the Imperial German public are emphasized in Wolfgang J. Mommsen, "Kultur als Instrument der Legitimation bürgerlicher Hegemonie im Nationalstaat," in *"Der Deutschen Kunst . . ." Nationalgalerie und nationale Identität 1876–1998,* ed. Sven Kuhrau and Claudia Rückert (Amsterdam and Dresden: Verlag der Kunst, 2001), 15–29; see also Sabine Beneke, *Im Blick der Moderne: Die "Jahrhunderausstellung deutscher Kunst (1775–1875)," in der Berliner Nationalgalerie 1906* (Berlin: Bostelmann und Siebenhaar, 1999), 30–60; and Birgit Kulhoff, *Bürgerliche Selbstbehauptung im Spiegel der Kunst: Untersuchungen zur Kulturpublizistik der Rundschauzeitschriften im Kaiserreich (1871–1914)* (Bochum: Brockmeyer, 1990).

44. Helen Lefkowitz Horowitz, *Culture and the City: Cultural Philanthropy in Chicago from the 1880s to 1917* (Chicago: University of Chicago Press, 1976). See also Vera L. Zolberg, "Conflicting Visions in American Art Museums," *Theory and Society* 10 (1981): 105.

45. Neil Harris, "The Gilded Age Revisited: Boston and the Museum Movement," *American Quarterly* 14 (1962): 550.

46. Peter Dobkin Hall, *The Organization of American Culture, 1700–1900: Private Institutions, Elites, and the Origins of American Nationality* (New York: New York University Press, 1982); Ronald Story, *The Forging of an Aristocracy: Harvard and the Boston Upper Class, 1800–1870* (Middletown, Conn.: Wesleyan University Press, 1980).

47. Paul DiMaggio, "Cultural Entrepreneurship in Nineteenth-Century Boston: The Creation of an Organizational Base for High Culture in America," *Media, Culture & Society* 4 (1982): 33–50; Paul DiMaggio, "Cultural Entrepreneurship in Nineteenth-Century Boston, Part II: The Classification and Framing of Art," *Media, Culture & Society* 4 (1982): 303–322.

48. Hall, *The Organization of American Culture.* Art museum philanthropy, as recent studies have shown, is still able to attract a succession of new donors from various segments of the American population. Francie Ostrower, *Why the Wealthy Give: The Culture of Elite Philanthropy* (Princeton, N.J.: Princeton University Press, 1995); Teresa Odendahl, *Charity Begins at Home: Generosity and Self-Interest among the Philanthropic Elite* (New York: Basic Books, 1990).

49. Barry D. Karl and Stanley N. Katz, "The American Private Philanthropic Foundation and the Public Sphere, 1890–1930," *Minerva* 19 (1981): 236–270.

50. Quoted in Constable, *Art Collecting in the United States;* see Calvin Tomkins, *Merchants and Masterpieces: The Story of the Metropolitan Museum of Art* (New York: E. P. Dutton, 1970), 95–110.

51. Burt, *Palaces for the People,* 252.

52. Quoted in Bernard Berenson to Aline Saarinen, September 23, 1957, Microfilm Roll 2069, Archives of American Art, Smithsonian Institution, Washington, D.C.

53. Tomkins, *Merchants and Masterpieces,* 107.

54. Walter Muir Whitehill, *Museum of Fine Arts Boston: A Centennial History,* 2 vols. (Cambridge Mass.: Belknap Press, 1970), 1: 172–217. The "battle of the casts" refers to a controversy regarding the aesthetic value of cast copies of sculptures, which some felt lacked the emotional force of the original.

55. Theodore Lewis Low, *The Educational Philosophy and Practice of Art Museums in the United States* (New York: Columbia University, 1948), 28–52; see also Laurence Vail Coleman, *The Museum in America: A Critical Study,* 3 vols. (Washington, D.C.: American Association of Museums, 1939).

56. *Communications to the Trustees Regarding the New Building,* 4 vols. (Boston, 1904–1906). The museological thoughts of the MFA curator mentioned here, Matthew Stewart

Prichard, are exceptionally well documented in his correspondence to Isabella Stewart Gardner in "Prichard on Museums," Microfilm Roll 389, Archives of American Art, Smithsonian Institution, Washington, D.C. The Boston "aesthetic movement," whose central figures included Prichard, MFA president Sam Warren, and Isabella Stewart Gardner, is portrayed by Martin Green in *The Mount Vernon Street Warrens: A Boston Story, 1860–1910* (New York: Charles Scribner's Sons, 1989).

57. "Prichard on Museums."

58. The guiding principles of Gilman's essays on museum theory were published by the Museum of Fine Art in 1918 in *Museum Ideals of Purpose and Method* (Cambridge, Mass.: Museum of Fine Art, 1918). Gilman contributed to the annual meetings of American Association of Museums, founded in 1906, on a regular basis.

59. Barry D. Karl, "Philanthropy and the Maintenance of Democratic Elites," *Minerva* 35 (1997): 207–220.

60. Fox, *Engines of Culture*, 45.

61. Paul J. DiMaggio, "Constructing an Organizational Field as a Professional Project: U.S. Art Museums 1920–1940," in *The New Institutionalism in Organizational Analysis*, ed. Walter W. Powell and Paul J. DiMaggio (Chicago: University of Chicago Press, 1991), 267–292.

62. Thomas Ritchie Adam, *The Museum and Popular Culture* (New York: American Association for Adult Education, 1939).

63. See Else Biram, *Die Industriestadt als Boden neuer Kunstentwicklung* (Jena: Diederichs, 1919), 51–53; Hans Schröter, "Maler und Galerie: Das Verhältnis der Maler zu den öffentlichen Galerien Deutschlands im 19. Jahrhundert" (Ph.D. thesis, Free University, Berlin, 1954).

64. Ludwig Justi, *Werden—Wissen—Wirken: Lebenserinnerungen aus fünf Jahrzehnten*, edited by Thomas W. Gaehtgens and Kurt Winkler, 2 vols. (Berlin: Nicolai, 2001), 1: 221ff.

65. See Frey's overview of the development of upper-class philanthropy in *Macht und die Moral des Schenkins*, 71–124. Philanthropy is analyzed by Dieter Hein in "Das Stiftungswesen als Instrument bürgerlichen Handelns im 19. Jahrhundert," in Bernhard Kirchgässner and Hans-Peter Brecht, eds., *Stadt und Mäzenatentum* (Sigmaringen: Thorbecke, 1997), 75–92.

66. Justi, *Werden—Wissen—Wirken: Lebenserinnerungen aus fünf Jahrzehnten*, 1: 221ff.

67. See Gustav Pauli, *Alfred Lichtwark* (Hamburg: Kunsthalle zu Hamburg, 1920), 7ff.

68. Irma und Gisela Richter, eds., *Italienische Malerei der Renaissance im Briefwechsel von Giovanni Morelli und Jean Paul Richter: 1876–1891* (Baden-Baden: Grimm, 1960); see Wilhelm Bode and Robert Dohme, *Katalog der Ausstellung von Gemälden älterer Meister im Berliner Privatbesitz: Veranstaltet zu Ehren der silbernen Hochzeit Ihrer K. u. K. Hoheiten des Kronprinzen und der Frau Kronprinzessin des Deutschen Reiches und von Preußen im Jahre 1883* (Berlin, 1884).

69. Bernd Behrendt, *Zwischen Paradox und Paralogismus: Weltanschauliche Grundzüge einer Kulturkritik in den neunziger Jahren des 19. Jahrhunderts am Beispiel August Julius Langbehn* (Frankfurt am Main: Lang, 1984); Gerhard Kratzsch, *Kunstwart und Dürerbund: Ein Beitrag zur Geschichte der Gebildeten im Zeitalter des Imperialismus* (Göttingen: Vandenoeck und Ruprecht, 1969); Fritz Stern, *Kulturpessimismus als politische Gefahr: Eine Analyse nationaler Ideologie in Deutschland* (Bern, Stuttgart, and Vienna: Scherz, 1963), 127–221.

70. Wilhelm v. Bode, "Das Kaiser Friedrich-Museum in Berlin. Zur Eröffnung am 18. Oktober 1904," *Museumskunde* 1 (1904): 1–16.

71. E. S., "Kaiser-Friedrich-Museum," *Der Vorwärts. Zentralorgan der Socialdemokratischen Partei Deutschlands* (October 19, 1904).

72. Justi, *Werden—Wissen—Wirken*, 238–245; Beneke, *Im Blick der Moderne*, 60–75; Sabine Beneke, *Hugo von Tschudi—Nationalcharakter der Moderne um die Jahrhundert-*

wende, in Rückert and Kuhrau, *Nationalgalerie und nationale Identität,* 44–60; Barbara Paul, *Hugo von Tschudi und die moderne französische Kunst im Deutschen Kaiserreich* (Mainz: von Zabern, 1993).

73. See Justi, *Werden—Wissen—Wirken,* 456; Kurt Winkler, *Tradition und Zeitgenossenschaft: Zu Ludwig Justis Memoiren,* in Justi, *Werden—Wissen—Wirken,* 1: 1–12, 2.

74. In 1937, Joseph Goebbels ordered the exhibition in Munich of a collection of what the Nazis called "degenerate art" (*Entartete Kunst*), a term that referred to any type of art that deviated from an imagined "realistic" ideal.

THREE

Self-Help and Philanthropy: The Emergence of Cooperatives in Britain, Germany, the United States, and Canada from Mid-Nineteenth to Mid-Twentieth Century

BRETT FAIRBAIRN

INTRODUCTION:
COOPERATION AND PHILANTHROPY

This chapter is a preliminary excursion into a little-examined territory, the overlap between two different categories of social action. A cooperative is a democratic association of people who operate an enterprise for their own use.[1] In cooperatives, people help themselves and others like them in mutual acts of self-help. By contrast, philanthropy is a personal act of aid to others; more narrowly, it is often seen as aid from the better-off for the general good of a community or for the specific well-being of less-privileged individuals. Most definitions of philanthropy would exclude cases in which the giver of aid derives a material benefit from giving it. With these definitions, it would appear that cooperatives differ from the idea of philanthropy in two basic respects. First, it is typically presumed that the persons involved in cooperatives derive personal material gain from their involvement. Second, mutual self-help in cooperatives is normally conceptualized as self-help among equals, not from those of higher social rank to those of a lower rank. These abstract distinctions become muddy in practice, however. Cooperatives have often been seen as serving wider causes of social reform and improvement, so it is not always clear that individuals who join and support them do so for direct personal benefits alone. Moreover, cooperatives have often been aided by or patronized from outside the circle of those for whom they have been intended. In important cases in many countries, this aid has unquestionably been philanthropic in character.

Cooperatives originated in Britain, and the British consumer cooperative movement was the world's leader and the model for other countries until well into the twentieth century. It is appropriate, therefore, to begin a consideration of philanthropy and cooperatives by looking at the original British case. Other kinds of cooperatives first originated in Germany—credit cooperatives and agricultural cooperatives—and these eventually became the most widely spread and biggest worldwide arms of the cooperative movement. Here, too, the role of philanthropic aid and inspiration is relevant. Based on such European examples, cooperatives spread internationally, including to North America. This chapter will examine the histories of the cooperative movements in Britain, Germany, the United States, and Canada in order to highlight the role of philanthropy in popular social and economic reform in the four countries.

MIDDLE-CLASS FOUNDERS OF
BRITISH COOPERATIVE INSTITUTIONS

Britain is well known as the country where the modern cooperative movement originated. Those who examine the British model of cooperation usually cite the example of the Rochdale Society of Equitable Pioneers, created in 1844 by a group of weavers and Owenite socialist activists. In fact, cooperatives started in the 1760s and Rochdale was built on a foundation of three generations of experimentation, but Rochdale came to sum up the British movement. The term "Rochdale" denotes a localist and social-reformist strain of cooperation, one considered more authentic and more transformative than others because of its emphases on democratic participation and education as well as economic success. In its context, the Rochdale tradition also meant a concentration on working-class participation through consumer-owned cooperative stores; ultimately, Rochdale and its successors and imitators became identified with labor politics and the vision of a new society in the form of a "co-operative common-wealth."[2] Whenever cooperators in other countries invoked the spirit and example of Rochdale, they were calling for genuine and democratic cooperatives and were usually stressing one aspect or another of the British movement's traditions and structures. People often overlook the facts that the British cooperative movement did not begin and end with Rochdale and that in certain critical respects it was helped along by the philanthropic assistance of notables who were not from working-class backgrounds. Even the paradigmatic British case has embedded within it strains of philanthropy.

When one looks at the institutionalization of cooperatives in nine-teenth-century Britain, all roads lead to Robert Owen. Owen, the reform-ing factory owner of the New Lanark mills, critic of industrial society, advocate of social improvement, and patron of utopian communities, was one of the emblematic personalities of the nineteenth century. Historian John F. C. Harrison sees Owenism as part of a complex of ideas that emerged in the context of North Atlantic industrial civilization.[3] Owen mirrored the ambiguities of a transitional age, combining in his person many contradictory elements. Owen was, among other things, a transat-lantic philanthropist who used his money and his name to support cooper-ation in both Britain and the United States. He was one of the first people to whom the term "socialist" was applied. E. P. Thompson saw the doctrine to which Owen gave his name as the culmination of the process in which the English working class became conscious of itself as a class.[4] Nine-teenth-century cooperators honored him as the father of cooperation.[5] All of these characterizations are deceptively simplistic.

Owen's own great interest was in criticizing the dehumanizing aspects of industrialism and in promoting "Villages of Co-operation" in which better human beings could be raised. His promotion of cooperative com-munities (of which four major ones were founded in Scotland, Ireland, England, and the United States) was ultimately unsuccessful in that such communities did not last long or multiply and they cost Owen a great deal of money, although as social experiments they continue to fascinate.[6] His largely working-class followers, who referred to themselves as Owenites, ap-pear to have shared Owen's communitarian ideal as well as his belief in the transformative power of education, but in other important respects they differed from him. Owenites in various parts of Britain were impatient about waiting for a wealthy philanthropist to provide them with a ready-made community and initiated hundreds of educational and economic self-help projects and organizations, including cooperatives. As Thompson wrote, "The notion of working-class advance, by its own self-activity to-wards its own goals, was alien to Owen, even though he was drawn . . . into exactly this kind of movement."[7] According to one of the cooperative labor movement's historians, George Jacob Holyoake, Owen's dreams were too large and impractical: "The world admired but did not subscribe, and it was left to chequeless enthusiasts to find funds to diffuse a knowledge of the new views."[8] These "chequeless enthusiasts" turned to cooperatives as a vehicle for their projects.

The complicated relationship between Owen and his followers is epito-mized by the Third Cooperative Congress held in 1832 in London. Owen had convened nationwide congresses and sought to dominate them; at the London congress, the cooperative delegates rejected his domination and distanced themselves from his controversial religious and political beliefs. "Whereas the co-operative world contains persons of every religious sect and of every political party," the delegates affirmed, "it is resolved that co-operators as such, jointly and severally, are not pledged to any political, religious or irreligious tenets whatsoever; neither those of Mr. Owen, nor of any other individual."[9] This declaration of intellectual autonomy became the standing motto on the cooperative movement's publications and served as the basis for the later articulation of a principle of neutrality in politics and religion among cooperatives. Owen's movement wore as a badge its disavowal of those of his ideas it did not like. In light of Owen's case, we have to wonder to what extent middle-class founders and patrons of cooperative movements were primarily figureheads. This is not to say that such individuals were "mere" figureheads, for in early nineteenth-century European society, and perhaps later, legitimate figureheads were very important. "Robert Owen carried Co-operation into good company," wrote Holyoake.[10] It is a possibility worth keeping in mind that the most important contribution of philanthropists may not have been either their ideas or their money, but rather their names, their social standing and connections, their respectability.

The model of cooperative shopkeeping that spread among Owen's followers was articulated and codified by another non-working-class person, Dr. William King of Brighton. King was a local notable, a progressive provincial physician, and a promoter of children's and adult education as well as thrift societies before he discovered cooperatives. King was involved in launching a new cooperative association in Brighton in the 1820s, and he codified its experiences in a monthly journal, *The Co-operator*, which he wrote from 1828 to 1830. After the journal folded, the collected issues continued to circulate as a kind of bible of cooperative storekeeping. In them, King set out the plan later incorporated into the bylaws of the Rochdale Pioneers: that working people could accumulate capital by operating and patronizing a shop and that this capital could then be used to initiate further projects in manufacturing, employment of members, housing construction, and in due course a full cooperative colony resembling Owen's model. King, in other words, laid out a plan for achieving Owen's goal by gradualism and self-help without philanthropic investment.[11]

Edward Vansittart Neale provides another compelling example of a philanthropist who promoted the development of the British cooperative movement in its critical stages. Neale was a lawyer, a Christian socialist, a member of the gentry, and a well-connected Tory who helped the movement obtain new legislation and national institutions in the 1840s and 1850s. He persuaded his Christian socialist colleagues—for the most part clerics who turned after the unrest of 1848 to promoting self-help for workers—to support the growing Rochdale movement of consumer cooperatives. Neale also helped the movement obtain the Industrial and Provident Societies Act of 1852, the first legislation designed for cooperatives; he encouraged cooperatives to band together to form cooperative wholesaling companies; and he struggled to educate the cooperative movement and draw it together into national meetings and institutions. His legal work for the movement was virtually pro bono (he sent the Rochdale Pioneers an invoice for £7.7.0 to pay for his work in guiding the new act through the House of Commons, of which £5.5.0 was to be paid to the Cotton Famine Relief Fund), and he lost something like £40,000–60,000 of his own money, and eventually his family's London house and country estate, in ill-fated investments in cooperative projects and companies. Most of his projects failed, yet they presaged the successful founding of new institutions only a few years later. The founding of the Cooperative Wholesale Society in 1863, the revival of the cooperative congresses in 1869–1871, and the eventual creation of the Cooperative Union in 1873 owed a great deal to Neale's work. Although he had a considerable impact, his work did not persuade cooperators to embrace either Christian socialism or Toryism; most of the friends Neale found were indeed Liberals. According to Philip N. Backstrom, "The great irony of Neale's life was that he ultimately became the leader of a powerful movement which benefited from the organisations he designed, while rejecting the purpose behind them."[12]

Philanthropists clearly played significant roles in the British movement. What Owen, King, and Neale contributed was a combination of ideas, legitimacy, and models; they especially furthered the development of national movements and institutions. They invested their time and, in the cases of Owen and Neale, large sums of money, though it is not clear that the money had much of an effect. The Rochdale myth is one of working-class self-help and is not inaccurate as myths go, but it is also true that the self-help of the Rochdale weavers was inspired by ideas of the entrepreneurial philanthropist Owen, following a model spelled out in detail by provincial philanthropist King and replicated in national institutions with the aid of Christian-inspired gentry Tory Neale. The development of English cooperatives was less unlike the development in Germany than is commonly supposed.

THE INVENTION OF
COOPERATIVES IN GERMANY

One of the clearest connections of philanthropy to cooperatives can be found in Germany, where those credited with being the great founders of cooperatives were middle-class social reformers. The creation of cooperatives issued from, overlapped with, and differed from philanthropic projects in a variety of ways and invites detailed examination.

Associations flourished in nineteenth-century Germany and provided a framework for the constitution of civic life as absolutism gave way to a liberalized economy and society. Many of the associations of the time had clear charitable or philanthropic elements: food associations, winter-help associations, and eventually, credit associations. Prominent individuals and groups organized these associations to help those who were less well-off; as time went on, a number of the latter began to appreciate the potential of self-help as a component, articulation, or replacement for charity. The credit associations created for people on poor relief by G. S. Liedke in Berlin in the 1840s were near the cusp of change, still predominantly charitable but beginning to stress the moral significance of self-help.[13] Some benevolent associations, such as the Gesellschaft zur Beschaffung von billigen Winterbedürfnissen created by "democrats" in Frankfurt am Main, later transformed themselves into cooperatives. In the Frankfurt case (where the Gesellschaft was converted to a cooperative in 1855), the city government, which had previously subsidized the distribution of potatoes to the poor, continued the subsidy by providing interest-free loans to the cooperative.[14]

But these reformers did not invent cooperatives, even though they were groping toward them in the 1840s. It was workers and perhaps peasants who appear to have taken the decisive steps to create the first fully member-directed cooperatives. These may have included communal village bakeries in the Hunsrück and on the Rhine, various kinds of cooperative or proto-cooperative credit associations, and—by the 1850s at the latest—communal wine cellars in the Rhineland, which were among the first to describe themselves using the modern term for cooperative, *Genossenschaft*.[15] At the very latest, the first modern cooperatives can be seen by mid-1849, issuing from the revolutions of the previous year and the activities of the General German Workers' Fraternity (Allgemeine Deutsche Arbeiterverbrüderung). Scores of workers' consumption or production/marketing associations were created during 1849.[16] Cooperatives, in Germany as other countries, were created by scattered and autonomous impulses that appeared to issue from the working classes and from peasants. German cooperatives were not, in fact, invented by middle-class thinkers. However, more so than in most other countries they were assimilated into a framework shaped by middle-class reformism and philanthropy.

The task of defining, categorizing, and Germanizing the concept of the cooperative association was taken up by a series of middle-class intellectuals and organizers. Victor Aimé Huber was perhaps the first German writer to formally present the idea of cooperatives, though he created none himself.

Huber was a college professor, an educated man from an educated background, and a monarchical conservative. His interest in social reform began with a trip to England in 1844, when he visited Manchester, observed British industrial development, and made contact with some of the Christian Socialists. Writing from the mid-1840s to the 1860s, he publicized the cooperative movements in England and France and defined various kinds of cooperatives, or (as he called them) *Assoziationen*, in Germany.[17] The link between cooperatives and conservatism, in Huber's case, was the moral improvement of the worker and the social peace that would be achieved through the stabilization and integration of the working classes. He saw "the solution to one of the most pressing tasks of the fateful, unsettled present" in "the transformation of propertyless workers into working owners."[18] This would bring the workers not only material advantages but also "a corresponding increase in moral and intellectual energies . . . while respecting the independence, self-sufficiency and sacredness of family life."[19] This tendency to see the cooperative as a lower-class institution embodying bourgeois values—therefore worthy of promotion—was shared by Hermann Schulze-Delitzsch, the great founder of cooperatives, despite the partisan differences between the two men.

Schulze-Delitzsch, like Huber, was a member of the educated middle classes; he was a member of the legal profession, an estate-court judge in Saxony from a family that had produced a number of judges and local officials.[20] Unlike Huber, he was a Liberal. A formative experience for Schulze-Delitzsch was his election to the Prussian National Assembly in 1848, where he emerged as a spokesperson for artisans and was involved in committees that heard their grievances. Schulze-Delitzsch's first involvement in creating an association was a sickness and death fund created in 1849 in Delitzsch, which however was not fully democratic and egalitarian in character. Late in 1849 he helped create two associations to purchase raw materials for furniture-makers and cobblers, which are recognized in standard histories (which, curiously, ignore the Arbeiterverbrüderung's workers' organizations) as "the first two co-operatives in Germany."[21] These were followed by his first *Vorschußverein*, or credit association, in 1850. By about 1852, the classic form of Schulze-Delitzsch association—the self-help credit association based on unlimited liability—had taken form. His ideas began to circulate and he became a well-known public figure in the mid-1850s through his publications, notably his *Assoziationsbuch für deutsche Handwerker und Arbeiter* (1853) and his periodical *Die Innung der Zukunft* beginning in 1854. He was recognized for his efforts at the Kongreß Deutscher Volkswirte in Gotha (September 1858), where participants voted unanimously to urge Germans to support his organizations. It was at that congress that the proposal was made to replace the foreign term "*As-*

soziation" with the German word *"Genossenschaft."*[22] The name change had nationalistic appeal, it helped legitimate cooperatives in Germany, and it distanced them from socialist production societies in France.

Schulze-Delitzsch was a tireless publicist and activist for his cooperatives, and he systematically created an organizational structure to support them as they multiplied in number. In 1859 he convened the first cooperative congress in Weimar and founded a central business office to facilitate business exchanges and discussions among the credit cooperatives. These developments culminated in the creation in 1861 of a federation that was eventually known as the Allgemeiner Verband. The leader of the movement was of course Schulze-Delitzsch until his death in 1883. He secured, through the assistance of Liberal colleagues, the creation of a bank in 1864, the Deutsche Genossenschaftsbank von Soergel, Parisius & Co., which served the needs of the multiplying cooperatives. These institutions jealously guarded the movement's autonomy from the state. Schulze-Delitzsch and a number of his Liberal colleagues created an umbrella under which self-help cooperatives were nurtured and protected from state interference. In a diffuse but significant sense, a relationship of patronage is implied in the sponsorship of cooperatives by Liberals. Concerning Schulze-Delitzsch's dominant role, Huber wrote: "This predominant general influence of a single person, this decisive participation by people of higher classes in the individual cooperatives, is entirely of a voluntary, moral, and intellectual nature and does no damage to the character of self-help."[23] Schulze-Delitzsch derived no adequate income from all his endeavors; he lived humbly for his class and depended on gifts from better-off Liberal friends. And yet this was not entirely a disinterested philanthropy but one that promoted the social and political values of Liberalism. Cooperatives were expected to reflect Liberal notions of economic rationalism, antisocialism, opposition to state intervention, and nationalism as well as values of thrift, self-improvement, and self-education to create worthy citizens. Moreover, while initially Schulze-Delitzsch wrote about cooperatives helping "workers," and while occasionally he or his followers referred to possibilities for peasants to form cooperatives, it was increasingly the *Mittelstand,* or lower middle class—artisans and later shopkeepers—that was the focus of the Schulze-Delitzsch movement. This focus on the *Mittelstand* reflected Liberal priorities and social theory. So while it is true that Schulze-Delitzsch argued for his cooperatives to be nonpartisan, and this perspective was written into the Prussian cooperative law of 1867, they were nevertheless political.

A similar mixture of philanthropy, political and cultural values, and assistance for self-help imbued the thinking of the other great founder of German cooperatives, Friedrich Wilhelm Raiffeisen. Raiffeisen belongs, unlike Schulze-Delitzsch, in the category of the conservative communal officials who sponsored charitable projects in the 1840s. Raiffeisen's administrative role as a rural junior Prussian official led him to organize citizens for community improvement projects that were initially public or philanthropic in character but later focused on cooperative self-help. Several characteristics distinguished Raiffeisen from other founders of social-welfare associations in the 1840s. First, his activities focused on rural areas, most immediately on the impoverished Westerwald on the right bank of the Rhine and its struggling peasant farmers. A second distinguishing feature was his energy and tenacity in founding and driving associations; a characteristic that later in his life, at least to critics, looked more like obstinacy. Finally, and perhaps most important, Raiffeisen learned by doing, and discovered against his own better judgment that cooperation seemed to work better than charity. His career as a developer of organizations encapsulates the gradual and complicated transition from philanthropy to self-help.[24]

Raiffeisen's organizing zeal seems to have cooled after his initial experiences in 1846–1854. According to his own account, he was disillusioned about the way his charitable ventures fell apart without constant effort and about how reluctant citizens were to increase their contributions over time or to assume greater risk. In the following years, Raiffeisen seems to have heard of Schulze-Delitzsch's experiments and to have decided to imitate or adapt them. In 1862 he founded four new associations, credit cooperatives he referred to as *Darlehenskassenvereine* (DKV), around Neuwied. For the first time Raiffeisen introduced the idea that the recipients of financial assistance were also to be members of the association and to help run it—the essential notion of self-help that makes a cooperative. Raiffeisen's Anhausen association of 1862 was the first to put this principle into practice; his 1864 Heddesdorf DKV (which built on people involved in one of his earlier charitable associations) was the first to write it into the statutes.

In 1865 Raiffeisen retired from the civil service due to ill health—an old eye injury that eventually left him blind and dependent on his daughter Amalie to conduct his correspondence—and devoted himself fully to the promotion of his new movement. He published his ideas in book form in 1866, essentially a manual that showed how to found and operate rural credit cooperatives.[25] He made contact with the Rhineland Agricultural Association, which began to promote his ideas; with members of the clergy; and with the agriculture ministry in Berlin, where some officials gradually became supporters. Geographically the Raiffeisen movement spread outward from the Rhineland into neighboring provinces and states, then throughout Germany by means, primarily, of the networks of agricultural reformers, local officials, and the clergy. Like Schulze-Delitzsch, Raiffeisen struggled to support himself while developing central institutions for his growing movement. Compared with the Liberal parliamentarian, Raiffeisen was both more ambitious and less successful. Raiffeisen created his own federation of cooperatives, later known as the Generalverband. He also made a series of attempts in the late 1860s and 1870s to create central banking institutions, which were bitterly criticized on technical grounds by Schulze-Delitzsch and his followers; in the end, Raiffeisen was able to set up only a weak and scaled-down set of regional cooperative central banks. Raiffeisen also set up a wholesaling company to supply his cooperatives with goods for sale to rural people (unlike those of Schulze-Delitzsch, Raiffeisen's associations were generally multipurpose cooperatives that also handled farm and consumer goods) and attempted to provide a living for himself and other organizers from the company's profits.

Having adapted the idea of self-help from Schulze-Delitzsch, Raiffeisen went about redesigning it, in effect reintroducing as many elements of charity and communal solidarity as he could—ideas that were similar to those of his pre-1862 organizations. Raiffeisen preferred cooperatives that had no shares and no share capital, hence also no dividends—they were strictly collective and nonprofit, with any surplus going into indivisible reserves.

The term "indivisible" means that profits were not distributed annually to members (as in patronage refunds in the Rochdale model) and that accumulated multiyear reserves would never be paid out to individual members, not even if the cooperative was dissolved. Essentially the word "indivisible" carries the connotation that individual members could not receive individual benefits from the funds. The surplus provided reserves for the cooperative and could be used for collective purposes determined by the administrative council and/or membership—usually reinvestment in expanded cooperative services, projects for the benefit of the wider community (benefits not limited to members—public goods, in effect), donations to charitable causes, and the like. In the case of the dissolution of such a cooperative, the accumulated net reserves would typically be donated to some nonprofit cause.

Raiffeisen cooperatives were happy to accept interest-free loans from notables as a way of capitalizing their operations—an unbusinesslike approach of which Schulze-Delitzsch disapproved, considering it a compromising of self-help and autonomy. Raiffeisen also preferred cooperatives that had no paid leaders or management: Everything was to be done, if possible, by volunteer officers. In legal and political disputes with Schulze-Delitzsch, Raiffeisen was forced to compromise on some of these matters, but his underlying vision remained an idealistic one of solidaristic cooperation with a minimum of individualism and formalism. These statutory features were complemented by practices that accentuated the communitarian character of the Raiffeisen cooperatives. It was common, for example, for a local official to convene the founding members, instigate the formation of a cooperative, and perhaps serve as its chairperson. It was even more common for the local priest to serve as the bookkeeper. This gave the authority of both state and church to the resulting cooperatives. Raiffeisen exhorted all local citizens to join his cooperatives, even or especially the wealthy, who would thereby demonstrate their practical support for their poorer neighbors. All of these elements of social solidarity or philanthropy coexisted with rigorous formal democracy in which each peasant borrower had one vote that was exactly equal to the vote of the official, the priest, or the landowner sitting at the same table.

Raiffeisen chose to open his book with a pessimistic view of society's moral decay:

> The struggle for existence is being conducted with an earnestness and restlessness that was previously unknown. . . . A wild chase for greater earning and greater possession dominates among the productive classes. . . . In the lower classes an ever increasing addiction to life and pleasure is similarly widespread; envy and hate against the propertied are ominously winning the upper hand in their ranks; the party of social revolution, despite legal hindrances, finds growing support for its plans for the subversion of our whole state and social system.[26]

Raiffeisen saw his projects as primarily directed toward the moral regeneration of the lower classes, and of the upper classes as well, through an idealistic communitarian solidarity between the two groups. The economic aspect of his associations was a means to an ideological end. As he put it:

> It is well known that spiritual well-being cannot be separated from material well-being. . . . Poverty and material corruption are undoubtedly the most favorable seedbeds for crime and burdens of all kinds. . . . Insofar as one awakens among the needy the desire to work themselves upward and to attain a better living station, one also calls forth in them the urge to increase their moral and physical energies to the highest levels. Hard work and thrift are produced, qualities that bring many others in their train.[27]

As we have seen, Raiffeisen was not alone in such sentiments.

The dominant formulations of cooperative self-help issued from the moral and political visions of mid-nineteenth-century, middle-class liberalism and conservatism; it was, however, implicit in the idea of mutual self-help that the lower classes might take their self-determination in other directions than the ones intended. By the early twentieth century, most of the associations inspired by Schulze-Delitzsch did not support his political creed; breakaway federations had formed for conservative Mittelstand cooperatives and for Social Democratic consumer cooperatives. Similarly, most cooperators who praised Raiffeisen's example shied away from his particular moral, conservative, and religious teachings; a more secular and statist Imperial Federation of Agricultural Cooperatives had a far larger membership than Raiffeisen's old Generalverband. Middle-class reformers were effective at starting cooperative movements but not at sustaining them. It is important to consider to what extent the role of great founders such as Schulze-Delitzsch and Raiffeisen may be a constructed national myth. If the role of middle-class—we might say philanthropic—reformers is exaggerated in Germany, it is downplayed in England. The role of notables in sponsoring cooperatives was not peculiar to Germany. It was, rather, a recurring pattern in transatlantic society from the mid-nineteenth to the early twentieth centuries.

SPONSORS OF U.S. COOPERATION

On the other side of the Atlantic, cooperative development was less marked by Old World social realities of class, hierarchy, and ideology, and yet things were not as different as one might think. One of the intriguing patterns of the emergence of cooperatives in the United States is that while farm cooperatives issued primarily from farmers, extension service educators, and government officials, most kinds of consumer cooperatives received a decisive early impetus from middle-class patrons, propagandists, and reformers. The United States may indeed epitomize the philanthropic promotion of cooperatives by the wealthy.

One interesting type that is present in several countries is that of the employer who organized consumer cooperatives for his employees. N. O. Nelson, a self-made St. Louis manufacturer known for profit-sharing experiments in his own company in the 1880s, organized a successful consumer cooperative among his employees in 1892. In the years that followed, Nelson became the largest single force behind a movement that turned the Midwest into a center of cooperative storekeeping.[28] Impatient to promote the schemes, he founded Nelson Cooperative Stores in the New Orleans and St. Louis areas and used his own money to buy a chain of retail stores, inviting his customers to buy shares and take them over. By 1917, there were sixty-one stores, meat markets, a bakery, a dairy, a coffee-roasting plant, and a large farm. Nelson's stores followed a policy of price-cutting competition rather than the more staid Rochdale practice of year-end refunds to patrons; it was this price-cutting policy that led to price wars with competitors and finally, after thirty years, destroyed his cooperatives and bankrupted him.[29] While Nelson stood out for his role in the region, he was not the only businessman who promoted cooperatives; he was, however, the most clearly philanthropic.

Nelson's projects ultimately failed because he did not create institutions that were self-sustaining. Two other individuals, however, succeeded on a national scale in promoting particular groups of cooperatives and in creating central organizations for them.

Dr. James Peter Warbasse was chief surgeon of the German Hospital in Brooklyn, New York, for thirteen years. He edited a medical journal, wrote a surgery textbook, and was a prominent and respected member of his profession. He became interested in cooperatives after observing them in Germany during his medical studies there and found himself involved when a small number of New York City cooperators wanted to create a new organization. In 1916 Warbasse hosted a meeting in his home where the Cooperative League of the United States was founded. Three years later, at the age of fifty-three, Warbasse resigned from his career in surgery to devote himself full-time to the promotion and organization of cooperatives. He went on to serve as the league's president for twenty-five years and as a director for forty-one years.[30] During this time he established himself as the leading propagandist in North America for consumer cooperation. He and his wife Agnes, who was the league's education director, worked without pay; in addition, by his own estimation, he spent $150,000 of his own money supporting the league.[31] During Warbasse's years, consumer cooperatives of various types multiplied across the United States and grew in strength to the point where the league could become a self-sustaining cooperative federation.

Warbasse's enthusiasm for consumer cooperation was visionary, radical, and well suited to intense social and political conflict of the interwar years. Warbasse believed consumer cooperatives could gradually expand until they assimilated every branch of the economy, resulting in the creation of a new kind of economic system and a new social order. In a period when capitalism appeared to be failing and communism and fascism seemed to be the alternatives, Warbasse held out cooperatives as the economic basis for the survival and renewal of democracy. These stirring ideas were put forth in his classic *Cooperative Democracy* and in countless articles, editorials, and speeches. But although Warbasse advocated democracy on a grand scale, he was reluctant to practice it in his own organization. He kept the Cooperative League tightly focused as an agency of education and development, promoting his own distinctive ideas. As cooperatives multiplied, he resisted sharing control with them and resisted the evolution of the league into a federation that would be more open, more inclusive, and necessarily more diffuse. He was suspicious of agricultural cooperatives, seeing them as agents of individualistic and particularist farm interests that would dilute the universal transformative power of consumer cooperation; he would have preferred consumer control of farmland, too. Warbasse's thinking and approach are probably causes of the deep division between agricultural and consumer cooperatives that has characterized the U.S. movement. His successor as president of the league in 1941, Murray Lincoln, came from the farm movement and agreed to join only after being assured that Warbasse's ideas were not the official policy of the league—a distancing from the founder's ideas somewhat reminiscent of Owen's legacy.

The idea of philanthropy with respect to cooperatives brings to mind one American more than all others: Boston department store owner Edward A. Filene. Filene inherited a prominent Boston family enterprise, taking it over when his father suffered ill health. Filene was a thoughtful and innovative entrepreneur who became known as a leader in the development of modern merchandising, but his lifelong concern was with the social role of business and the social obligations of businesspeople. He undertook experiments in his own stores to share power and profits with employees, set up numerous charitable foundations to promote innovative social and economic reforms, and wrote and spoke widely on social issues. He felt that the emerging mass consumer economy offered the potential for social progress and that businesses played a role in such progress. Filene saw that credit for ordinary people would be a key issue in a new age of mass production and mass consumption. The credit union was a mechanism to meet this need. By making the economy work more smoothly and more efficiently, credit unions would help create a new era of mass prosperity.[32]

Filene became interested in credit unions during a visit in 1907 to India. He encountered a British civil servant who had dedicated himself to introducing credit societies in India—by this time, hundreds, possibly thousands, had been created in that country, based on the Raiffeisen model and influenced by British colonial officials.[33] He became involved with North American credit cooperatives in 1909, when he was one of a group of industrialists and merchants who lobbied successfully to have credit union legislation passed by the state of Massachusetts. This initiative was organized by well-connected Bostonian Pierre Jay, the state commissioner of banks. In 1908, Jay invited *caisse populaire* (people's bank) founder Alphonse Desjardins of Québec to meet Boston citizens and discuss his ideas of cooperative credit. Based on adaptations of Desjardins's model, the credit union movement began to develop slowly in the United States.[34]

Credit unions had been conceived, had been established, and were slowly spreading; Filene's contribution was to accelerate this process rapidly. In 1921 he established a Credit Union Extension Bureau based in Boston, financed from his own personal resources, and hired cooperative organizer

Roy F. Bergengren to travel the country. From 1921 until 1934 (when it was replaced by the self-supporting Credit Union National Association, C.U.N.A.), Filene and Bergengren's bureau laid the groundwork for what became a rapidly growing movement of mutual financial self-help. The bureau had four central objectives: to legalize credit unions in all states; to "Americanize" the credit union idea by experimenting in forms appropriate to the United States; to form state leagues to promote and guide credit unions; and to organize a national association. By 1934 Filene and Bergengren had largely succeeded in all objectives. The number of credit unions had increased twelvefold from about 200 in 1920 to about 2,500 in 1934; credit union legislation was passed in most states and in 1934 the Roosevelt administration passed a federal credit union act; and the credit unions were strong enough to take over their own affairs through C.U.N.A.[35] Unlike Warbasse, Filene planned for and welcomed this development.

In support of his ideas, Filene financed the development of credit unions with, over his lifetime, nearly 1 million dollars of his own funds. Although Bergengren did most of the organizing work, Filene's money, his speeches, and his overall sponsorship were important factors in the movement's growth. In addition, he founded a number of charitable and nonprofit institutions, including the Edward A. Filene Good Will Fund, Inc.; the Twentieth Century Fund, Inc.; and the Consumer Distribution Cooperative (CDC). The latter was an ambitious attempt to create a chain of cooperatively owned department stores. Previously, Filene had experimented with worker control of cooperatives by trying to turn over the operations of his own Boston store to an employee-run Filene Cooperative Association. Both of these attempts ended in failure. Through his writings and speeches as well as through his foundations, Filene sponsored many other reformist causes, including improved health care, shorter workdays and workweeks, cheap mass vacation travel, old-age benefits, and more. Filene was a model philanthropist, a wealthy bachelor who could devote his full time and attention to his chosen projects. He once justified his support for credit unions thus: "I appropriate to the credit union just about what it costs a rich man to own and enjoy a steam yacht. I do not like steam yachts. I do like credit unions. Why should anyone be surprised because I spend my money the way that gives me the most pleasure and satisfaction?"[36] The credit union movement in the United States, which in 2002 had something in excess of 82.5 million members, benefited significantly in its early stages from the fact that Filene took such pleasure in helping other people help themselves.[37]

In assessing the role of exceptional individuals such Warbasse and Filene, two points are noteworthy. First, they did not create the idea of cooperatives, nor did they introduce the very first of them. Cooperatives issued and were driven substantially from popular circles. But second, Warbasse and Filene made large contributions to bring these cooperatives together into a more unified movement and to publicize the model for more systematic development in more locations. Their efforts succeeded in the sense that the movements did become self-sustaining.

PHILANTHROPY AND COOPERATIVES IN CANADA

In cooperatives, as in other fields, Canada shows strong influence from and similarities to both the United States and Britain while it also follows unique paths of development in various respects. Canadian history does offer at least one example of a great founder, much in the mold of Schulze-Delitzsch or Raiffeisen.

Alphonse Desjardins was a citizen of Lévis, a town across the river from Québec City. In the late nineteenth century Desjardins made his career and became involved in public life in a variety of ways, including as a journalist and publisher, as a Conservative with good connections, as a member of a variety of community associations, and professionally as a parliamentary recorder. He was not wealthy, but he was educated, reasonably prosperous, and well connected—a respectable middle-class person, a local notable. Desjardins's work eventually took him to Ottawa, where he served as a clerk in the House of Commons when it was in session. His concern with social issues, fed by social Catholicism, gained a new focus in 1897 when he heard a Member of Parliament make a speech about the evils of usury. Desjardins was appalled by what he heard. He saw that banks were not serving the common people, and he began to study mechanisms for providing wholesome and beneficial popular credit. He studied cooperatives and corresponded with European leaders such as Hans Crüger (Schulze-Delitzsch's successor at the Allgemeiner Verband) and international figures such as Henry Wolff of the International Cooperative Alliance, an advocate of cooperative banks. Over a period of several years, Desjardins gradually designed a form of financial cooperative that he thought would be suited to the circumstances of the Catholic French population in small-town Québec. He called this a *caisse populaire,* or people's bank.[38]

Desjardins organized a meeting of about 100 local citizens in December 1900 to found the Caisse Populaire de Lévis. He arranged for the parish priest and the principal of the local Catholic seminary to address the crowd in support of the new institution. For many years, the *caisse populaire* was run out of the Desjardins home. Depositors and borrowers stopped by in the evenings to make their transactions and have them recorded in the society's ledgers. Since Alphonse Desjardins was away for months at a time in Ottawa, his wife Dorimène played a large role in the society's management and was frequently the main person in charge of its affairs. While the Desjardins did not have a large fortune to use in supporting the bank's development, they did have time, respect, and connections in the community, which they used to good effect. The *caisse* prospered in no small part because it conformed to the hierarchies and structures of the Catholic parish milieu: It captured a sense of community solidarity; benefited from the good offices of the clergy, local notables, and associations; and met a perceived economic need with a unique service.

Desjardins also worked to spread his model beyond Lévis and throughout Catholic and Francophone areas of Canada. His main instruments in this task were legislation, which after a difficult struggle he finally obtained from the government of Québec in 1906, and the network of the Catholic clergy. In parishes across French Canada, it was frequently the priest who informed parishioners what a *caisse populaire* was; the priest who convened a founding meeting; the priest who served as the secretary or treasurer of the new bank, a personal guarantor of its honesty and legitimacy. Effectively the *caisses populaires* became institutions of the Franco-Canadian nationalism of the day, which was insular, conservative, small-town, and Catholic. An interesting aspect of this vision was that Desjardins firmly insisted that each *caisse* be very autonomous and strongly rooted in its own milieu. While he emphasized good management, he did not promote centralization or federation, which developed only weakly during his lifetime. His vision was very localist, reflecting his experience in Lévis and his idea of the *caisses* as projects of parish communities to assist their poorer members. Only as his health was failing, shortly before his death in 1920, did he begin to push for his *caisses* to federate together into a common organization.

Clearly the work of Alphonse and Dorimène Desjardins was itself philanthropic, both in the loose sense of helping others and in the more narrow sense of middle-class individuals working for the good of the community, particularly for people of lower rank than themselves. Also, the model of the *caisse populaire* and the way it spread implied or evoked a similar philanthropic impulse in many communities. As a project for community betterment and for credit for the disadvantaged, sponsored usually by local elites, the foundation model of the *caisse populaire* had an inherent philanthropic element. Ronald Rudin has argued that the efforts by small-town clerical-nationalist elites to promote *caisses populaires* should be seen not as a disinterested public cause but rather as a way for these groups to maintain their social power over their communities. He feels that this took place even at the economic expense of the working classes, who capitalized the *caisses* with their savings while artisans and small businessmen received this capital in the form of loans.[39] Rudin's argument is interesting and relevant, but even if he is right, it does not mean the promotion of *caisses* was not philanthropic. Indeed, if helping *caisses* increased the social standing of those giving the aid, this may make it more like classic bourgeois philanthropy, not less.

Desjardins and his *caisses populaires* movement constitute a Canadian example of cooperative philanthropy—promotion of cooperatives for a group by someone of higher social rank using personal resources—but what is striking is how few other such examples there are. Anglophone regions of Canada had no Desjardins or Schulze-Delitzsch, and Canada as a whole offers no examples of a wealthy Warbasse or Filene. Clearly the different modes of leadership or sponsorship, and their legitimacy, vary from one region, culture, or milieu to another.[40] If one casts about for an Anglophone Canadian example of philanthropic promotion of cooperatives on a regional or national level, a close fit might be George Keen of Brantford, Ontario, who poured immense and largely unremunerated effort into building up the Cooperative Union of Canada (now Canadian Cooperative Association) when he was its general secretary from 1909 to 1945.[41] Prairie farmer, utopian, and socialist visionary E. A. Partridge, organizer and critic of cooperatives in the early twentieth century, would be another candidate.[42] Perhaps the best-known visionary and popular leader would be the charismatic Atlantic Canadian priest Moses Coady, who organized fishing and farm communities in the 1920s and 1930s.[43] But to include such activist individuals, who are present in almost all cooperative movements, is to stretch the definition of philanthropy.

BOUNDARIES OF PHILANTHROPY

The concept of self-help, especially self-help in groups, is more complex than it at first appears and conceals a variety of cross-class, institutional, and community relationships that can, as we have seen, amount to philanthropic patronage. It is clear enough that the benefactors of cooperatives can be considered philanthropists when they earn wealth and power from unrelated sources and charitably dedicate this to the support of cooperatives for others of lesser social rank. But what do we call it when their office or calling is partly related to the promotion of cooperatives, as it was in the case of reforming members of the clergy? Promoting cooperatives was not necessarily in the job description of any particular member of the clergy, but social Catholicism (or for Protestants the social gospel) was a part of the church's tradition that an individual cleric might choose to implement in his or her work. Individuals in certain sorts of institutional offices had latitude to interpret what their work entailed. If they chose to devote their position to supporting cooperatives were they (partial) philanthropists? Several categories of individuals stand out in this regard: members of the clergy, academics, and government officials. If this is philanthropy, then most cooperative movements benefit from countless acts of philanthropy.[44]

There is also another kind of semiphilanthropist: the cooperator who, although a member of the group for whom self-help is intended, does not personally require it. Many are the tales from the farm cooperative movements of directors who saved the cooperative by pledging their farms to its creditors or of members who joined and invested even though they themselves needed no personal gain. Such a person joins, supports, and participates in a cooperative in order to help out friends, neighbors, and peers. This category would take in many of the volunteers, activists, and reformers who help out cooperatives, sometimes as formal leaders and sometimes in background roles. This raises a question: Is every leader in such an organization then a philanthropist? If we extend "philanthropy" to mean the same as "voluntarism," then indeed the cooperative movement is a mass movement of tens and hundreds of thousands of small philanthropists. Indeed, if we are willing to stretch the word so far, cooperatives can be seen as a characteristic form of philanthropy for the less well-off, for those who have no money to speak of, but rather have time to give: the "chequeless" people, to recall Holyoake's characterization of the activists who gave associational life to Owen's ideas in Britain.[45] There is a clear gender dimension to this discussion, since if we define philanthropy as a function of wealth and power it was the preserve primarily of men, whereas if voluntary activism is central, then female philanthropy was essential to many cooperative movements. Depending on our definition, then, we can regard almost all the cooperative movement as a generally philanthropic endeavor or we can reserve the word for the exceptional roles of the Owens, Schulze-Delitzsches, Warbasses, and Desjardins. Certainly there is something to be gained from considering the meaning of these individuals' roles.

Perhaps in thinking about philanthropy more narrowly conceived as a charitable and at least partly financial transaction between social classes, we can from the examples above loosely speculate about some possible transatlantic patterns. Britain and Germany hint at an Old World model in which the social status of educated individuals, professionals, and officials was key to their role and in which the promotion of cooperatives was defined in a received and ordered framework of social relations that preserved and honored these elite groups. If we accept this characterization, Germany fulfills it more clearly; while in Britain, Owen as a self-made industrialist constitutes a bridge to the U.S. pattern. Precisely because sponsorship of cooperatives was often so bound up with office and community in Europe, it is less clearly philanthropy in the sense in which the word is typically used. Over against this is the U.S. example, in the cases of Warbasse and Filene fully philanthropic: wealthy businessmen who chose cooperative self-help as a good cause to be subsidized from their personal fortunes. Canada is a slightly different case; Desjardins's role conforms more to the European pattern. Apart from him, sponsorship for cooperatives in Canada came more from institutions—church, government, university—than from individuals, perhaps reflecting a certain conservatism and lack of American-style individualism in early-twentieth-century Canadian society.

Despite such differences between the two sides of the Atlantic and among different countries, there are also commonalities: not only the fact of middle-class patronage of cooperatives but also some of the modalities of the movement. Philanthropists were effective when they concentrated on defining models, bringing legitimacy, and creating umbrella institutions to tie together growing movements: This was Owen's partial success, King's and Neale's contribution, Schulze-Delitzsch's and Raiffeisen's strength, and the forte of Filene, Warbasse, and Desjardins. There are fewer examples of successful direct ongoing philanthropy in the affairs of *primary* (community-level) cooperative societies. One can contrast N. O. Nelson's heavy-handed and ultimately unsuccessful philanthropic activities in the U.S. Midwest or, for that matter, Filene's department store reorganizations with the more hands-off approach in other more successful cases. Successful cooperative philanthropy or external aid often concentrated on ideas and umbrella institutions, a sort of indirect support to local cooperators; respect for self-help meant respect for local autonomy and experience in the primary cooperatives.

Several of the examples touch on the fundamental ambiguity of the meaning of philanthropic aid to self-help endeavors: The aid must not only be given, but accepted; the meaning of the action is constructed not only by the giver, but by the recipients; and the aid can only be successful if it becomes unnecessary and the movement escapes dependency. The impact of the founders is limited precisely to the extent that they succeed in initiating self-sustaining movements. Cooperatives grew out of philanthropic associational initiatives of the nineteenth and early twentieth centuries and were for a time an alternative realm for the exercise of middle-class reformist zeal. Social reformers sought to experiment with adaptations of the idea of association to meet the needs of the lower classes. In the process, some of them came to believe that self-help was more lasting and effective than charity and that self-help was more compatible with the prevailing notions of civic virtue. This can be interpreted as a diffusion of institutions of civil society to the lower classes, indeed, an active philanthropic transmission of such institutions. The reformers who promoted this adaptation and diffusion hoped thereby to spread their own values to the masses. In some respects they were successful, as broad groups of the population certainly took up the orderly practice of associational life—of membership, self-gov-

ernment, administration, and property ownership. Yet successful cooperative movements were by definition changeable and member directed. Cooperatives were fully capable of drawing on the ideas, resources, or legitimacy offered by philanthropic individuals when it suited them to do so
while disassociating themselves actively or passively from whatever they dis-
liked. Particularly where individuals are remembered and honored—Raiffeisen, Desjardins—we may wish to regard this memorialization as an
invention of tradition by the movement itself for its own symbolic and ritual purposes and not as simply a factual tale of one-way philanthropic assistance. The overlap between cooperatives and philanthropy is a complex
area where the meaning of actions depends on their construction and perception. Somewhere in this complexity, philanthropy encounters a fuzzy
boundary with self-help.

NOTES

1. More fully, "A co-operative is an autonomous association of persons united voluntarily to meet their common economic, social, and cultural needs and aspirations through a
jointly-owned and democratically-controlled enterprise." "The ICA Statement on the Cooperative Identity," from Ian MacPherson, *Co-operative Principles for the 21st Century*
(Geneva: International Co-operative Alliance, 1996), 1. This definition is the product of
more than a century of scholarly debate and political discussion.

2. On the British cooperative movement, see the excellent recent work of Peter Gur-
ney, especially *Co-operative Culture and the Politics of Consumption in England, 1870–1930*
(Manchester: Manchester University Press, 1996). A recent international survey is provided
in Johnston Birchall, *The International Co-operative Movement* (Manchester: Manchester
University Press, 1997). Older works are still useful, including particularly G. D. H. Cole,
A Century of Co-operation (Manchester: Co-operative Union, 1944); and Arnold Bonner,
*British Co-operation: The History, Principles, and Organisation of the British Co-operative
Movement* (Manchester: Co-operative Union, 1961).

3. A good short summary of Owen's complexities is in John Fletcher Clews Harrison,
"In Search of Robert Owen," in *Robert Owen and the World of Co-operation*, ed. Chushichi
Tsuzuki (Tokyo: Robert Owen Association of Japan, 1992), 175–180. See also John Fletch-
er Clews Harrison, *Robert Owen and the Owenites in Britain and America: The Quest for the
New Moral World* (London: Routledge and Kegan Paul, 1969).

4. E. P. Thompson, *The Making of the English Working Class* (Harmondsworth, U.K:
Penguin Books, 1980).

5. "Out of Owenism came the ideals, doctrines, myths, and much of the inspiration,
which are associated with the Co-operative Movement"; Bonner, *British Co-operation*, 1–2.
George Jacob Holyoake's landmark history of the cooperative movement referred to Owen
as "the originator . . . undoubtedly" of the modern cooperative movement. George Jacob
Holyoake, *The History of Co-operation in England: Its Literature and Its Advocates*, 2 vols.
(1875; reprint, New York: AMS Press, 1971), 1: 52.

6. Among many works on utopian and intentional communities, see Ronald George
Garnett, *Co-operation and the Owenite Socialist Communities in Britain, 1825–1845* (Manchester: Manchester University Press, 1972).

7. Thompson, *The Making of the English Working Class*, 859.

8. Holyoake, *The History of Co-operation in England*, 1: 55 and 65 (two quotations).

9. Quoted in Bonner, *British Co-operation*, 30.

10. Holyoake, *The History of Co-operation in England*, 1: 59.

11. On King, see any of the general works on British cooperation; see also Thomas William Mercer, *Co-operation's Prophet: The Life and Letters of Dr. William King of Brighton* (Manchester: Co-operative Union, 1947).

12. Philip N. Backstrom, *Christian Socialism and Co-operation in Victorian England: Edward Vansittart Neale and the Co-operative Movement* (London: Croom Helm, 1974), 64.

13. On these early associations, see Michael Prinz, *Brot und Dividende: Konsumvereine in Deutschland und England vor 1914* (Göttingen: Vandenhoeck & Ruprecht, 1996), 120–128; Helmut Faust, *Geschichte der Genossenschaftsbewegung: Ursprung und Aufbruch der Genossenschaftsbewegung in England, Frankreich und Deutschland sowie ihre weitere Entwicklung im Deutschen Sprachraum*, 3rd ed. (Frankfurt am Main: Fritz Knapp, 1977), 31.

14. *Jahre Konsum-Verein Frankfurt a.M. und Umgegend eGmbH* (Frankfurt am Main: Union-Druckerei, 1925), 5–6. This and many other consumer cooperative Festschriften can be found in Bundesarchiv Berlin, Materialsammlung "Geschichte der Konsumgenossenschaften," here No. 114.

15. N. Blesius, "Entstehungsgeschichte des neuzeitlichen Genossenschaftswesen," typescript of lecture held on January 25, 1929, at the Seminar für Genossenschaftswesen und Handelskunde der landwirtschaftlichen Hochschule in Berlin. The typescript is in Geheimes Staatsarchiv Preußischer Kulturbesitz HA I Rep 87 B (Ministerium für Landwirtschaft, Domänen und Forsten), Nr 9790.

16. On the Arbeiterverbrüderung and cooperatives, see Christiane Eisenberg, *Frühe Arbeiterbewegung und Genossenschaften: Theorie und Praxis der Produktivgenossenschaften in der deutschen Sozialdemokratie und den Gewerkschaften der 1860er/1870er Jahre* (Bonn: Neue Gesellschaft, 1985), Anhang A.

17. On Huber, see Wolfgang Schwentker, "Victor Aimé Huber and the Emergence of Social Conservatism"; and Hermann Beck, "Conservatism and the Social Question in Nineteenth-Century Prussia," both in *Between Reform, Reaction and Resistance: Studies in the History of German Conservatism from 1789 to 1945*, ed. Larry Eugene Jones and James Retallack (Providence, R.I.: Berg, 1993), 95–121 and 61–94, respectively, and the literature they cite.

18. From a document written by Huber and sealed in the cornerstone of the first building constructed by the Berlin Gemeinnützige Baugesellschaft in March 1849; cited by Rudolf Elvers, *Victor Aimé Huber. Sein Werden und Wirken, Erster Teil* (Bremen: C. Ed. Müller, 1872), 272–273.

19. Huber, "Allgemeine Charakteristik des Genossenschaftswesens (from 1855–63)," in Victor Aimé Huber, *Ausgewählte Schriften über Socialreform und Genossenschaftswesen. In freier Bearbeitung hrsg. von Dr. K. Munding* (Berlin: Pionier, n.d. [1894]), 731.

20. On Schulze-Delitzsch, see Rita Aldenhoff, *Schulze-Delitzsch: Ein Beitrag zur Geschichte des Liberalismus zwischen Revolution und Reichsgründung* (Baden-Baden: Nomos, 1984).

21. Faust, *Geschichte der Genossenschaftsbewegung*, 207–208.

22. See Aldenhoff, *Schulze-Delitzsch*, 107ff.

23. Huber, *Die genossenschaftliche Selbsthülfe der arbeitenden Klassen* (n.p.: Rheinisch-Westf. Provinzial-Ausschuß für innere Mission, n.d. [1864]), 47. Copy of a lecture delivered in Bonn.

24. There are a number of biographies, though few of them attempt to be critical in a scholarly sense—the myth of "Father Raiffeisen," the good Christian, the blind visionary leading a movement by inspiration and willpower, is alive and well. A good recent biography is Ludwig Hüttl, *Friedrich Wilhelm Raiffeisen: Leben und Werk. eine Biographie* (Mün-

chen: Bayerischer Raiffeisenverband, 1988). Walter Koch, *F.W. Raiffeisen: Dokumente und Briefe, 1818–1888* (Vienna: Genossenschaftliche Zentralbank, 1988) provides documents and commentary. See also Faust, *Geschichte der Genossenschaftsbewegung*, 323–367.

25. Raiffeisen, *Die Darlehnskassen-Vereine*, 7th ed. (Neuwied: Verlag der Raiffeisendruckerei, 1887) (1st ed. 1866).

26. Ibid., 17.

27. Ibid., 31.

28. Joseph G. Knapp, *The Rise of American Cooperative Enterprise, 1620–1920* (Danville, Ill.: Interstate, 1969), 396.

29. Emil Sekerak and Art Danforth, *Consumer Cooperation: The Heritage and the Dream* (Santa Clara, Calif.: Consumers Cooperative Publishing Association, 1980), 37–38.

30. Wallace J. Campbell, "James Peter Warbasse: Founder of the Cooperative League," in *Great American Cooperators: Biographical Sketches of 101 Major Pioneers in Cooperative Development*, ed. Joseph G. Knapp and Associates (Washington, D.C.: American Institute of Cooperation, 1967), 520–523.

31. Joseph G. Knapp, *The Advance of American Cooperative Enterprise, 1920–1945* (Danville, Ill.: Interstate, 1973), 572n2.

32. Tom J. Hefter, "Edward A. Filene: U.S. Father of Credit Unions," in Knapp and Associates, *Great American Cooperators*, 165–171.

33. Following a study tour to Europe and a report in 1893, cooperatives were organized and eventually a Co-operative Credit Societies Act was passed in 1904. Within ten years, 15,000 cooperative societies were formed in British India. See Margaret Digby, *Agricultural Co-operation in the Commonwealth* (Oxford: Blackwell, 1951), 78.

34. J. Carroll Moody and Gilbert C. Fite, *The Credit Union Movement: Origins and Development 1850–1980*, 2nd ed. (Dubuque, Iowa: Kendall/Hunt, 1984), 25–27.

35. Knapp, *The Advance of American Cooperative Enterprise*, 196ff.; Sekerak and Danforth, *Consumer Cooperation*, 46, 61; Moody and Fite, *The Credit Union Movement*, 120, 123.

36. Quoted in Hefter, "Edward A. Filene," 169.

37. Credit Union National Association, "Credit Union Report for 2002," available online at http:/www.cuna.org. Accessed January 29, 2003.

38. Pierre Poulin, "The Origins of Savings and Credit Co-operatives in North America: The Work of Alphonse and Dorimène Desjardins," in *Canadian Co-operatives in the Year 2000: Memory, Mutual Aid, and the Millennium*, ed. Brett Fairbairn, Ian MacPherson, and Nora Russell (Saskatoon: Centre for the Study of Co-operatives, 2000), 28–38. There is surprisingly little available in English about Desjardins.

39. Ronald Rudin, *In Whose Interest? Quebec's Caisses Populaires 1900–1945* (Montreal: McGill-Queen's University Press, 1990).

40. Some brief reflections on the lack of Anglophone Canadian equivalents of great founders can be found in Brett Fairbairn, "Raiffeisen and Desjardins: Co-operative Leadership, Identity, and Memory," in *Canadian Co-operatives in the Year 2000*, 13–26, esp. 23–24.

41. Ian MacPherson, "'In These Pioneers Days': George Keen and Leadership through Sacrifice and Determination," in Fairbairn, MacPherson, and Russell, *Canadian Co-operatives in the Year 2000*, 40–54. Georgina Taylor's portrait of prairie leader Violet McNaughton and MacPherson's of Alexander Laidlaw, both in the same volume, provide additional examples of individuals who played similar roles as voluntary activists.

42. Murray Knuttila, *"That Man Partridge": E. A. Partridge, His Thoughts and Times* (Regina: Canadian Plains Research Centre, 1994).

43. A recent biography is Michael R. Welton, *Little Mosie from the Margaree: A Biography of Moses Michael Coady* (Toronto: Thompson Educational, 2001).

44. Many of the exceptional individuals portrayed in Knapp's *Great American Cooperators* turn out to be officials and professionals, particularly in government offices, universities, and the like. These include Oliver H. Kelley, founder of the Grange agrarian movement; professor Edwin G. Nourse; and lawyer Aaron Sapiro (who was paid for his services).

45. Then there are the organized charitable activities of the cooperative movements in all the countries mentioned, who operate development foundations and agencies to help poor people form cooperatives in other countries and sometimes in their own. This is certainly organized cooperative philanthropy; I have not covered it in this chapter because it falls mostly outside my chosen time period of the mid-nineteenth to mid-twentieth centuries.

FOUR

Patronage and the Great Institutions of the Cities of the United States: Questions and Evidence, 1800–2000

DAVID C. HAMMACK

INTRODUCTION

The United States has produced many notable patrons and major donors, many of them famously memorialized in the names of universities, hospitals, and museums: Hopkins, Carnegie, Rockefeller, Stanford, Duke, Guggenheim, Mellon, Ford, Lilly, Kellogg, Sloan, Kettering, Eastman, Walters, Frick, Gardner.[1] Big donors continue to appear: Gates, Packard, Hewitt, Annenberg, Turner, Soros.[2] These donors have attracted attention from historians and other scholars as well as from the general public.

But to what extent have wealthy individual Americans or families succeeded in using patronage to exert their will on society? To what extent has their success varied from city to city or from time to time?

Those who wish to explore these questions must closely consider several general points:

Some donors have certainly made very large gifts, but in relation to the economy as a whole, or even to the fields of education, health care, and social service, the amount of money devoted to patronage has never been very large. Wealthy patrons have had their greatest influence in the fields of religion—where large donations are balanced by small ones—and the arts.

Nearly all large gifts go to nonprofit corporations (directly or via foundations) or to state universities and public schools.[3] Public institutions depend heavily on taxes and must respect policies established by elected state legislatures and school boards.

Nonprofit corporations have always depended more on earned income than on private gifts and have also enjoyed significant direct and government subsidies. Patrons or donors have thus always had to compete for influence with voters, paying customers, and government officials. Almost all large nonprofits—hospitals, colleges and universities, libraries, even orchestras, museums, and libraries—receive support from many wealthy donors, who often disagree with one another.[4] In the twentieth century, most of the leading nonprofits have built up fairly substantial endowments and physical plants, so that current donors must also compete with the preferences of past donors and with the accumulated decisions of past boards. Nonprofit corporations have always been subject to a certain degree of legal and political control; since the 1960s, this control has both decreased and increased and has become much more concentrated in the federal government. Nonprofit organizations, like other organizations, are also shaped by organizational dynamics other than dependence on resources.

Those who have controlled significant amounts of wealth have never pursued a unified policy. In the last third of the twentieth century, the trustees of the leading nonprofit organizations in the United States have become much more diverse in religious background than ever in the past. Very important groups, most notably evangelicals and other religious conservatives, remain apart—and support their own arrays of organizations and activities.

These points, especially the unusual role of nonprofit corporations in the United States, must be taken into consideration in any attempt to compare patronage in U.S. cities with patronage in the cities of other nations.

HISTORICAL PERSPECTIVES ON PATRONAGE IN U.S. CITIES

These points stand as a challenge to several influential views. Writing at the depth of the Great Depression in 1937, Ferdinand Lundberg offered an acerbic view of patronage by the wealthy in the United States that is still widely held. In the following passage, Lundberg focused on the patronage of higher education, which, according to the thorough analysis of Eduard C. Lindemann, had absorbed 25 percent of foundation grants during the 1920s.[5] Elsewhere Lundberg applied a similar analysis to health care and medicine, the arts, and religion. Lundberg wrote:

As control of the colleges and universities in America slipped from the hands of the clergy after the Civil War, the pecuniary element eased itself into dominance. The overwhelming presence of bankers as trustees and regents became only logical, however, once the inner pecuniary motivation of the American university was granted, because the endowments, in combination with the philanthropic foundations and church endowments (supervised by essentially the same persons), conferred upon the trustees a large amount of industrial control and voting power as well as strategic supervision over research and studies. The university endowments are really instruments of industrial as well as social control; and, like other endowments, are tax-exempt, making possible an ever-enlarging concentration of authority in the hands of the rich.[6]

In Lundberg's view, one of the chief purposes of endowments was to enable "America's 60 Families" to exert continuing control over the nation's largest business firms. On the basis of his examination of the business careers and affiliations of trustees, he wrote,

The American Telephone and Telegraph Company appears to hold more university trusteeships through its directors than any other big corporation; J. P. Morgan and Company appears to hold more than any other banking house; the Rockefeller philanthropic endowments control more than any other so-called philanthropic enterprises. The coalitions of wealth which exercise the greatest direct influence in American higher education are the Morgan, Rockefeller, DuPont, and Mellon groups.[7]

Congressman Wright Patman of Texas picked up on Lundberg's criticism in the 1960s. Foundations, Patman asserted, were "agents of concentration" contributing to a "rapidly increasing concentration of economic power in foundations which . . . is far more dangerous than anything that has happened in the past in the way of concentration of economic power."[8]

What—in addition to control of industrial corporations—did these groups seek from higher education? According to Lundberg, they had always sought to educate "the young of their own class"; scholarships to expensive Ivy League colleges helped only "the lower fringe of the well-to-do."[9] The wealthy gave disproportionately to institutions in the Northeast, providing advantages to that region at the expense of the West and South. From the last third of the nineteenth century, industrialists helped "the discernibly brightest intellects of the poorer classes" to gain technical skills relevant to their industries and to advance technology in general. Wealthy donors also sought to suppress "the social scientists—men preoccupied with economics, sociology, history, and political science"—who were inclined to "criticize, to analyze, or to explore the society" that had allowed some to become rich. And they used colleges and universities to support both applied scientists whose work benefited their businesses and articulate defenders of the existing order.[10]

In general, Lundberg asserted, America's wealthy patrons sought to enhance their own prestige, power, and personal interests. Gifts for religious purposes he did "not regard as philanthropies."[11] He dismissed the bulk of gifts to "churches, hospitals, and conventional charities" as of slight cultural importance. "Culture" implied, in this modernist view, "ways for organizing emotional experience, experiments in tone or quality of living" and thus "culture cannot be merely something which conserves but must . . . become dynamic."[12] Medical gifts (one-third of foundation grants in the 1920s) were, Lundberg insisted, "undependable, haphazard, egocentric," serving donors' personal health and business interests.[13] "Social welfare" work, with the exception of some studies by the Russell Sage Foundation, some grants to African-American institutions by the Rosenwald Fund, and some support of liberal weekly papers and liberal organizations, was "wholly static." Contributions to the arts enabled the wealthy to avoid taxes and enshrine the art of the past but failed to encourage living artists.[14] Foundations and other wealthy patrons sought social power. "Without expending any money they can influence the attitudes of professional and technical people who need money to go on with their work," Lundberg concluded. "These people, hoping that the lightning of a foundation grant will strike them, consciously or unconsciously shape their attitudes so as to please potential donors, who passively achieve their objective of inducing these prospective recipients to speak out in defense of the social *status quo* or to maintain silence."[15]

In the seventy-five years since Lundberg wrote, historical understanding of patronage in the United States has changed. Some historians have continued to insist that there is evidence that U.S. patrons (and their biggest foundations) have successfully advanced narrow class interests.[16] Others assert such conclusions on the basis of their theoretical analysis of "capitalism." But since World War II, foundations (and some other patrons) have come in for more criticism from the political right than from the left. E. Digby Baltzell pointed out in the early 1960s that Senator Joseph McCarthy railed against the views and acts of Ivy Leaguers who had benefited from the patronage to which Lundberg objected. McCarthy complained to the United States Senate about what he called

> the traitorous actions of those who have been treated so well by this nation. It is not the less fortunate or members of minority groups who have been selling this nation out but rather those who have had all the benefits the wealthiest nation on earth has had to offer—the finest homes, the finest college educations, and the finest jobs in the government.[17]

Others, ranging from the Cox and Reece and Patman Committees of the U.S. Congress to Marvin Olasky (the publicist who has been closely aligned with Congressman Newt Gingrich and others) to the Capital Research Center and the Bradley Foundation's National Commission on Philanthropy and Civic Renewal, have complained that foundations and other donors have supported too many causes of big government and economic redistribution.[18]

Foundations and other patrons also won a reputation for combating racial and religious discrimination. Lindemann emphasized the Protestant origins of the foundation donors. Baltzell campaigned against the exclusion of Jews—and often Catholics—from the clubs and other institutions dominated by upper-class Protestants. He emphasized the role of some of those institutions, especially certain foundations and other patrons, in moderating and eventually ending Protestant hegemony.

Although postwar trends diversified formerly Protestant suburbs, country clubs held the line. In Philadelphia, Boston, Pittsburgh, and Chicago, Jews were excluded from the top ranks of business corporations and when, rarely, a Jewish leader did emerge at the top in the world of business, he was still denied membership in the leading local club. "They'll call on me to lead their Community Chest campaign," Baltzell quoted a Jewish civic leader as saying. "But when it comes to the country club, I'm not good enough for them."[19]

Yet Baltzell believed that bigoted religious discrimination was beginning to decline. Patronage constituted one weapon in the campaign against discrimination, as Baltzell's Community Chest example suggests. Key institutions were also changing their policies. By the early 1960s, Harvard's board of overseers included a number of Jews. Key observers were asserting that New York City's most "vital" clubs selected members on "aristocratic" grounds of achievement, rather than clannish grounds of birth and religion. Secure in their own status, successful and intelligent people—and some of those who hoped to hold key federal offices—could not only resign from clubs that excluded Jews, Catholics, and African Americans but sometimes they felt they had no choice but to do so.

Writing in the immediate aftermath of the McCarthy period, Baltzell argued that the organizations patronized by an "establishment" served a most important role in a democratic society:

> There is little empirical evidence in history to support the theory that either a free people or a free press is, in the long run, sufficient, though both are indeed necessary, guarantors of freedom against the rise of dictatorial demagoguery. Though economic security may be valued and understood by the many, there is good reason to believe that civil liberties and freedom of expression are more highly valued by the few. McCarthy was feared far more in the university than on the assembly line.[20]

The "pluralist" approach that came to dominate empirical studies of local power structures in the 1970s and 1980s incorporated this perspective. Generalizing on the basis of work such as Baltzell's, Robert A. Dahl argued in *Polyarchy* (1971) that an effective democracy required the presence of eight factors, including "alternative sources of information, freedom to form and to join organizations, eligibility for public office, right of political leaders to compete for support, [the] right to vote, free and fair elections, freedom of expression, and institutions for making government policies depend on voters' preferences." Young political scientists such as Kelly McMann are currently renewing this perspective through their studies of the countries that have emerged from the former Soviet Union, in which nongovernment leaders and organizations can provide a sustainable basis for independent speech, press, and political organization only if they enjoy economic autonomy.[21]

In the early 1980s, Frederic C. Jaher published a massive study, *The Urban Establishment: Upper Strata in Boston, New York, Charleston, Chicago, and Los Angeles.* He concluded with a comprehensive and sophisticated review of serious work on the history of wealth, power, and status in American and European cities. "If a solitary ruling elite or class exists" in American cities, he concluded,

> it is territorially fluid and culturally adaptive. Nor is its personnel . . . constant. Outside of the descendants of a few persistent clans . . . the great post–World War II statesmen and capitalists do not come from the old urban aristocracy, or even from their successors, the late-nineteenth-century captains of industry. Whether the contemporary power structure is pyramidic or polycentered, it is fixed neither geographically, culturally, nor hereditarily. Those who assert the existence of a national power elite do not claim that it depends upon recruitment from a narrow range of families or localities. If there is such a group, however, it has shifting geographical bases, high turnover in personnel, and great responsiveness to social and economic change. . . . Such conditions render this putative enclave either so amorphous that it cannot in a systematic and all-inclusive manner mobilize and therefore monopolize power, or so shrewd and comprehensive that its omnipotence is unchallengeable.[22]

Others have concluded that the influence U.S. elites exert, through patronage or other devices, is limited. In congressional testimony on foundations in 1965, John Simon asked whether these patrons "have the capacity to or do they in fact, coerce other institutions—notably universities—to conform to the orthodoxy of what the Reece Committee used to call a foundation 'interlock'?" Simon doubted that they did.

For many years the general disinterest of most foundations in such subjects as preschool education, civil rights, and most aspects of the urbanization hindered progress in these areas. But . . . their neglect of these problems reflected a failure of imagination and compassion on the part of an entire nation, not only a few chosen trustees.

It is also true that most foundations accept and act upon certain major premises when they deal with higher education. Probably most of them do favor international cooperation and empirical research and probably all do shy away from contemplative metaphysics. But these same premises would be shared, I venture to say, by much smaller foundations in the same field. These preferences are too widely held by educated men to be charged to a few foundation executives alleged to wield dominant power.[23]

Like Simon, many historians and other scholars—as well as many critics of social reform—have emphasized efforts of wealthy donors to influence public opinion and to shape government policy. The most careful scholars have concluded that although such patrons of ideas have more than their share of influence, they are rarely able to shape policy as they wish.[24]

Much of the scholarship of the 1990s put analyses such as these to one side in order to emphasize the fact that much earlier research had focused on white men, leaving out of direct discussion the general exclusion of women and members of racial minorities.[25] These are important points, although to be fair we should note that Lundberg, Baltzell, Dahl, and Jaher were all vigorous critics of racial discrimination. And that, like feminists who acknowledge the impact of class, they assumed that women of wealth and status shared (and generally sought to defend) most of the advantages held by their husbands, fathers, and brothers.[26] What the scholarship of the 1990s has successfully emphasized is that property-owning white Protestant men enjoyed significant legal and cultural advantages that earlier scholars took for granted—or ignored. Patterns of patronage built on these advantages but played little role in establishing or maintaining them.[27]

THE AMOUNT OF MONEY DEVOTED TO PATRONAGE HAS NEVER BEEN VERY LARGE

Undermining much of his own argument about the power of patronage, Ferdinand Lundberg noted that wealthy Americans had not, in fact, devoted much money to philanthropy. He quoted two contemporary studies as concluding independently that between 1909 and 1932 Americans gave less than 2 percent of their incomes to charitable institutions of all kinds. A few wealthy people (notably Andrew Carnegie, Mrs. Russell Sage, Julius Rosenwald, John D. Rockefeller, James B. Duke, and a few others) had made very large donations. But "ninety-four percent of the wills" of New York City's wealthiest people "transferred ninety-four percent of the wealth to relatives and friends."[28] The most recent estimates, surveyed by Colin B. Burke for the forthcoming millennial edition of *Historical Statistics of the United States*, come to a similar conclusion: Voluntary gifts to religious and nonprofit organizations ranged from under 1 to just over 2 percent of national income over the course of the twentieth century.[29] Jaher notes that late-nineteenth-century wills left by men named Astor, Vanderbilt, and Sage left less than 1 percent of their fortunes to public projects and that J. P. Morgan's will left less than 2 percent.[30]

Even Rockefeller's very large gifts amounted only to a very small share of government spending on "the welfare of mankind." Government expenditures have always been significantly lower in the United States than in Western Europe, but in 1900 they already approached 8 percent of the total U.S. economy, reached more than 20 percent by 1950, and more than 30 percent by 1990.[31] Until the mid-1930s the federal government had almost no direct role in the activities relevant to ordinary welfare.[32] Profit-seeking organizations and individuals have always provided much or even most of the performing and visual arts, nursing home care, and vocational education. Local governments provided most elementary education and public health, most welfare support, much medical care, and most of the support that U.S. governments provide for the arts. Thus one measure of the scale of the resources required for influential patronage is the cost of local government. One set of estimates puts the cost of local government at 5 percent of the gross national product of the United States in 1902 and shows that it rose to nearly 10 percent by 1929 and nearly 20 percent by 1990.[33] If individual contributions amounted to 1 percent of the U.S. economy in 1900, that equaled just one-fifth of local government spending. If individual contributions grew to 2 percent of the U.S. economy in 2000, they added up to one-tenth of local government spending.

Most private giving has gone to support activities that local and other U.S. governments will not support. Half or more of all private giving has gone to religious activity (which has received almost no direct government funding in the United States since Massachusetts ended tax support for churches in 1833).[34] These figures date from the middle of the twentieth century; in earlier periods, when health care and higher education commanded smaller shares of U.S. resources, the share religious endeavors received was even higher. The nonprofit sector probably accounted for about 1 percent of the national labor force in 1900. At that time clergy and religious women accounted for just over half of 1 percent; teachers in the mostly religious private schools and colleges accounted for perhaps one-sixth of 1 percent; others worked in church-sponsored orphanages, old age homes, and clinics.[35] Through the nineteenth century, before the era of comprehensive public education, private gifts supported secondary and collegiate education; with the expansion of public schools and colleges, private gifts have gone to selective schools, "centers of excellence," and schools devoted to religious and other special purposes that do not command public support. Private gifts advanced science until the expansion of the National Institutes of Health and the creation of the National Science Foundation. At present, private gifts are most important to the arts.

Even in the United States, home of "small government," government spending has always overshadowed private giving, and it has done so to a greater and greater degree over the last 100 years.

NONPROFIT ORGANIZATIONS BLUNT THE IMPACT OF INDIVIDUAL PATRONS

Under U.S. law, patrons usually work through nonprofit organizations, and these, too, have almost always overshadowed even the greatest fortunes.

Patrons can rarely provide all the resources a nonprofit needs. U.S. nonprofit organizations have always relied on earned income above all—on tuition and fees for schools[36] and orphanages,[37] fees for hospital services,[38] admissions fees for arts events and exhibits, and offerings and pledges for religious organizations.[39] U.S. nonprofits have also always relied on government subsidies and tax exemptions.[40] Gifts have always provided a minor part of the income of most nonprofits, and nonprofits almost always seek gifts from many donors rather than rely on single individual or family patrons.[41] Large donors find that because U.S. nonprofits receive resources from many sources, nonprofit leaders respond to a variety of interests.

Most of the largest nonprofit organizations in the United States have worked to accumulate assets—land, buildings, equipment, libraries, endowments—from their earliest years. Earned income, government grants of land and money, and gifts from donors all combine to pay for these assets. New donors find that assets are usually tied to ongoing programs, making it difficult for even the wealthiest new patron to transform a nonprofit.[42]

Legally, nonprofit organizations are almost always required to have multi-member boards governed by state law; those boards are ordinarily required to adopt bylaws that require them to act by consensus. The boards select their own members, hire top leaders and set policies, and are responsible for their organizations' finances.[43] It has always been very difficult for individual U.S. patrons, even very wealthy patrons, to control the nonprofit organizations through which they must usually work. Even a very large donor does not provide all the resources, cannot control other trustees, and cannot control the general arrangements under which the trustees operate.

A great patron may control for a time the board of an organization he or she starts but is likely to find it very difficult to maintain control over a longer span or to gain full control over an existing board.[44]

SOME USES OF PATRONAGE IN THE U.S. CONTEXT

The nonprofit organization system has directed U.S. patronage to religious and cultural causes at least as much as it has advanced class interests. Throughout the nineteenth century, patronage was most effective in creating distinct worlds of Protestant and Catholic, and in some places Jewish, institutions. In the last seventy years, patronage has created an extraordinary array of arts organizations, promoted research universities, and gone far to reduce formerly strong distinctions among Protestants and between Protestants, Jews, and Catholics.

Throughout the nineteenth century and for much of the twentieth, most donors sought to advance their own religious communities. The nonprofit sector arose in the U.S. polity as a means of institutionalizing the separation of church and state. Protestants developed nonprofit organizations in their effort to maintain denominational commitments forged in the colonial period and to convert a largely areligious U.S. population; one measure of their success is that the proportion of church members rose from 17 percent at the time of the Revolution to 51 percent by 1906.[45] The nonprofit sector persisted in large part because it helped manage the conflicts produced by the great and increasing religious diversity of the United States.[46] Private nongovernmental nonprofit organizations sponsored by Protestant denominational and interdenominational groups, as well as by Catholics and Jews, provided most educational, health care, and social services in the nineteenth-century United States.

Early in the nineteenth century, these arrangements helped manage conflicts among Episcopalians, Presbyterians, Congregationalists, and Baptists.[47] Rather than battle within the state legislatures over the religion of state institutions, the major Protestant sects in the southern and middle states, and then in New England, agreed to sponsor their own clinics, schools, and colleges. They frankly used these institutions to convert others to their faiths, first from the vaguely Protestant "unchurched" population, then from the population of non-Protestants.[48] As large numbers of Catholics arrived during the middle decades of the nineteenth century, to be joined by increasing numbers of Eastern Orthodox and Jewish immigrants who came after 1880, protests against the aggressive proselytizing of Protestant organizations grew.[49] To protect their traditions and commitments, Catholics and Jews quickly built their own schools, hospitals, and other institutions.[50]

In the nineteenth century and well into the twentieth, most large donations went to support nonprofits that worked within specific religious communities. Members of "mainline" Protestant religious denominations—especially the Episcopalians, Presbyterians, Congregationalists, Lutherans, Reformed, and Methodists—and Catholics[51] organized the largest numbers of nonprofit organizations in the nineteenth-century United States.[52] The Masonic Order and a few other fraternal movements provided similar, though more modest, support for some organizations, and some notable gifts went to nonsectarian libraries, museums, and adult education institutions.[53] But the practical reasons for the success of the religious institutions—their formal governing arrangements, informal processes for evaluating leaders and attracting students and other clients, and numerous donors—all served to reduce the influence of individual patrons. By 1900, America's cities and college towns sported a remarkable array of schools, colleges, hospitals, clinics, orphanages, training schools, and old age homes as well as many churches, synagogues, and convents.[54]

Religious conflicts by no means provided the only lines of commitment and contention among wealthy patrons. The abolitionist movement had notable patrons, many of whom gave to Protestant schools and colleges for African Americans in the South after the Civil War.[55] Southern Presbyterians, Methodists, and Baptists did much to rebuild southern institutions for whites after the Civil War, sometimes in order to maintain substantial aspects of antebellum life. Despite very difficult conditions, African Americans succeeded, more often than not through sweat equity, in building hundreds of churches, dozens of small colleges, and a few hospitals.[56] Working usually within the framework of religious institutions, members of many immigrant groups used their donations to advance cultural and national aims. In Cleveland, for example, Czechs, Poles, Hungarians, Slovaks, Croats, and Slovenians struggled with one another to shape Catholic institutions and to advance national ambitions in their homelands.[57] Women's patronage sometimes advanced the cause of women's rights in general and women's education in particular; Catholic women's patronage gave an essential impetus to many Catholic institutions.[58]

Within the range permitted by regulations and regulators,[59] American nonprofits and their patrons long pursued particularistic parochial purposes. But it is expensive to maintain a cultural tradition and much more expensive to convert people. Nineteenth-century colleges were chronically short of funds. Often, as Colin B. Burke has demonstrated, they had to lay religious courses aside in order to offer practical courses in bookkeeping and surveying for which students were willing to pay.[60]

The massive immigration of Catholics, Jews, and Orthodox Christians after the Civil War made it more and more difficult to sustain the dominance of Anglo-Saxon Protestant ideas and institutions in the cities and states of the industrial and increasingly heterogeneous Northeast and upper Midwest.[61] By the end of the nineteenth century, conflicts among competing Protestant sects seemed to Carnegie, Rockefeller, and like-minded donors to have grown beyond all bounds. And leaders of more than a few of the institutions that existed in the framework of Protestant denominationalism and Catholicism placed themselves in opposition to science even as scientific research made it possible for the first time to combat infectious disease in a systematic way. The result was what Thomas Haskell has called a late-nineteenth-century "crisis of authority."[62] Haskell does not put it this way, but it is clear that this crisis of authority frustrated the ambitions of many wealthy patrons. Some responded with funds that helped to transform America's great eleemosynary institutions, especially its universities. Twentieth-century patronage, channeled through the U.S. nonprofit sector, advanced scientific research and the professions; created remarkable arts organizations; helped reduce conflict among Protestants, Jews, and Catholics; and played a small role in advancing opportunities for women and African Americans.

Liberal Protestantism had already produced important interdenominational, nondenominational, and scientific social service, health care, and moral uplift societies by the end of the nineteenth century. Some scholars have even concluded that religious belief became less salient to public life as the nineteenth century wore on.[63] But it remained true that most of the "nonsectarian" institutions retained close ties to Protestantism and that nearly all local schools, poverty-relief organizations, and clinics and hospitals drew their support through religious networks.[64]

Wealthy Protestant donors such as John D. Rockefeller, Andrew Carnegie, and Mrs. Russell Sage and many others responded to the late-nineteenth-century crisis of Protestant authority by providing significant amounts of money outside the channels of the religious establishments, enabling many nonprofits to shift from a Protestant denominational (or interdenominational or nondenominational) basis to nonsectarianism and "science."[65] The result was a thoroughgoing reorganization of the nonprofit sector early in the twentieth century and the creation of a new set of nonsectarian coordinating organizations for nonprofits. As Haskell points out, new specialized professional disciplinary associations in the fields of economics, history, political science, sociology, and statistics displaced the liberal Protestant American Social Science Association (ASSA). In many ways, the leading national foundations replaced the ASSA.[66] The new research universities, which housed the new academic disciplines, became the favorite objects of America's wealthiest donors to the 1970s.[67]

I can best make the case for the role of patronage directed toward non-profit organizations in reducing the distances between Protestants, Jews, and Catholics with a case study from Cleveland, Ohio. The Program on Non-Profit Organizations at Yale University has collected a good deal of information on all trustees of fifteen leading Cleveland nonprofits in 1931, 1961, and 1991.[68] Overall, we have been able to obtain some information on the religious allegiance of more than 1,100 trustees in the three years we studied.[69] Newspapers, directories, and other sources contain information on 79.1 percent of all trustees for 1931, 75.6 percent in 1961, and 66.1 percent in 1991. Clearly, religious affiliation has always been important and a matter of public record for most of Cleveland's trustees. It may be that religion had become less salient by 1991, but the somewhat lower proportion for that year may also reflect the fact that obituaries and death notices are often our source of information about religion, and most 1991 trustees are still living.

To some extent, Cleveland certainly had a "Protestant establishment" through much of the twentieth century. In 1931, 76 percent of all trustees whose religion we have been able to learn something about were Protestant. The Protestant share remained high, at 63 percent, in 1961 (Cleveland dominates Cuyahoga County, and in the mid-1950s active Protestants accounted for perhaps 20 percent or 25 percent of the county's population). Of the trustees about whose religion we know something, Protestants held 90 percent of the trusteeships in "nonsectarian" organizations in 1931; they held 84 percent in 1961. Most Protestant trustees were Episcopalians or Presbyterians—36 percent and 32 percent, respectively, of those whose religion we know in 1931, and 35 percent and 30 percent in 1961.

But Cleveland also had Jewish and Catholic establishments through the middle of the twentieth century. Almost without exception trustees of Jewish organizations have always been Jews, and through 1961 all trustees of Catholic organizations were Catholic. Catholics and Jews were included on the boards of some of the city's leading "nonsectarian" institutions—the Community Chest and the Musical Arts Association (Cleveland Orchestra)—as early as 1931. They held 15 percent of the seats on those boards in 1961. But their participation increased greatly in the next thirty years. In 1991, Catholic and Jewish trustees together held about half of all seats on the "nonsectarian" boards; in that year, Episcopalians and Presbyterians held 31 percent.

As Cleveland became more "cosmopolitan" in this way, evangelical "fundamentalist" Protestants did not move into leadership positions on the boards of its leading institutions. That matter calls for additional consideration, especially in the light of the rise of fundamentalist influence in the Republican Party in national affairs.

We are gathering comparable data for six other cities—Boston, Philadelphia, Atlanta, Minneapolis, St. Paul, and Los Angeles. So far that effort is less complete, but the preliminary evidence points in the same direction. In Minneapolis–St. Paul, for example, we have data for about half of all trustees: Of those whose religion is known, in 1931, half were Episcopalians, Presbyterians, and Congregationalists—but in 1991, about half were Catholic or Jewish. We have data for about a third of the trustees in Boston. In 1931, nearly half were Episcopalian, Unitarian, or Congregationalist. In 1991, according to very preliminary data, 80 percent were Catholic or Jewish.

These data suggest that any long-term effort of a "Protestant Establishment" to solidify and perpetuate its influence through patronage of non-profit organizations failed. Perhaps the great increase in federal funding that followed the Civil Rights movement and the Great Society programs of the 1960s led major northern nonprofits to move rapidly away from the tradition of Protestant control. Whatever their motives, Americans have clearly used nonprofit organizations to negotiate conflicts among religious groups and to reallocate responsibility and status one institution at a time.

This evidence does not contradict the argument of those who insist that the divisions in U.S. society are now based on class, race, or gender far more than on religion, but neither does it support their conclusion. Other studies will be required to demonstrate that patrons have actively sought such results and that they were able to achieve what they sought. To judge from the evidence at hand, patrons have consciously sought diverse results. Working through nonprofit organizations as they must in the United States, no patron can entirely control the outcome. Every patron must contend with consumer preferences and government policies as well as with the preferences of other patrons who wish to advance different views.

NOTES

1. Big donors in earlier periods of U.S. history are discussed in Kathleen S. Kennedy, *Effective Fund-Raising Management* (Mahwah, N.J.: Lawrence Erlbaum Associates, 1998); Robert Bremner, *American Philanthropy* (Chicago: University of Chicago Press, 1988); Waldemar A. Nielsen, *The Golden Donors: A New Anatomy of the Great Foundations* (New York: E. P. Dutton, 1985); Nathaniel Burt, *Palaces for the People: A Social History of the American Art Museum* (Boston: Little, Brown, 1977); Helen Lefkowitz Horowitz, *Culture and the City: Cultural Philanthropy in Chicago from the 1880s to 1917* (Chicago: University of Chicago Press, 1976); and Merle Curti and Roderick Nash, *Philanthropy in the Shaping of American Higher Education* (New Brunswick, N.J.: Rutgers University Press, 1965).

2. For a list of several hundred reported gifts of $50 million or more made by U.S. donors since 1966 maintained by the Indiana University Center on Philanthropy, see http://www.philanthropy.iupui.edu/studies.htm#million. By far the largest donations have

come from Bill and Melinda Gates; others who gave more than $350 million include David and Lucille Packard, Bill Daniels, Ted Turner, Walter Annenberg, the Albertsons, Charles A. Feeney, the Intel and Microsoft corporations, Alisa Bruce Mellon, Sir Harold Acton, George Soros, Patrick J. McGovern, and Lore Harp.

3. The very large gifts listed in note 2 went to foundations and targeted efforts established by the donors, including Gates's Global Fund for Children's Vaccines and the Annenberg National Institute for School Reform; to fund-raising intermediaries, including the United Nations Foundation, the Hispanic Scholarship Foundation, the United Negro College Fund, the American Indian College Fund, and United Way of King County; to a number of U.S. public school districts; and to nonprofit corporations, including the Massachusetts Institute of Technology, New York University, the Metropolitan Museum of Art, the International Planned Parenthood Federation, the American Red Cross, CARE, and Save the Children. The next 120 gifts of $100 million to $350 million similarly went to nine foundations established by the donors or their families, thirty-three private universities and medical schools, twenty-odd private art museums, the Seattle Symphony and the Seattle Children's Museum, six private scientific research institutes, four or five health charities, the Atlanta Salvation Army and six other humanitarian charities, three charities devoted to United Nations agencies, six other international efforts ranging from Central European University to Planned Parenthood, two private boarding schools, and thirty-one state universities. Funds from these large gifts also went to three of the museums of the Smithsonian Institution, the National Science Foundation, the New York State Library, and large numbers of public schools and public libraries, usually to pay for computers or computer training.

4. Institutions endowed and controlled by single individuals have often encountered severe problems in maintaining their facilities and programs, especially over time: notable examples include the Barnes Foundation's art museum, the Isabella Stewart Gardner Museum, and—in a very different way—the Moody Foundation. *The Philadelphia Inquirer,* October 28, 2001, 10; Waldemar Nielsen, *The Big Foundations* (New York: Columbia University Press, 1972), 151–157. Organizations supported by numbers of individuals also get into serious trouble, of course.

5. Eduard C. Lindemann, *Wealth and Culture* (New York: 1936).

6. Ferdinand Lundberg, *America's 60 Families* (New York: The Citadel Press, 1938), 381.

7. Ibid., 384. As John Simon pointed out in testimony before Congress in 1965.

8. "Tax-Exempt Foundations and Charitable Trusts: Their Impact on Our Economy," Chairman's Report to the Select Committee on Small Business, House of Representatives, 87th Congress, 2nd Session (U.S. Printing Office, 1962), 1.

9. Lundberg, *America's 60 Families,* 338, 386. For a widely cited recent critique of endowments that strikingly echoes Lundberg's, see Gilbert M. Gaul and Neill A. Borowski, *Free Ride: The Tax-Exempt Economy* (Kansas City: Andrews and McMeel, 1993).

10. Lundberg, *America's 60 Families,* 386–407.

11. Ibid., 332–333.

12. Ibid., 322.

13. Ibid., 338–344, 354.

14. Ibid., 364–371.

15. Ibid., 353.

16. Robert F. Arnove, *Philanthropy and Cultural Imperialism: The Foundations at Home and Abroad* (Bloomington: Indiana University Press, 1980); Ronald Story, *The Forging of an Aristocracy: Harvard and The Boston Upper Class, 1800–1870* (Middletown, Conn.: Wesleyan University Press; distributed by Columbia University Press, 1980); Edward H. Berman, *The Ideology of Philanthropy: The Influence of the Carnegie, Ford, and Rockefeller*

Foundations on American Foreign Policy (Albany: State University of New York Press, 1983); E. Richard Brown, *Rockefeller Medicine Men: Medicine and Capitalism in America* (Berkeley: University of California Press, 1980); Donald Fisher, "The Role of Philanthropic Foundations in the Reproduction and Production of Hegemony," *Sociology* 17 (1983); Donald Fisher, "Boundary Work: Toward a Model of the Relation of Power/Knowledge," *Knowledge* 10 (1988): 156–176; Donald Fisher, "Philanthropic Foundations and the Social Sciences: A Response to Martin Bulmer," *Sociology* 18 (1984): 581–587; Magali Sarfatti Larson, "The Production of Expertise and the Constitution of Expert Power," in *The Authority of Experts: Studies in History and Theory*, ed. Thomas Haskell (Bloomington: Indiana University Press, 1984).

17. E. Digby Baltzell, *The Protestant Establishment: Aristocracy and Caste in America* (New York: Random House, 1964), 357.

18. John E. Lankford, *Congress and the Foundations in the Twentieth Century* (River Falls: Wisconsin State University, 1964); Thomas C. Reeves, *Freedom and the Foundation: The Fund for the Republic in the Era of McCarthyism* (New York: Knopf, 1969); Thomas C. Reeves, ed., *Foundations under Fire* (Ithaca, N.Y.: Cornell University Press, 1970); Marvin Olasky, *The Tragedy of American Compassion* (Washington, D.C.: Regnery Publishing, 1992); Peter Dobkin Hall, *Inventing the Nonprofit Sector and Other Essays on Philanthropy, Voluntarism, and Nonprofit Organizations* (Baltimore: Johns Hopkins University Press, 1992); David C. Hammack, "History and Myth: Marvin Olasky's *The Tragedy of American Compassion*," *Nonprofit and Voluntary Sector Quarterly* 25 (June 1996): 259–268; Capital Research Center, available online at http://www.capitalresearch.org; National Commission on Philanthropy and Civic Renewal (the Bradley Commission), *Giving Better, Giving Smarter: Renewing Philanthropy in America* (Washington, D.C.: The Commission, 1997).

19. Baltzell, *The Protestant Establishment*, 356; Rovere quoted in Baltzell, *The Protestant Establishment*, 284, from Richard Rovere, *Senator Joe McCarthy* (New York: Meridian Books, 1960), 82.

20. Baltzell, *The Protestant Establishment*, 292–293. Baltzell exaggerated the independence of establishment institutions if not of some individuals; see, for example, Sigmund Diamond, *Compromised Campus: The Collaboration of Universities with the Intelligence Community, 1945–1955* (New York: Oxford University Press, 1992).

21. Kelly McMann, "From the Street to the Ballot Box: How Different Forms of Participation Interact," paper presented at the 2001 Annual Meeting of the American Political Science Association, 2001; McMann's restatement of Dahl's eight factors is on page 1.

22. Frederic C. Jaher, *The Urban Establishment: Upper Strata in Boston, New York, Charleston, Chicago, and Los Angeles* (Urbana: University of Illinois Press, 1982), 730.

23. John Simon, "Statement," in U.S. Congress, House, Committee on Ways & Means, *Written Statements by Interested Individuals and Organizations on Treasury Department Report on Private Foundations*, issued February 2, 1965 (Washington, D.C.: U.S. Printing Office, 1965), vol. 1, pp. 458–462.

24. Simon, "Statement." The most influential contribution on this line of thought is Barry D. Karl and Stanley N. Katz, "The American Private Philanthropic Foundation and the Public Sphere, 1890–1930," *Minerva* 19 (1981): 236–270; one of the most recent is Alice O'Connor, *Poverty Knowledge: Social Science, Social Policy, and the Poor in Twentieth-Century U.S. History* (Princeton, N.J.: Princeton University Press, 2001). Simon went on to add that, *contra* Patman, foundations were not different from other stockholders in advancing concentration of ownership. Foundations care just as much as other stockowners about returns on their investments, he added, so they do not welcome the diversion of income from dividends to other corporate purposes—and hence, foundation ownership of corporations does not increase the concentration of economic power. Historians who have concluded that foundations and individual patrons of ideas usually find it impossible to control

events and policy include Ellen Condliffe Lagemann, *Private Power for the Public Good: A History of the Carnegie Foundation for the Advancement of Teaching* (Middletown, Conn.: Wesleyan University Press, 1983); Martin Bulmer, "Philanthropic Foundations and the Development of the Social Sciences: A Reply to Donald Fisher," *Sociology* 18 (1984): 572–579; Steven Wheatley, *The Politics of Philanthropy: Abraham Flexner and Medical Education* (Madison: University of Wisconsin Press, 1988); David C. Hammack, "Community Foundations: The Delicate Question of Purpose," in *An Agile Servant,* ed. Richard Magat (New York: The Foundation Center, 1989), 23–50; Ellen Condliffe Lagemann, *The Politics of Knowledge: The Carnegie Corporation, Philanthropy, and Public Policy* (Middletown, Conn.: Wesleyan University Press, 1989); and Judith Sealander, *Private Wealth and Public Life: Foundation Philanthropy and the Reshaping of American Social Policy from the Progressive Era to the New Deal* (Baltimore: Johns Hopkins University Press, 1997). Several of the best-informed foundation insiders have argued that foundations rarely take bold or clearly considered action: Waldemar A. Nielsen, *The Golden Donors: A New Anatomy of the Great Foundations* (New York: E. P. Dutton, 1985); Merrimon Cuninggim, *Private Money and Public Service: The Role of Foundations in American Society* (New York: McGraw-Hill, 1972).

25. James Anderson, *The Education of Blacks in the South, 1860–1935* (Chapel Hill and London: University of North Carolina Press, 1988).

26. See, notably, Lori Ginzberg, *Women and the Work of Benevolence* (New Haven, Conn.: Yale University Press, 1990); Linda Gordon, *Pitied But Not Entitled: Single Mothers and the History of Welfare* (Cambridge, Mass.: Harvard University Press, 1994); and Suzanne Mettler, *Dividing Citizens: Gender and Federalism in New Deal Public Policy* (Ithaca, N.Y.: Cornell University Press, 1998).

27. See, for example, Rogers M. Smith, *Civic Ideals: Conflicting Visions Of Citizenship in U.S. History* (New Haven, Conn.: Yale University Press, 1997); William E. Nelson, *The Legalist Reformation: Law, Politics, and Ideology in New York, 1920–1980* (Chapel Hill: North Carolina University Press, 2001).

28. Lundberg, *America's 60 Families,* 322–323.

29. Colin B. Burke, "Nonprofit History's New Numbers: And the Need for More," in a special symposium on "The Growth of the Nonprofit Sector," *Nonprofit and Voluntary Sector Quarterly* (June 2001): 187.

30. Jaher, *The Urban Establishment,* 274.

31. Data on government expenditures can be found in *Historical Statistics of the United States* and the *Statistical Abstract of the United States;* for influential discussions of the changing proportion of the economy involved in government expenditures, see Robert Higgs, *Crisis and Leviathan: Critical Episodes in the Growth of American Government* (New York: Oxford University Press, 1987); and Ballard C. Campbell, *The Growth of American Government: Governance from the Cleveland Era to the Present* (Bloomington: Indiana University Press, 1995), 34.

32. With the important exception of the Civil War veterans' pensions and the less important but notable exception of the Sheppard-Towner Act; see Theda Skocpol, *Protecting Soldiers and Mothers: The Political Origins of Social Policy in the United States* (Cambridge, Mass.: Belknap Press of Harvard University Press, 1992).

33. Robert Higgs, *Crisis and Leviathan: Critical Episodes in the Growth of American Government* (New York: Oxford University Press, 1987); and Campbell, *The Growth of American Government,* 34.

34. For an estimate of the share of giving that went to religious organizations in the 1990s, see Virginia A. Hodgkinson and Murray S. Weitzman et al., *The Nonprofit Almanac 1996–97: Dimensions of the Nonprofit Sector* (San Francisco: Jossey-Bass, 1996). All but the New England states of Massachusetts, Connecticut, and New Hampshire, where taxes supported the dissenting Congregational Church, ended direct tax support for religious activ-

ity in the 1780s. See William G. McLoughlin, *New England Dissent, 1630–1833: A Chapter in the History of Individual Freedom* (Cambridge, Mass.: Harvard University Press, 1971); Jacob C. Meyer, *Church and State in Massachusetts from 1740 to 1833: A Chapter in the History of the Development of Individual Freedom* (Cleveland: Western Reserve University Press, 1930); Richard J. Purcell, *Connecticut in Transition, 1775–1818* (Washington, D.C., 1918); Susan Martha Reed, *Church and State in Massachusetts, 1691–1740,* University of Illinois Studies in the Social Sciences, vol. III, no. 4 (Urbana: University of Illinois, 1914).

35. Susan Carter, Scott Gartner, Michael R. Haines, Alan Olmstead, Richard Sutch, and Gavin Wright, eds., *Historical Statistics of the United States on CD-ROM: Millennial Edition* (New York: Cambridge University Press, forthcoming); for a discussion, see David C. Hammack, "Growth, Transformation, and Quiet Revolution in the Nonprofit Sector: Law, Policy, and Commerce," *Nonprofit and Voluntary Sector Quarterly* 30 (June 2001): 160–163.

36. George Frederick Miller, for example, argued that tuition fees provided the "principal source of revenue" of nineteenth-century academies. See George Frederick Miller, *The Academy System of the State of New York* (Albany: J. B. Lyon Co., 1922), and Colin B. Burke shows the importance of tuition to early colleges in *American Collegiate Populations: A Test of the Traditional View* (New York: New York University Press, 1982).

37. Timothy A. Hacsi, *Second Home: Orphan Asylums and Poor Families in America* (Cambridge, Mass.: Harvard University Press, 1997), 103, reports that in 1910 fees provided about 10 percent of income for non-Catholic orphanages and 20 percent of income for Catholic orphanages.

38. The best account of the funding of hospitals at the end of the nineteenth century and the beginning of the twentieth that I know is David Rosner, *A Once Charitable Enterprise: Hospitals and Health Care in Brooklyn and New York, 1885–1915* (Princeton, N.J.: Princeton University Press, 1982).

39. On current church funding arrangements, see Dean R. Hoge, Charles Zech, Patrick McNamara, and Michael J. Donahue, *Money Matters: Personal Giving in American Churches* (Louisville, Ky.: Westminster John Knox Press, 1996). On the general history of religious congregation-building in the United States, see Roger Finke and Rodney Stark, *The Churching of America: Winners and Losers in Our Religious Economy* (New Brunswick, N.J.: Rutgers University Press, 1992).

40. The 1910 U.S. Census of Benevolent Institutions, for example, found that half or more of the nonprofit benevolent institutions in Maryland, New York, California, Pennsylvania, and Kansas depended to a considerable extent on direct government subsidies, as did at least a third in the District of Columbia, New Hampshire, Connecticut, New Jersey, Indiana, Oregon, Utah, Idaho, and Mississippi. See Burke, "Nonprofit History's New Numbers," 193–194.

41. The exceptions are notable, often for the difficulties in covering costs they have encountered over time: the Isabella Stewart Gardner Museum in Boston, the Frick Collection and the Morgan Gallery in New York, the Barnes Museum near Philadelphia, and Black Mountain College in North Carolina. Black Mountain College closed and the Gardner and Barnes Museums have found it very difficult to maintain their facilities.

42. The late Richard Shatten, an exceptionally capable advisor to some of Cleveland's leading business firms and wealthiest entrepreneurs during the 1980s and 1990s, once protested to me in conversation that it was frustrating to find foundation, hospital, university, and arts organization administrators using money "earned by those who are dead" to thwart the plans of "those who have earned money through their own efforts."

43. For the general argument, see David C. Hammack, *Making the Nonprofit Sector in the United States: A Reader* (Bloomington: Indiana University Press, 1999).

44. One of the great cases is that of the Ford Foundation: Henry Ford II eventually resigned from the board of the foundation his family had created because while "the Foundation is a creature of capitalism it is hard to discern recognition of this fact in anything the Foundation does." William E. Simon, "Reaping the Whirlwind," *Philanthropy Monthly* 13 (1980): 5–8, quoted in Peter Dobkin Hall, *Inventing the Nonprofit Sector and Other Essays on Philanthropy, Voluntarism, and Nonprofit Organizations* (Baltimore: Johns Hopkins University Press, 1992), 95. On the general point, see also Cuninggim, *Private Money and Public Service.*

45. Finke and Stark, *The Churching of America.*

46. See Hammack, *Making the Nonprofit Sector in the United States.* An early approximation of this argument can be found in Merle Curti, "American Philanthropy and the National Character," in *America's Voluntary Spirit: A Book of Readings,* ed. Brian O'Connell (New York: The Foundation Center, 1983), 167; this essay was originally published in *American Quarterly* 10 (Winter 1958): 420–437.

47. For the Virginia background, see Buckley, *Church and State in Revolutionary Virginia;* for an account of the background in the middle states, see Sally Schwartz, *"A Mixed Multitude": The Struggle for Toleration in Colonial Philadelphia* (New York: New York University Press, 1988); for the New England background, see William G. McLoughlin, *New England Dissent, 1630–1833: A Chapter in the History of Individual Freedom* (Cambridge, Mass.: Harvard University Press, 1971); for the colonies in general, see Patricia U. Bonomi, *Under the Cope of Heaven: Religion, Society, and Politics in Colonial America* (New York: Oxford University Press, 1986).

48. Ray Allen Billington, *The Protestant Crusade, 1800–1860: A Study of the Origins of American Nativism* (New York: Macmillan, 1938); Clifford S. Griffen, *Their Brothers' Keepers: Moral Stewardship in the United States, 1800–1965* (New Brunswick, N.J.: Rutgers University Press, 1960); Carol Smith Rosenberg, *Religion and the Rise of the American City: The New York City Mission and Tract Society* (Ithaca, N.Y.: Cornell University Press, 1971).

49. The classic account of increasing religious conflict in late-nineteenth-century America is John Higham, *Strangers in the Land: Patterns of American Nativism, 1860–1925* (New Brunswick, N.J.: Rutgers University Press, 1955). To emphasize the late-nineteenth-century crisis is not to downplay the significance of early-nineteenth-century bigotry and strife, as documented many years ago in Ray Allen Billington's *The Protestant Crusade, 1800–1860* (New York: Macmillan, 1938).

50. Mary J. Oates, *The Catholic Philanthropic Tradition in America* (Bloomington: Indiana University Press, 1995); Dorothy M. Brown and Elizabeth McKeown, *The Poor Belong to Us: Catholic Charities and American Welfare* (Cambridge, Mass.: Harvard University Press, 1997); Timothy A. Hacsi, *Second Home: Orphan Asylums and Poor Families in America* (Cambridge, Mass.: Harvard University Press, 1997).

51. The pioneering study of Catholic parish human-service efforts is Jay Dolan, *The Immigrant Church: New York's Irish and German Catholics, 1815–1865* (Baltimore: Johns Hopkins University Press, 1975); the fullest account of the development of a big city's Catholic schools is James W. Sanders, *The Education of an Urban Minority: Catholics in Chicago, 1833–1965* (New York: Oxford University Press, 1977). The most comprehensive account of Catholic institution-founding is Oates, *The Catholic Philanthropic Tradition in America.* Dorothy M. Brown and Elizabeth McKeown's *The Poor Belong to Us: Catholic Charities and American Welfare* (Cambridge, Mass.: Harvard University Press, 1997) is exceptionally thoughtful and provocative. An earlier and unusually extensive dissertation treatment is Susan Scharlotte Walton, "To Preserve the Faith: Catholic Charities in Boston, 1870–1930" (Ph.D. diss., Boston University, 1983). Walton's dissertation was published by Garland Press in 1993.

52. Perhaps the most useful general study relevant to this generalization is Frederick Rudolph, *The American College and University: A History* (New York: Alfred A. Knopf, 1962). For interpretations that place more emphasis on the political, economic, and regional interests of the builders of nineteenth-century institutions in the framework of the Protestant denominations, see Peter Dobkin Hall, *The Organization of American Culture, 1700–1900: Private Institutions, Elites, and the Origins of American Nationality* (New York: New York University Press, 1984); and Griffen, *Their Brothers' Keepers*. A comprehensive contemporary account of efforts by Calvinist Presbyterians and Congregationalists is Robert Baird, *Religion in the United States of America* (Glasgow and Edinburgh: Blackie and Son, 1844; reprint, New York: Arno Press, 1969).

53. Steven C. Bullock, *Revolutionary Brotherhood: Freemasonry and the Transformation of the American Social Order, 1730–1840* (Chapel Hill: University of North Carolina Press, 1996) documents the difficulty faced by nineteenth-century Masons as they sought to define and honor their obligations to members of their order and their heirs and thus to build lasting institutions for public benefit. An effort to identify early institutions that reflected a nonsectarian Enlightenment spirit indirectly provided considerable evidence of their weakness: Frank Warren Crow, "The Age of Promise: Societies for Social and Economic Improvement in the United States, 1785–1815" (Ph.D. diss., University of Wisconsin, 1952). Notable individual institutions that did not emphasize commitment to a religious tradition included the Boston Public Library, the Lowell Institute, the New York Public Library and its predecessors, the Cooper Union, the Franklin Institute, and the Carnegie Institution. Formally nonsectarian donations also created the Boston Museum of Fine Arts, the Worcester and Hartford Athenaeums, the Metropolitan Museum of Art, the American Museum of Natural History, the Philadelphia Museum of Art, the Walters Art Museum, and the Corcoran Gallery.

54. In most cities and towns, the most impressive buildings housed these institutions. See, for example, Elliot Wilensky and Norval White, *AIA Guide to New York City,* 3rd ed. (New York: Harcourt Brace Jovanovich, 1988); The Foundation for Architecture, *Philadelphia Architecture: A Guide to the City,* 2nd ed. (Philadelphia: The Foundation for Architecture, 1994); Franklin Toker, *Pittsburgh: An Urban Portrait* (University Park: Penn State University Press, 1986); Francis R. Kowsky et al., eds., *Buffalo Architecture: A Guide* (Cambridge, Mass.: MIT Press, 1981); Robert C. Gaede and Robert Kalin, eds., *Guide to Cleveland Architecture* (Cleveland: Cleveland Chapter, American Institute of Architects, 1990).

55. Bertram Wyatt-Brown, *Lewis Tappan and the Evangelical War against Slavery* (Cleveland: Press of Case Western Reserve University, 1969); James McPherson, *The Abolitionist Legacy: From Reconstruction to the NAACP* (Princeton, N.J.: Princeton University Press, 1975); James D. Anderson, *The Education of Blacks in the South, 1860–1935* (Chapel Hill: University of North Carolina Press, 1988).

56. W. E. B. DuBois, *Economic Co-operation among Negro Americans* (Atlanta, Ga.: Atlanta University, 1907).

57. David C. Hammack, John Grabowski, and Diane Grabowski, eds., *Identity, Cooperation, and Competition: Central European Migrants in Cleveland, 1870–1930* (Cleveland: Western Reserve Historical Society/Kent State University Press, forthcoming).

58. Kathleen D. McCarthy, *Noblesse Oblige: Charity and Cultural Philanthropy in Chicago, 1849–1929* (Chicago: University of Chicago Press, 1982); Kathleen D. McCarthy, *Lady Bountiful Revisited: Women, Philanthropy, and Power* (New Brunswick, N.J.: Rutgers University Press, 1990); Kathryn Kish Sklar, *Florence Kelley and the Nation's Work: The Rise of Women's Political Culture, 1830–1900* (New Haven, Conn.: Yale University Press, 1995); Mary J. Oates, *The Catholic Philanthropic Tradition in America* (Bloomington: Indiana University Press, 1995). Lori Ginzberg (*Women and the Work of Benevolence: Morality, Politics, and Class in the Nineteenth-Century United States* [New Haven, Conn.: Yale University

Press, 1990]) and Helen Lefkowitz Horowitz (*Culture and the City*) see women's philanthropy as often advancing the agenda of class rather than gender.

59. An important qualification; see Norman I. Silber, *A Corporate Form of Freedom: The Emergence of the Nonprofit Sector* (Boulder: Westview Press, 2001). State legislators have also often changed the rules for voluntary associations and mutual benefit societies, including the rules under which they are allowed to hold property; see Elizabeth Clemens, "The Encounter of Civil Society and the States: Legislation, Law, and Association, 1900–1920," paper presented at the Social Science History Association Annual Meeting, Pittsburgh, Pa., November 2000.

60. Burke, *American Collegiate Populations.*

61. This is one of the overriding messages of John Higham's *Strangers in the Land* and one of the key points of Sydney Ahlstrom's magisterial *A Religious History of the American People* (New Haven, Conn.: Yale University Press, 1972).

62. Thomas L. Haskell, *The Emergence of Professional Social Science: The American Social Science Association and the Nineteenth-Century Crisis of Authority* (Urbana: University of Illinois Press, 1977). The American Social Science Association served as the peak association and chief forum for the managers of private as well as many public schools, hospitals, orphanages, and other social institutions in the 1880s and 1890s. By the early twentieth century it had lost its ability to play those roles, in part because the programs of so many organizations have shifted from a religious to a scientific basis.

63. See, for example, Charles Rosenberg, *The Cholera Years: The United States in 1832, 1849, and 1866* (Chicago: University of Chicago Press, 1962); and James Turner, *Without God, without Creed: The Origins of Unbelief in America* (Baltimore: Johns Hopkins University Press, 1985).

64. This is a large topic that deserves far more exploration than it has yet received, but see, for example, Griffen, *Their Brothers' Keepers;* Carol Smith Rosenberg, *Religion and the Rise of the City: The New York City Mission Movement* (Ithaca, N.Y.: Cornell University Press, 1971); Higham, *Strangers in the Land;* John Webb Pratt, *Religion, Politics, and Diversity: The Church-State Theme in New York History* (Ithaca, N.Y.: Cornell University Press, 1967); and James M. McPherson, *The Abolitionist Legacy: From Reconstruction to the NAACP* (Princeton, N.J.: Princeton University Press, 1975).

65. The most important book on this topic is Thomas Haskell's *The Emergence of Professional Social Science: The American Social Science Association and the Nineteenth-Century Crisis of Authority* (Urbana: University of Illinois Press, 1977). Albert Schenkel makes the related argument that John D. Rockefeller played a dominant role in funding the nonsectarian and interfaith religious organizations that came to constitute what Schenkel calls the "Protestant Establishment": Albert F. Schenkel, *The Rich Man and the Kingdom: John D. Rockefeller Jr. and the Protestant Establishment* (Minneapolis: Fortress Press, 1995). On Rockefeller, see Raymond B. Fosdick, *The Story of the Rockefeller Foundation* (New York: Harper, 1952); on Carnegie's charities, see Ellen Condliffe Lagemann, *Private Power For the Public Good: A History of the Carnegie Foundation for the Advancement of Teaching* (Middletown, Conn.: Wesleyan University Press, 1983); and *The Politics of Knowledge: The Carnegie Corporation, Philanthropy, and Public Policy* (Middletown, Conn.: Wesleyan University Press, 1989); on Mrs. Sage, see David C. Hammack and Stanton Wheeler, *Social Science in the Making: Essays on The Russell Sage Foundation, 1907–1972* (New York: Russell Sage Foundation, 1994).

66. David C. Hammack, "Foundations in the American Polity," in *New Scholarship on the History of American Foundations,* ed. Ellen Condliffe Lagemann (Bloomington: Indiana University Press, 1999), 43–68.

67. Merle Curti and Roderick Nash, *Philanthropy in the Shaping of American Higher Education* (New Brunswick, N.J.: Rutgers University Press, 1965); Roger Geiger, *To Ad-*

vance Knowledge: The Growth of American Research Universities, 1900–1940 (New York: Oxford University Press, 1986); Roger Geiger, *Research and Relevant Knowledge: American Research Universities Since World War II* (New York: Oxford University Press, 1993). Detailed data on amounts raised by field over time is included in *Historical Statistics of the United States: Millennial Edition* (forthcoming).

68. Data for this study derive from the multiyear "Six Cities" study funded by the Lilly Endowment through the Program on Non-Profit Organizations at Yale (PONPO) and from additional work on the study of trusteeship also funded by the Lilly Endowment through PONPO. An unpublished report on the initial dataset by Rikke Abzug and Joseph Galaskiewicz, "Nonprofit Boards: Crucibles of Expertise or Symbols of Local Identities," September 2000, is based on data on about one-quarter of all trustees and on a different sense of the role of nonprofit boards. I want to thank Shilpa Damle and Ruth Milne, graduate students in the Case Western Reserve University Department of History, and the Mandel Center for Nonprofit Organizations for assistance in gathering and compiling the data that I report here.

69. Of these, eight were "nonsectarian": University Hospitals of Cleveland, the Cleveland Museum of Art, the Musical Arts Association (the Cleveland Orchestra), United Way Services, the Junior League of Cleveland, The Cleveland Foundation, and Case Western Reserve University. Two were Catholic: St. Vincent Charity Hospital and Catholic Social Services. Two were Jewish: Mt. Sinai Hospital and the Jewish Family Service Association. And four were Protestant: St. Luke's Hospital, the Center for Human Services, the YMCA, and the YWCA.

PART TWO

Between Market and State:
Philanthropy and Social Elites

FIVE

Philanthropy and Science in Wilhelmine Germany

ECKHARDT FUCHS AND DIETER HOFFMANN

" A round 1910 German industrialists were not used to donating money for scientific purposes. Of course, there were exceptions, such as the Göttingen Society for Applied Physics and Mathematics (Göttinger Gesellschaft für angewandte Physik und Mathematik) and since 1905 the Imperial Institute of Chemistry (Chemische Reichsanstalt), but these were relatively small organizations. The vast majority of German industrialists kept their distance from such ideas, especially since they did not grasp their purpose. . . . Philanthropy for science without any expectations about its practical use, as had been common in the United States for a long time, was completely unusual within this circle."[1] This quote reflects the general assumption among historians of science that in Wilhelmine Germany, science was promoted and funded only by the government and state institutions. Only in recent years has new research on German philanthropy revealed the existence of a wide range of private sponsorship for science which began at the end of the eighteenth century. Various local case studies indicate that scientific philanthropy has a much longer tradition in Germany than was previously thought.[2]

In the context of the modern philanthropic movement, scientific philanthropy developed late. Only when, in the last decades of the nineteenth century, science and technology became major agents for the industrial, social, and military development of nations and scientific research, and enterprises reached new dimensions that exceeded the financial resources of the state did philanthropists realize the high social potential that donations in the field of science and industrial research offered them. As the German government faced the rise of science and technology during a phase of economic growth and tried to use both for its political purposes, it was confronted with a dilemma. On the one hand, it sought to maintain its monopoly over education and science. On the other hand, it needed financial resources to match the demands of science and industry. Scientific philanthropy seemed to be the only way to solve this dilemma, even if it meant a limitation of the state's influence on science and—in the case of the Frankfurt University—on educational institutions. Bernhard vom Brocke lists forty-seven foundations with scientific purposes that were founded in Germany between 1894 and 1914 for which the foundation capital was in the six-digit range.[3] The Prussian Academy listed in its *Statutes and Regulations* (1907)[4] more than thirty foundations that were connected with the academy and that played an important role in organizing the scientific life of this important scientific institution in Germany. The broad spectrum of scientific philanthropy in Germany that developed before World War I was by no means a countercurrent to state-funded science but a complementary form that was still closely intertwined with the government.

In this chapter we will introduce two leading representatives of scientific philanthropy, Werner von Siemens and Leopold Koppel. These two individuals are excellent examples of the specific bourgeois (and Jewish) milieu of private funding for science in Germany. They not only demonstrate that there indeed existed a scientific philanthropy in Germany comparable to that in the United States but—in the case of Koppel—that this scientific philanthropy reached beyond Germany. As we will show, the institutionalized scientific relations between Germany and the United States before the Great War were mainly based on private sponsorship in Germany as well as in the New World.

WERNER VON SIEMENS AND THE
FOUNDING OF THE IMPERIAL INSTITUTE
OF PHYSICS AND TECHNOLOGY

The Franco-Prussian War in 1870–1871 and new technological developments in the civilian sector revealed a lack of precision instruments and other technical devices—especially for military purposes—in Germany. It is not surprising, therefore, that a group of Prussian army officers and scientists proposed the establishment of a government-sponsored institute for precision mechanics in Berlin in 1872. However, this proposal was only partially implemented. A commission consisting of leading scientists and technicians was appointed, but no more than informal discussions resulted from its work. Since the Prussian government was not able to finance the project, the institute was never founded. This failure deeply worried Werner von Siemens, who was delegated to the commission by the Prussian Academy of Science, of which he had been a member since 1873.

Siemens, born in 1816 near Hanover, was not only an eminent scientist but, more important, a pioneer of electrical engineering. Together with Georg Halske he had founded his own company, the Telegraphenbauanstalt Siemens & Halske in 1847; Siemens can be seen as the "father" of the German electro-technical industry. When he decided to take over the commission in the early 1880s, he gave it a new direction. For him, the new institute had to serve the interests of the new and innovative electrical industry. He was convinced that "scientific research is the safest ground for technical progress, and the national industry cannot reach and keep a leading position in the world if it is not—at the same time—on top of scientific progress."[5] It was for that reason that, first, the institute had to become the basis for the establishment of precise and secure electrical components and, second, its research should create the scientific foundation for new technical and industrial developments. For Siemens, "The important question of electrical components makes it absolutely necessary to accelerate the founding of a research organization with its own buildings and equipment."[6] Siemens found an excellent ally in Hermann von Helmholtz in his pursuit of both of these goals. The "chancellor of German physics," as his contemporaries called Helmholtz in a respectful yet ironic way, became "Siemens' right hand man . . . and acted as Siemens' plenipotentiary."[7]

When Siemens realized that this idea required more money than the Prussian state could provide, he increased his contributions in the summer of 1883.[8] In a letter to the Prussian minister of culture, Gustav von Gossler, he revealed his fear that the Prussian government would not provide enough money and offices necessary for an institute of such importance. This fear was the reason why Siemens, who expected important results for science and technology from the work of the institute, undertook an additional step. He offered the Prussian government some of his land under the condition that the government use it to build and maintain an institute of experimental physics that included labs and other facilities. He argued that his own professional success as an industrialist was founded on the close relationship between experimental research and its practical scientific and technical use.[9]

Although Gossler responded positively and praised Siemens's gift as new evidence of his "patriotic and unselfish disposition to contribute to the state for the well-being of the fatherland and in the interest of science," the plan was not realized.[10] Prussia could not afford to match Siemens's funding. Therefore, Siemens turned to the German government. His new and extended offer not only included the announced gift but also his willingness "to take care of the construction of the necessary buildings."[11] In a letter to the minister of the interior, Heinrich von Boetticher, he described the scientific importance of the planned institute and underlined his own patriotic motives. He stated "that in offering $1/2$ million marks in real estate or capital for the founding of the planned institute my purpose is only to perform a service for my fatherland and to prove my love for science, which alone is responsible for my prosperity in life."[12]

Siemens's initiative coincided with the Reich's efforts to turn Berlin into a leading center of Germany's political, cultural, and scientific life. His efforts led finally to the founding of an Imperial Institute despite many financial and political problems.[13] During the spring of 1887, the *Reichstag* approved the first budget of the new Imperial Institute of Physics and Technology (Physikalisch-Technische Reichsanstalt, PTR), which was formally opened in October. In the end, the cost for the establishment of the new institute had added up to about 3.7 million reichsmark. The value of Siemens's gift of land—about 20,000 square meters —was 566,157 reichsmark. Hermann von Helmholtz was appointed the first president of the Reichsanstalt, as Siemens had wanted. During his presidency from 1887 to 1894, Helmholtz integrated the new institute into the German scientific community, and its laboratories soon became the foremost scientific institutions for physical research in Germany and the world.[14] Siemens and Helmholtz did not focus exclusively on modern metrology and electrical measurement but based the work of the institute on a wide range of research that sought to provide scientific and technological knowledge in a very general sense. As the center of highly technical research and as the main metrological institute in Germany, the Imperial Institute quickly gained recognition in the fields of science, technology, and economy, since it contributed to the expansion of scholarship into the areas of society and industry. In addition, the precision measurements involved in this applied research became the starting point for excellent scientific developments, discoveries, and inventions that established the reputation of the PTR as an institute of advanced research. There are many examples of such scientific and technical outputs; most famous are the light measurements during the last decade of the nineteenth century, which were rooted in the need for a precise and useful light standard.[15] This research not only created such a light standard but led to the discovery of Max Planck's quantum hypothesis and the birth of quantum theory in 1900—one of the central theories of modern physics.[16] This example demonstrates not that Siemens's philanthropic efforts directly affected his own enterprise; rather, the founding of the Imperial Institute was very significant and influential for the industrialization and modernization of Germany in general and for the development and reputation of German science in particular.

LEOPOLD KOPPEL AND THE FOUNDING
OF THE KAISER WILHELM SOCIETY

The founding of the Reichsanstalt was a big success and became a model for the birth of similar institutions—at least in the way their establishment was financed. In 1905, the chemical industry founded the Society for the Imperial Institute of Chemistry with the aim of collecting money for a chemical research institute.[17] This project eventually led to the founding of the Kaiser Wilhelm Society (Kaiser-Wilhelm-Gesellschaft) and its research institutes in 1910.[18] The Society was established as a nongovernmental institution and financed its scientific activities through membership fees, grants, and donations. With an initiation fee of 2,000 reichsmark, an annual membership fee of 1,000 reichsmark, and the donation of several hundred thousand reichsmark, the Kaiser Wilhelm Society represented a new dimension of scientific philanthropy in Germany, a dimension that was comparable with the philanthropic practice in the United States. The beneficiaries of the new Society were not only the bourgeoisie but also the German economic elite of bankers and industrialists, such as Eduard Arnhold, Heinrich Theodor Böttinger, Ludwig Delbrück, Gustav Krupp, Franz von Mendelssohn, and James Simon.[19]

Leopold Koppel played a central role in founding the Kaiser Wilhelm Society. Koppel was born in 1854 in Dresden, Saxony. Raised in poverty, he started a career as a businessman in the 1870s, and in the late 1880s he founded a bank in his home town. In 1890, he moved from Dresden to Berlin, where he soon became one of the richest people in Prussia. "There are probably only a few people in Berlin who had earned so much money during the last twenty years," or so read the *Yearbook of Berlin's Millionaires*.[20] Among the Jewish millionaires of the Empire there were only two self-made men: Rudolf Mosse and Leopold Koppel.[21] The basis of Koppel's extraordinary success was his role as financier of the Deutsche Gasglühlicht AG (German Gaslight Company), the so-called Auer Company, a very successful enterprise in the new and growing electrical industry and in chemical production. Furthermore, Koppel was also a partner of the very successful Hotel Betriebsgesellschaft and a member of the board of trustees of several other enterprises. In addition to his business activities, Koppel was interested in science and art and in the scientific and artistic communities. In 1903, he began his philanthropic career by planning to establish a foundation for homeless people (Bekämpfung des Schlafstellenunwesens). While this plan failed, Koppel was more successful in promoting science and international academic exchange. Banker and industrialist Emil Jacob introduced Leopold Koppel to the influential science advisor in the Prussian ministry of culture, Friedrich Althoff, in 1905. Althoff convinced Koppel to create a foundation, and Koppel established his Koppel Foundation for the Promotion of Scientific Relations Abroad (Koppel-Stiftung zur Förderung geistiger Beziehungen mit dem Ausland) in the same year.[22]

Because the Koppel Foundation was already involved in various international scientific projects, it was no surprise that Koppel became involved in the plans for the founding of a society for the advancement of science under the patronage of the German emperor, William II. In fact, Koppel became one of the society's biggest financiers. The volume of his donations totaled about 1 million reichsmark—an amount topped only by several founders of other institutes of the Kaiser Wilhelm Society which were established later.[23] In the framework of this Society, Koppel saw the chance to realize one of his older ideas: What Helmholtz was for Siemens, one could say, Fritz Haber was for Koppel. Koppel had already tried to create employment for Fritz Haber, whom he saw as one of the leading German chemists, before the Society was founded. In 1909 he offered Haber the position of director of the Auer Company. This idea failed, but a new chance arose with the founding of the Kaiser Wilhelm Society. In the summer of 1910, Koppel made an official proposal to completely finance the founding of an institute for physical chemistry under the condition that Fritz Haber become its director. Although such complete financing and the preappointed directorship were very unusual, the plan succeeded. With the money from the Koppel Foundation—a total of about 1 million reichsmark—the Kaiser Wilhelm Institute for Physical and Electrical Chemistry was founded and constructed. In October 1912 the institute opened, making it one of the first new institutes of the Kaiser Wilhelm Society. The emperor himself was present at the opening, and he honored the sponsor in his inaugural speech and met him personally. In the ensuing years, the Koppel Foundation financed a large portion of the Institute's budget with about 30,000 marks annually.[24]

Koppel's philanthropic activities were not exhausted with the establishment of Haber's Institute for Physical and Electrical Chemistry. Just before the outbreak of World War I, the Kaiser Wilhelm Society developed a new plan; it was again connected with an extraordinary scientist. During this time the scientific community of Berlin—in particular Fritz Haber, Max Planck, and Emil Warburg—discussed plans to bring the "new genius of physics," Albert Einstein, to Berlin. In 1914, Einstein was appointed as a "paid" member of the Prussian Academy of Sciences. His salary was partly paid by Koppel himself.[25]

Moreover, the Kaiser Wilhelm Society tried to use the Koppel Foundation to realize another plan, namely the establishment of an Institute for

Physical Research, which was originally planned when the Society was founded. But only after the successful establishment of the Institute for Physical Chemistry and the funding of Einstein's membership at the Prussian Academy of Sciences could the plan be revived in 1913. The project quickly came to fruition. By the end of that year Koppel had approved the promotion and funding of such an institute under Einstein's directorship through his foundation. In the beginning of 1914, the "Proposal for the Establishment of a Kaiser Wilhelm Institute for Physical Research" stated that Koppel would finance the construction of the buildings and partly finance the annual maintenance costs. Unfortunately, the outbreak of World War I stopped the construction, and postwar inflation prevented the founding of the institute in its original form. Under completely new conditions and with the sponsorship of the Rockefeller Foundation, it was finally opened in 1938.[26] Nevertheless, another project was more successful. In 1916, Koppel sponsored the founding of the Kaiser Wilhelm Foundation for Military-Technical Science.[27]

THE INTERNATIONAL DIMENSION
OF SCIENTIFIC PHILANTHROPY

In the context of international cultural politics and the attempts of the German government to establish a so-called world politics at the turn of the twentieth century, the German ministry of culture began to incorporate science and education into foreign politics. As mentioned above, it was the collaboration between state (Althoff) and industry (Koppel) that enabled the German government to inaugurate scientific and educational institutions abroad. The Koppel Foundation, which was integrated into Althoff's network, promoted various scientific and educational projects of the German government, beginning with the German Medical School in Shanghai, the German-Chinese College in Tsingtau, and, in 1907, the journal *Internationale Zeitschrift für Wissenschaft, Kunst und Technik*.[28] However, in correlation with international politics, the most desired partner in these activities to promote international cultural and scientific transfer was the United States, which was mainly pursued by Althoff. The establishment of an exchange of professors and the founding of the America Institute in Berlin became the primary means of this institutionalized bilateral academic and scientific exchange.

In 1905, the German government initiated an exchange of German and U.S. professors between Harvard University and Berlin University; from 1906 onward this also included exchanges between the Berlin University and Columbia University.[29] Every year until the outbreak of World War I, the Berlin University exchanged a professor with both of the U.S. universities. Altogether twenty-nine professors crossed the Atlantic Ocean. The German side was completely financed by the Koppel Foundation, which provided 1 million marks, and two German-American philanthropists financed the U.S. professors. New York banker James Speyer gave an endowment of $50,000 to Columbia University to fund the Roosevelt Professorship at Berlin University.[30] The exchange professor received an annual scholarship of $2,000 to $2,400. In 1911, when Speyer's endowment no longer sufficed, the Division of Intercourse and Education of the Carnegie Endowment of International Peace donated the necessary amount.[31] Jacob H. Schiff, the director of the bank Kuhn, Loeb & Co. in New York, founded the Jacob H. Schiff Professorship at Cornell University in 1913 with an endowment of $10,000.

The Koppel Foundation also played a decisive role in founding the second institution, the America Institute in Berlin in 1910. Originally suggested by the Americans in order to institutionalize the international exchange of academic literature, it soon became the center of German-American cultural and scientific relations.[32] The main sponsors were Koppel (20,000 reichsmark), Speyer (interest on an endowment of 500,000 reichsmark), and Schiff (100,000 reichsmark). Representatives of the Koppel Foundation were members of the board of the Institute.[33]

One cannot overlook the large number of German Americans in the United States who were very interested in maintaining close relations with their home country. It is, therefore, not surprising that many wealthy German Americans sponsored cultural and scientific relations between the two countries on the local and the national levels. For example, the Germanistic Society, founded in New York in 1904, organized and sponsored a lecture series of German scholars in the United States. The famous German-American brewer Adolphus Busch from St. Louis and businessman Hugo Reisinger from New York financed the Germanic Museum at Harvard University in 1910. As these examples show, the Koppel Foundation was one of many private foundations that sponsored the academic and scientific exchange between Germany and the United States. Yet it was the only German foundation involved in the project and the one which donated the most money.

To be sure, this program of academic exchange would not have become a reality without U.S. sponsorship. At this point we cannot go into detail about U.S. scientific philanthropy, except to say that their most important representatives before World War I were John D. Rockefeller in conjunction with the Spelman Seminary in Atlanta (1886), the University of Chicago (1889), the Institute for the Advancement of Medicine (1901), and the Rockefeller Foundation (1913); and Andrew Carnegie, whose Carnegie Institute in Pittsburgh (1895) and Carnegie Institution in Washington, D.C.

(1902), supported art and science.[34] While their activities are widely known, the role U.S. foundations played in sponsoring German science and academic exchange in the years before the Great War is not known. A few examples illustrate this interchange. In 1904, the Marine Biology Laboratory of the Carnegie Institution gave a scholarship to German zoologist Ludwig Plate. This was unusual, since the scholarships of the Institution were restricted to U.S. citizens. The procedure was negotiated through diplomatic channels, and it was some time before Plate could go to the Tortugas Islands for zoological studies.[35] The German government was very well informed about the Carnegie Institution by its Ambassador Sternburg and through the travels of the president of the Institution, Daniel C. Gilman, in 1902. Carnegie's philosophy of easing social tensions through private charity was attractive in Germany, and the emperor was eager to obtain a copy of the founding statutes of the Carnegie Institution.[36] Similarly, Carnegie's invitation to the German government to send several famous scientists as official German delegates to the founding celebrations of the Carnegie Institute in Pittsburgh in April 1907 demonstrates the importance of German science to him. In fact, this institute was modeled after the Technical College in Berlin-Charlottenburg. In his opening speech, Carnegie stated that "we cannot forget what we owe Germany as the teacher of industrial educations for all nations."[37] It is therefore not surprising that Carnegie sponsored scientific institutions and research in Germany. In 1908, he gave $500,000 to the Robert Koch Foundation for research on tuberculosis in Berlin. This was the first scientific donation made by an American for a cause outside the United States.[38] The Rockefeller Institute for Medical Research also donated money to German scientists. In 1909, for example, it donated $10,000 to the Institute of Experimental Therapy in Frankfurt, directed by Paul Ehrlich.[39]

Whereas the academic exchange between the two countries was mainly financed by Jewish-German and German-American bankers, another—hitherto forgotten—transatlantic philanthropist is worthy of mention. Count Joseph Florimond von Loubat from New York lived most of his life in Paris. After the International Congress of Americanists which took place in Berlin in 1889, he offered to finance a foundation and a prize for the promotion of American studies at the Berlin Academy of Sciences. Famous Berlin scholars, such as Gustav von Schmoller, Rudolf Virchow, and Heinrich von Sybel, created the statutes of the Count Loubat Foundation. The first prize was awarded to Eduard Georg Seler in 1895 for his research on Aztec hieroglyphs.[40] More important, however, was the creation of the first Chair for Pre-Columbian History endowed by Loubat at Berlin University. In 1899, Loubat gave 300,000 marks for the creation of this professorship, and its first professor was Seler one year later.[41]

SCIENTIFIC PHILANTHROPY REVISITED

The cases of Siemens, Koppel, and others show that scientific philanthropy has a longer tradition in Germany than has previously been stated in historical research. In the context of industrialization and modernization, private sponsorship reached its peak in the decades before World War I. Without any doubt, the German Empire was among the leading industrial nations at the end of the nineteenth century. However, the modernization of its economy did not produce concomitant results in its social structure, which remained complex and, to a large extent, premodern. Scientific research and technical education were the bases for economic growth. Industrial development and scientific and technological progress required the establishment of innovative scientific institutions and forms of scientific research. The state was not able to meet all of these challenges. This made cooperation between state, science, and industry necessary. This triad was at the core of what was called "science policy," and private sponsorship was an integral part of this alliance.

However, it was the specific social and political conditions that caused the late onset (compared to the United States) of modern scientific philanthropy. Although the German state claimed a monopoly over science and education, scientific philanthropists donated prizes and awards, financed professorships and research projects, and provided scholarships to students for most of the nineteenth century. In addition, the social distinction between the commercial and educated bourgeoisie (*Wirtschafts-* and *Bildungs-bürgertum*) prevented cooperation between economic elites and academic mandarins. The latter followed a specific German ideology that pure science (*Grundlagenforschung*) had to be pursued objectively, independently from political influence, and without any economic interest in order to maintain academic freedom. The hesitation of scientists to accept private sponsorship, on the one hand, and the lack of extremely rich industrialists, such as Carnegie and Rockefeller in the United States, on the other, delayed large-scale scientific philanthropy in Germany. The dramatic change in the social strata at the end of the nineteenth century, the changes in the educational system, and the rise of applied sciences and engineering that required new forms and institutions of research, in particular new forms of big science (*Großforschung*), created the conditions for scientific philanthropy. In most cases, though, scientific philanthropy never gained complete independence from the state.

An examination of the philanthropists themselves reveals that the vast majority of private sponsors were Jews. Twenty-five percent of the senators of the Kaiser Wilhelm Society were Jews. In Frankfurt, Louise von Rothschild and her daughter sponsored a public library and established the foundation called Carolinum, a dental clinic. Banker Georg Speyer and his wife sponsored professorships, scientific institutes, and laboratories. Other Jews, such as Ludwig Edinger and Richard Passavant, sponsored institutes for medical research. The most important case was the University of Frankfurt, whose establishment was based on funding by Jewish philanthropists. The chemist and owner of the Cassella Farben Company, Leo Gans, donated 1 million marks to establish the faculty of sciences of the new university.[42] In proportion to the population, Jews were also the biggest group of sponsors for the German Museum in Munich, founded in 1903. In Hamburg, the philanthropic interest of Jews was directed toward the Hamburg Scientific Foundation, founded in 1907.[43] The Jewish background of these private foundations was one reason why officials did not want to make the sponsorship public. This was especially the case with the Koppel Foundation. There are various cultural and social reasons for this phenomenon. In general, Jewish philanthropy can be seen as an attempt to gain social prestige and political influence on the local and the national levels and, as the result, to assist in their assimilation and integration into German society.[44]

Increasing social recognition played an important role for non-Jewish philanthropists as well. Of course, idealism, patriotism, a scientific ethos, religiously motivated duty, involvement in local affairs, or even economic interests can be considered individual motivations for scientific philanthropy.[45] In general, however, the new bourgeois elites, such as Siemens and Koppel, tried to establish a new social position, especially in order to distinguish philanthropists from the traditional military and noble elites. Since science became an important factor in exercising and representing power, it seemed socially worthwhile to invest in it. Philanthropy that would interest the emperor could only help. Neither Siemens nor Koppel was a singular case; they were part of a philanthropic movement that found its most visible expression in the founding of the Kaiser Wilhelm Society. Koppel and James Simon were awarded the very prestigious Wilhelm medal for their philanthropic activities. With this official recognition of their philanthropic activities and, therefore, the rise of their social prestige, Koppel, Siemens, and other philanthropists symbolize a phenomenon that Pierre Bourdieu has explained as a transformation of economic capital into social capital.[46] Philanthropy, therefore, became a means for the *Bürgertum* to express its self-confidence as a social elite and to contribute independently and under its own control to the reform of German society. Its specific cultural milieu made the rise of philanthropy—as an alliance between *Wirtschaftsbürgertum* and *Bildungsbürgertum*—possible.[47] In cases such as that of Siemens, the interests of both groups were combined.

Scientific philanthropy has always had an impact on urban development, as seen through Carnegie's influence on Washington and Pittsburgh and Siemens's and Koppel's influence on Berlin-Charlottenburg and Dahlem (the "German Oxford").[48] The Reichsanstalt was located in the city of Charlottenburg, which was an independent town until 1920, about two miles away from historic downtown Berlin. It was the favorite neighborhood of the wealthy and innovative upper class that lived there in a country-like atmosphere. Werner von Siemens and great financiers such as Gerson von Bleichröder or eminent academics such as Theodor Mommsen had their villas there. That Charlottenburg became the location of the Reichsanstalt was the result of Siemens's gift, but it was also an expression of the great self-confidence of its innovative bourgeois. Another modern institution of higher learning was housed in Charlottenburg: the Technical College, founded in 1789, which is now Berlin's Technical University. In fact, during its first years of existence, the laboratories of the Reichsanstalt were located at the Technical College before they could finally move into the newly constructed buildings in the 1890s. With the establishment of both scientific institutions and the growing industrialization during the last decades of the nineteenth century, Charlottenburg was poised to become Germany's technopolis. Siemens's philanthropy contributed significantly to this process.

Although social reform and the promotion of science, technology, and art were the main aims of scientific philanthropy, it always followed political agendas. On the one hand, philanthropists believed that it was their patriotic duty to serve their country by promoting science. On the other hand, and especially in the United States, the philanthropists wanted to promote international scientific projects whose goal was to create peace and international understanding among nations. Education and scientific progress were the buzzwords at international exhibitions, world's fairs, exchange programs, congresses, international institutions, and the like. The belief in the universal merits of international education and academic exchange led to the founding of many international institutions, most of them sponsored by private foundations. In general, it can be said that a main goal of the Rockefeller Foundation, as well as for other foundations such as the Carnegie Endowment for International Peace, was to promote international cooperation based on harmony and peace. For example, the Division of Intercourse and Education of the Carnegie Endowment for International Peace discussed several plans for an international educational cooperation that led to the founding of the Institute of International Education in 1919; the International Educational Board of the Rockefeller Foundation is another example. For this purpose, Carnegie contacted the leading politicians in Europe. In a letter to the German ambassador in Washington,

Count von Speck-Sternburg, he stated, "I am not less firm in my belief that His Majesty is destined to fulfill his mission which is, before long, to ask four leading powers to join Germany in proclaiming that the peace of the world is not to be disturbed."[49] This, of course, remained an ideal. For Germany, the academic exchange was embedded in the context of imperial foreign policy and followed specific political agendas. Even if the Koppel Foundation intended to bring different people closer together, it was doomed to fail because of its close relationship with the German government.[50] In contrast to U.S. foundations, German philanthropists were not as independent as their U.S. counterparts in defining the aims of their projects that would exceed scientific purposes.[51]

World War I and the ensuing economic crisis did not stop private scientific philanthropy in Germany, but it changed it in many ways. It turned to the state to create collective foundations in order to reestablish sponsorship of scientific research. The most important postwar example was the Stifterverband für die Deutsche Wissenschaft founded in 1920 and the Notgemeinschaft der Deutschen Wissenschaft.[52] German industry also helped establish societies to promote education and research. For instance, there were the Justus Liebig Society for the Promotion of Educational Instruction and the Emil Fischer Society for the Promotion of Chemical Research, both founded in 1920 and sponsored by the chemical industry. In the same year, the Helmholtz Society for the Promotion of Physical-Technical Research was established with the support of German industry. Nevertheless, inflation, political instability, and international isolation led to a decline of scientific philanthropy in Weimar Germany.

NOTES

1. Lothar Burchardt, "Zwischen Staat und Wissenschaft. Die Kaiser-Wilhelm-Gesellschaft bis zum Ende des ersten Weltkriegs," in *Formen außerstaatlicher Wissenschaftsförderung im 19. und 20. Jahrhundert,* ed. Rüdiger vom Bruch and Rainer A. Müller (Stuttgart: Steiner, 1990), 64.

2. On philanthropy in general, see Bernhard Kirchgässner and Hans-Peter Brecht, eds., *Stadt und Mäzenatentum* (Sigmaringen: Thorbecke, 1997); Manuel Frey, *Macht und Moral des Schenkens. Staat und bürgerliche Mäzene vom späten 18. Jahrhundert bis zur Gegenwart* (Zwickau: Fannei & Walz, 1999); Thomas W. Gaehtgens and Martin Schieder, eds., *Mäzenatisches Handeln. Studien zur Kultur des Bürgersinns in der Gesellschaft. Festschrift für Günter Braun zum 70. Geburtstag* (Zwickau: Fannei & Walz, 1998); and Jürgen Kocka and Manuel Frey, eds., *Bürgerkultur und Mäzenatentum im 19. Jahrhundert* (Zwickau: Fannei & Walz, 1998). On scientific philanthropy, see Gerald D. Feldman, "The Private Support of Science in Germany, 1900–1933," in vom Bruch and Müller, *Formen außerstaatlicher Wissenschaftsförderung,* 87–113; Dieter P. Herrmann, "Freunde und Förderer. Ein Beitrag zur

Geschichte der privaten Hochschul- und Wissenschaftsförderung in Deutschland" (Phil. Diss., Universität Bonn, 1990); and Michael Dorrmann, "Eduard Arnhold (1849–1925): Eine biographische Studie zu Unternehmer- und Mäzenatentum im Deutschen Kaiserreich" (Phil. Diss., Humboldt University Berlin, 2001). An excellent study on scientific philanthropy in Great Britain is Peter Alter, *Wissenschaft, Staat, Mäzene. Anfänge moderner Wissenschaftspolitik in Großbritannien 1850–1920* (Stuttgart: Klett-Cotta, 1982).

3. See Rudolf Vierhaus and Bernhard vom Brocke, eds., *Forschung im Spannungsfeld von Politik und Gesellschaft. Geschichte und Struktur der Kaiser-Wilhelm-Gesellschaft/Max-Planck-Gesellschaft* (Stuttgart: Deutsche Verlags-Anstalt, 1990), 110ff.

4. *Statuten und Reglements der Königlich Preußischen Akademie der Wissenschaften sowie der ihr angegliederten Stiftungen und Institute* (Berlin: Reichsdruckerei Berlin, 1907).

5. Werner von Siemens, *Wissenschaftliche und Technische Arbeiten* (Berlin: Verlag Julius Springer, 1891), 2: 568 and 580.

6. See Reichsministerium des Innern, Nr. 13144/8, Bl. 109, Bundesarchiv Berlin.

7. David Cahan, *An Institute for an Empire: The Physikalisch-Technische Reichsanstalt 1871–1918* (Cambridge and New York: Cambridge University Press, 1989), 43.

8. See Dieter Hoffmann, "Werner Siemens und die Physikalisch-Technische Reichsanstalt," in *Werner Siemens (1816–1892). Studien zu Leben und Werk,* ed. Dieter Hoffmann and Wolfgang Schreier (Braunschweig: PTB Verlag, 1995), 35–49.

9. Werner Siemens to Gustav von Gossler, July 7, 1883, Rep. 76 Vb, Sek. 1, Tit. X, Nr. 4, Bd. 1, Bl. 402–404, Geheimes Staatsarchiv Preußischer Kulturbesitz, Berlin.

10. Gustav von Gossler to Werner Siemens, July 13, 1883, 61/Lc 973, Siemens Archiv, Munich.

11. Werner Siemens to Gustav von Gossler, December 1, 1884, quoted in Conrad Matschoß, *Werner Siemens. Ein kurzgefaßtes Lebensbild nebst einer Auswahl seiner Briefe* (Berlin: Springer, 1916), 2: 805.

12. Werner Siemens to Heinrich von Boetticher, March 20, 1884, 61/Lc 973, Siemens Archiv, Munich.

13. See Gisela Buchheim, *Die Gründungsgeschichte der Physikalisch-Technischen Reichsanstalt 1872–1887,* Dresdener Beiträge zur Geschichte der Technikwissenschaften, Teil 3/4 (Dresden: Technische Universität Dresden 1981/1982).

14. See Cahan, *An Institute for an Empire.*

15. Dieter Hoffmann, "Die Physikalisch-technische Reichsanstalt. Zum 100. Gründungsjubiläum der bedeutenden Forschungseinrichtung," *Feingerätetechnik* 36 (1987): 558–562.

16. Dieter Hoffmann, "On the Experimental Context of Planck's Foundation of Quantum Theory," *Centaurus* 43, no. 3–4 (2001): 240–259.

17. See Jeffrey A. Johnson, *The Kaiser's Chemists: Science and Modernization in Imperial Germany* (Chapel Hill: University of North Carolina Press, 1990).

18. See Vierhaus and Brocke, *Forschung im Spannungsfeld,* 17ff.

19. Lothar Burchardt, *Wissenschaftspolitik im Wilhelminischen Deutschland* (Göttingen: Vandenhoeck & Ruprecht, 1975), 53ff.

20. Rudolf Martin, *Jahrbuch des Vermögens und Einkommens der Millionäre im Königreich Preußen* (Berlin: Martin, 1914), 146.

21. See Margit Szöllösi-Janze, *Fritz Haber: 1868–1934. Eine Biographie* (Munich: Beck, 1998), 213.

22. See Bernhard vom Brocke, "Der deutsch-amerikanische Professorenaustausch. Preußische Wissenschaftspolitik, internationale Wissenschaftsbeziehungen und die Anfänge einer deutschen auswärtigen Kulturpolitik vor dem Ersten Weltkrieg," *Zeitschrift für Kulturaustausch* 31 (1981): 144; Vierhaus and Brocke, *Forschung im Spannungsfeld,* 98ff.

23. Vierhaus and Brocke, *Forschung im Spannungsfeld,* 145ff. The highest single donation was 3 million reichsmark and was given by Marianne von Friedlaender-Fuld for the founding of the Kaiser Wilhelm Institute of Coal Research in 1917.

24. Vierhaus and Brocke, *Forschung im Spannungsfeld,* 144ff.

25. Christa Kirsten and Hans-Jürgen Treder, eds., *Albert Einstein in Berlin. Teil I. Darstellung und Dokumente* (Berlin: Akademie Verlag, 1979), 102ff.

26. See Horst Kant, "Albert Einstein, Max von Laue, Peter Debye und das Kaiser-Wilhelm-Institut für Physik in Berlin (1917–1939)," in *Die Kaiser-Wilhelm-/Max-Planck-Gesellschaft und ihre Institute. Studien zu ihrer Geschichte: Das Harnack Prinzip,* ed. Bernhard vom Brocke and Hubert Laitko (Berlin and New York: de Gruyter, 1996), 227–243. We would like to thank Giuseppe Castagnetti for further information on Koppel's involvement in the founding of the Kaiser Wilhelm Institute for Physical Research.

27. Manfred Rasch, "Wissenschaft und Militär: Die Kaiser-Wilhelm-Stiftung für kriegstechnische Wissenschaft," *Militärgeschichtliche Mitteilungen* 49 (1991): 73–120.

28. See Jürgen Kloosterhuis, *"Friedliche Imperialisten": Deutsche Auslandsvereine und auswärtige Kulturpolitik, 1906–1908* (Frankfurt am Main: Lang, 1981), 1: 1177ff.; Friedrich Schmidt-Ott, *Erlebtes und Erstrebtes, 1860–1950* (Wiesbaden: Steiner, 1952), 102.

29. Vom Brocke, "Der deutsch-amerikanische Professorenaustausch"; Ragnhild Fiebig-von Hase, "Die politische Funktionalisierung der Kultur: Der sogenannten 'deutsch-amerikanische' Professorenaustausch," in *Zwei Wege in die Moderne: Aspekte der deutsch-amerikanischen Beziehungen 1900–1918,* ed. Ragnhild Fiebig-von Hase and Jürgen Heideking (Trier: Wissenschaft Verlag Trier, 1998), 45–88; Schmidt-Ott, *Erlebtes,* 107ff.

30. *Yearbook of the Carnegie Endowment for International Peace* 10 (1911): 65.

31. Ibid., 64ff.

32. See Eckhardt Fuchs, "Schriftenaustausch, Copyright und Dokumentation: Das Buch als Medium der internationalen Wissenschaftskommunikation vor dem Ersten Weltkrieg unter besonderer Berücksichtigung Deutschlands und der Vereinigten Staaten von Amerika," *Leipziger Jahrbuch zur Buchgeschichte* 7 (1997): 136ff.

33. See Christian H. Freitag, "Die Entwicklung der Amerikastudien in Berlin bis 1945 unter Berücksichtigung der Amerikaarbeit staatlicher und privater Organisationen" (Phil. Diss., Free University Berlin, 1977), 39ff.; Bernhard vom Brocke, "Internationale Wissenschaftsbeziehungen und die Anfänge einer deutschen auswärtigen Kulturpolitik: Der Professorenaustausch mit Nordamerika," in *Wissenschaftsgeschichte und Wissenschaftspolitik im Industriezeitalter: Das System "Althoff" in historischer Perspektive,* ed. Bernhard vom Brocke (Hildesheim: Lax, 1991), 219.

34. See Andrew Carnegie, *Geschichte meines Lebens* (Leipzig: K. F. Koehler, 1922), 174ff.; Joseph F. Wall, *Andrew Carnegie* (New York: Oxford University Press, 1970), 855ff.; and Raymond B. Fosdick, *Die Geschichte der Rockefeller-Stiftung* (Vienna and Würzburg: Zettner, 1955). For a more recent study, see Karsten Borgmann, "Kultur des Reichtums: Philanthropy, Wohltätigkeit und Elite in den Vereinigten Staaten von Amerika," in Gaethgens and Schieder, *Mäzenatisches Handeln,* 216–235. On Rockefeller, see Allan Nevins, *John D. Rockefeller, Industrialist and Philanthropist,* vol. 1 (New York: Scribner, 1953); Theresa Richardson, "Evangelischer Protestantismus, wissenschaftliche Philanthropie und die Universität von Chicago: Theologische Grundlagen der säkularen Sozialwissenschaften," in *Lokale Wissenschaftskulturen in der Erziehungswissenschaft,* ed. Alfred Langewand and Andreas von Prondczynsky (Weinheim: Deutscher Studienverlag, 1999), 53–74.

35. The scholarship was $1,000 for a four-month period. See Auswärtiges Amt, Botschaft Washington, 3 F 2, 383, Politisches Archiv des Auswärtigen Amtes, Berlin; Auswärtiges Amt, 38612, Bundesarchiv Berlin.

36. Frey, *Macht und Moral des Schenkens,* 81.

37. See Auswärtiges Amt, 38613 and 38614, Bundesarchiv Berlin.

38. See *Tägliche Rundschau*, February 25, 1908; *New Yorker Staatszeitung*, April 12, 1908; Auswärtiges Amt, 38606, Bundesarchiv Berlin.

39. Auswärtiges Amt, 38606, Bundesarchiv Berlin.

40. See Kultusministeriums to Minister für Auswärtige Angelegenheiten, February 9, 1889, Auswärtiges Amt, 38604, Bundesarchiv Berlin; *Vossische Zeitung*, September 13, 1899. Seler and Loubat met at the Seventh International Congress of Americanists at Berlin in 1888. Loubat sponsored several of Seler's projects; among others, his second research trip to Mexico and Guatemala in 1895–1897. See Ursula Sachse, "Beiträge deutscher Gelehrter zur Erforschung der altmexikanischen Kulturen, und der zeitgenössischen Indianerproblematik. Untersuchen zur Entwicklung des bürgerlichen deutschen Mexiko-Bildes von der Entstehung Mexikos bis zum Ende des 19. Jahrhunderts," Phil. Diss., University of Rostock, 1968, 299ff. On Loubat, see *Le Duc de Loubat. Avec les hommages du Duc de Loubat 1831–1894* (Paris: Typ. Chamerot et Renouard, 1894); and George G. MacCurdy, "Duke de Loubat," *American Anthropologist* 29 (1927): 340. Loubat also donated similar prizes to the Academies of Sciences in Paris, Stockholm, and Madrid. He also gave an endowment to Columbia University in 1903, establishing a professorship for American anthropology. See Sally F. Moore, "The Department of Anthropology," in *The Bicentennial History of Columbia University: The History of the Faculty of Political Science*, ed. Dwight Carroll Miner (New York: Columbia University Press, 1955), 147–160.

41. See Rep. 76, Vc, Sekt. 2, Tit. 4, Nr. 64, Geheimes Staatsarchiv Preußischer Kulturbesitz; and *National-Zeitung*, November 9, 1899.

42. See Ralf Roth, "'Der Toten Nachruhm.' Aspekte des Mäzenatentums in Frankfurt am Main (1750–1914)," in Kocka and Frey, *Bürgerkultur und Mäzenatentum*, 102ff.

43. Gerhard Neumeier, "Bürgerliches Mäzenatentum in München vor dem Ersten Weltkrieg—Das Beispiel des Deutschen Museums," in Kocka and Frey, *Bürgerkultur und Mäzenatentum*, 152; Elisabeth Kraus, "Jüdisches Mäzenatentum im Kaiserreich: Befunde-Motive-Hypothesen," in Kocka and Frey, *Bürgerkultur und Mäzenatentum*, 45.

44. See Kraus, "Jüdisches Mäzenatentum"; Kraus, "Jüdische Stiftungstätigkeit: Das Beispiel der Familie Mosse in Berlin," *Zeitschrift für Geschichtswissenschaft* 45 (1997): 101–121; Simone Lässig, "Juden und Mäzenatentum in Deutschland. Religiöses Ethos, kompensierendes Minderheitsverhalten oder genuine Bürgerlichkeit?" *Zeitschrift für Geschichtswissenschaft* 46 (1998): 211–237; Cella-Margareta Girardet, *Jüdische Mäzene für die Preußischen Museen zu Berlin. Eine Studie zum Mäzenatentum im Deutschen Kaiserreich und in der Weimarer Republik* (Egelsbach, Frankfurt am Main, and Washington, D.C.: Hänsel-Hohenhausen, 1997); Derek Penslar, "Philanthropy, the 'Social Question,' and Jewish Identity in Imperial Germany," *Leo Baeck Institute Year Book* 38 (1993): 51–73; Wilhelm Treue, "Jüdisches Mäzenatentum für die Wissenschaft in Deutschland," in *Jüdische Unternehmer in Deutschland im 19. und 20. Jahrhundert*, ed. Werner E. Mosse and Hans Pohl (Stuttgart: Steiner, 1992), 284–308; Michael S. Cullen, "Juden als Sammler und Mäzene," in *Juden als Träger bürgerlicher Kultur in Deutschland*, ed. Julius H. Schoeps (Stuttgart and Bonn: Burg Verlag, 1989), 123–148. For a case study, see Olaf Matthes, *James Simon. Mäzen im Wilhelminischen Zeitalter* (Berlin: Bostelmann und Siebenhaar, 2000).

45. For the connection between philanthropy and religion, see Richardson, *Evangelischer Protestantismus*.

46. Pierre Bourdieu, *Die verborgenen Mechanismen der Macht. Schriften zu Politik & Kultur* (Hamburg: VSA Verlag, 1992), 49ff.

47. Kocka and Frey, *Bürgerkultur und Mäzenatentum*, 10; Thomas W. Gaethgens, *Der Bürger als Mäzen* (Opladen: Westdeutscher Verlag, 1998); Frey, *Macht und Moral des Schenkens*, 71ff.

48. On philanthropy in Berlin, see Günter and Waltraut Braun, eds., *Mäzenatentum in Berlin. Bürgersinn und kulturelle Kompetenz unter sich verändernden Bedingungen* (Berlin and New York: de Gruyter, 1993). See also Andreas Ludwig, "Die sozialen Stiftungen der Stadt Charlottenburg und ihre Träger im 19. und 20. Jahrhundert," in *Berlin in Geschichte und Gegenwart. Jahrbuch des Landesarchiv Berlin,* ed. Jürgen Wetzel (Berlin: Landesarchiv Berlin, 1993), 63–85.

49. Carnegie to Speck-Sternburg, 6 April 1908, in Auswärtiges Amt, 38606, Bundesarchiv Berlin.

50. For this political aspect, see Eckhardt Fuchs, "Erziehung in internationaler Dimension: Zur Rolle Deutschlands und der USA im Prozeß der Internationalisierung pädagogischen Wissens am Anfang des 20. Jahrhunderts," in Jürgen Schriewer, ed., *Internationalisierung pädagogischen Denkens* (Weinheim: Beltz, forthcoming).

51. For satirical comments, see "Ornamente," *Die Zukunft* (4 February 1911): 180ff.

52. Winfried Schulze, *Der Stifterverband für die Deutsche Wissenschaft 1920–1995* (Berlin: Akademie Verlag, 1995). See also Ulrich Marsch, *Notgemeinschaft der Deutschen Wissenschaft. Gründung und frühe Geschichte 1920–1925* (Frankfurt am Main: Lang, 1994).

SIX

The Serious Matter of True Joy: Music and Cultural Philanthropy in Leipzig, 1781–1933

MARGARET ELEANOR MENNINGER

This chapter discusses the structure and scope of cultural philanthropy as a social practice, an evolution that must be considered a central characteristic of the symbolic as well as the actual bourgeois domination of German society in the long nineteenth century. The nature of cultural philanthropy changed significantly throughout this period. Initially, it resembled the eighteenth century in terms the dominance of more or less socially exclusive voluntary associations (*Vereine*) as the mode of organization of cultural activities. By 1914, this picture had changed substantially; most cultural institutions had become publicly owned and operated concerns that were supported by tax revenues and administered by civil servants. Their buildings occupied an important place in each city's presentation of itself to the outside world in guidebooks, tourist guides, and postcards. Leipzig's urban patriciate had come to realize that cultural philanthropy, in order to be fruitful, would require new levels of cooperation between private and municipal organizations as well as a sharing of resources. This was not simply a reaction to rising construction costs but also a recognition that cultural institutions mattered greatly to the city's sense of self-worth.

PATRONAGE VERSUS PHILANTHROPY

I define the actions discussed here in terms of "cultural philanthropy" rather than "patronage" to highlight what I view as an important distinction between these two terms. Patronage emphasizes a specific act of purchase or acquisition of an object of art (broadly defined) without any reference to a larger public good (akin to the German *Stifter*).[1] Philanthropy, by contrast, connotes duty and responsibility to a greater cause; that is to say, it bears the characteristics of a social practice. What I have in mind here are actions associated with the funding of the fine and performing arts. I suspect we can all agree that the consumption of high culture was a basic element of the habitus of an educated German. However, it is my contention that this activity required that one be a supporter and protector of the arts as well. This was more than a reaffirmation of individual worth; it was also a collective acknowledgement of the importance of high culture to civil and civilized society. These semantic distinctions are complicated when dealing with a German case study. The term *Mäzenatentum* partially bridges the gap between the English terms discussed above.[2]

THE ORCHESTRA AND ITS DIRECTORS: A GROUP PORTRAIT OF THE PHILANTHROPISTS

This chapter focuses on one organization, the board of directors (*Konzertdirektion*) of the Gewandhaus Orchestra. The orchestra was the first founded in the German-speaking world without benefit of aristocratic or court patronage and was the most famous of Leipzig's public cultural treasures. It was also unique in Leipzig's associational history because of its small and elite board of directors who kept it independent from city control until after 1945. Board members were appointed for flexible terms, paid a yearly membership, oversaw the administration of the group, and spearheaded fund-raising activities for the support of the musicians (through pension funds) and the upkeep of the concert hall.[3]

The construction of the new concert hall (which was completed in 1884) for the sole use of the Gewandhaus symbolized the manner in which city interests gradually intertwined with those of the orchestra's *Konzertdirektion*. The history of the Gewandhaus also illustrates the evolution of an official musical culture in Leipzig, which had its highest expression in its concerts. There were outside challenges from other orchestras to the group's claim to be Leipzig's official orchestra (and thus retaining exclusive rights of performance in the new hall). These were vigorously and successfully countered by the *Konzertdirektion*. Thus, the history of this group persuasively demonstrates the manner in which cultural institutions gradually became more municipal and more generally accessible (in a symbolic if not in an actual sense), and yet it also shows us how the philanthropists on the board could consistently limit access to a newly acknowledged municipal treasure.

The Großes-Concert was founded on the 11th of March 1743, when "sixteen persons, some noble and some bourgeois," pledged themselves to support an orchestra of sixteen.[4] Most of the original founders and players remain unknown. The three named founders (*Stifter*) were Johann Friedrich Gleditzsch (or Gleditsch), the owner of a publishing company that had been founded in 1694 by his father and was bought in 1830 by F. A. Brockhaus; tobacco merchant Gottlob Benedict Zehmisch, also a great patron of the theater; and Bergrat Schwaben, probably the scion of a family long involved in mining in Saxony.[5] The organizational structure of the Großes-Concert did not fit the general patterns of civic musical associations, which tended to be founded by players and later acquire sponsorship from individuals who were not musicians. By contrast, the Großes-Concert always maintained a distinction between patrons and musicians.

The *Konzertdirektion,* as the directorial board was called after 1781, illustrated the elite tone of the organization; according to the original statutes, six of the twelve members were to be merchants and six were to be "intellectuals" (*Gelehrte*). The mayor was automatically a member of the directorate. Of the twelve founding members, two were bankers and four were merchants. Three were "doctors of law," although only one was listed as being on the law faculty of the University of Leipzig. The remaining three members were the mayor and two civil servants (Table 6.1).[6] Seven of these men were also members of the municipal administration. Richter (an indigo merchant) and Winckler both owned important art collections. Küstner's son became the first director of the Altes Theater, and the Frege family remained active in Leipzig banking and cultural life for many generations. This connection between municipal administrators and philanthropists remained strong until 1933.

A statistical overview of the entire roster of the men who served on the orchestra's board confirms the findings of that first group. The members of the *Konzertdirektion* continued to represent the most elevated strata of Leipzig's social life. Bankers, textile merchants, higher civil servants, and professors, they represented the most exclusive segment of Leipzig's upper bourgeoisie of any cultural association's governing board (Table 6.2).[7] The low level of participation of the industrial bourgeoisie underlines the point that the *Konzertdirektion* was the province of the old mercantile elite of Leipzig, not the newer industrial rich. This is another sign of the board's atypical structure and its older age; the directorial boards of Leipzig's museums, which were founded in and around 1860, were more heterogeneous in composition.

In nineteenth-century Leipzig, voluntary associations fostered an ideal of local and regional identity and served as the forcing ground for later municipal support and administration of the arts. The members of the *Konzertdirektion,* as Table 6.3 indicates, were active in many of these associations. Of these, two deserve special mention, the Vertrauten and the Gesellschaft Harmonie.

TABLE 6.1.
Founding Directorate of the Großes-Concert, 1781

Name	Profession
August Wilhelm Crayen (1751–1802)	Merchant
Jacob Marcus Anton Dufour-Pallard (1737–1805)	Merchant
Christian Gottlob Frege (1747–1816)	Banker, city councillor
Johann Samuel Traugott Gehler (1751–1795)	Civil servant, lawyer, councillor
August Friedrich Siegmund Green (1736–1798)	Professor of Law at the University of Leipzig, councillor
Friedrich Ludolph Hansen (1737–1803)	Merchant, councillor
Johann Heinrich Küstner (1752–1816)	Banker
Philipp Heinrich Lastrop (1748–1801)	Lawyer
Carl Wilhelm Müller (1728–1801)	Mayor
Johann Christoph Richter (1734–1801)	Civil servant, councillor
Friedrich Wilhelm Treitschke (d. 1800)	Merchant, councillor
Gottfried Winckler (1731–1795)	Merchant, councillor, civil servant

TABLE 6.2.
Social Distribution of *Konzertdirektion* Membership, 1781–1930

Profession	Numbers	Percent
Commercial Bourgeoisie (*Handelsbourgeoisie*)	43	38
Merchants (*Kaufmänner*)	17	
Bankers	13	
Booksellers (*Buchhändler*)	7	
Music publishers	6	
Industrial Bourgeoisie (*Industriebourgeoisie*)	10	9
Clothing/textile industries	7	
Chemical industries (including pharmaceuticals)	2	
Paper manufacturers	1	
State (or imperial) civil servants (*hohe Staatsbeamte*)	19	16
Liberal professions (lawyers, doctors, journalists)	22	19
Professors	11	10
No data	9	8

Die Vertrauten was one of Leipzig's oldest voluntary associations; it was founded in 1680, after plague had claimed over 2,500 lives. The original group of sixteen men met for mutual assistance, friendship, and charity work for others, which was to be undertaken anonymously.[8] Die Vertrauten continued to be active into the twentieth century, having established a reputation for being composed of men who, both as private citizens and as members of the communal administration, were centrally concerned with city affairs.

One important and consistent element in the membership profile of the Vertrauten was the high incidence of kinship, by blood and by marriage, among its members. Almost all of the original members were merchants, and all lived within one or two streets of the central marketplace in Leipzig. There were only 188 members total in the Vertrauten between 1680 and 1937, and the bulk of these were active before 1900; by 1913, the active membership had dwindled to only fifteen men.[9] Kinship was also an important form of continuity within the *Konzertdirektion.*

The imprimatur of the Vertrauten was clear to see in all significant political, commercial, economic, and cultural undertakings in Leipzig in the nineteenth century. Four of the six original backers of the Leipzig-Dresden railway were members.[10] Vertraute were also active in local politics either as members of the city council (an appointed position) or the municipal parliament (elected through limited suffrage).[11]

Less select than the Vertrauten, but more central to municipal life in Leipzig in terms of sheer numbers, the Gesellschaft Harmonie was founded in the winter of 1775–1776 as a social club and an organization to help the poor. Structured along the philosophical lines of Enlightenment associations, Harmonie drew its membership from two classes within Leipzig's social elite—the mercantile (*Kaufmannsstande*) and the educated (*Gelehrten-, Beamten-, und Künstlerstande*). Candidates could be "respectable and independent" members of either class. Bankruptcy required immediate resignation. Respectability was central to the gatherings as well; for instance, gambling was forbidden.[12]

All nineteenth-century descriptions of Leipzig mentioned the Gesellschaft Harmonie as one of the most prominent associations in the city. It was the group whose ranks made up the majority of men active in political and cultural matters in Leipzig throughout the nineteenth century. As in the Vertrauten, there was a strong tendency for sons to follow their fathers into membership, but Harmonie was also somewhat less exclusive, in part because of its larger numbers. For example, the Reformed Protestant French and Franco-Swiss who had settled in Saxony in the eighteenth century were admitted into the Harmonie a full generation before they became members

TABLE 6.3.

Other Associational Memberships of the Gewandhaus *Konzertdirektion*

Other Associations	*Konzertdirektion* members in other *Vereine* and city government	Percent of total membership, 1781–1930 (110)
Die Vertrauten	20	18
Gesellschaft Harmonie	92	84
Gesellschaft Erholung	18	16
Leipziger Kunstverein	41	37
Verein Museum für Völkerkunde	16	14
Verein Kunstgewerbemuseum Leipzig	16	14
Bondholders for the 1866 Neues Theater construction project	11	10
Dilletanten-Orchesterverein (inactive)	9	9
Member city parliament (Stadtverordneter)	12	11
Member city council (Stadtrat)	25	23

of the Vertrauten. And booksellers and publishers were present in the Harmonie as early as 1800; they did not gain entry into the Vertrauten until the mid-nineteenth century.

As a whole, Harmonie's politics were either center or right-wing National Liberal, and its religious orientation was strongly Christian and Protestant. Jews were not admitted until 1887. Membership was not cheap; fees in 1887 included an entrance fee of 100 marks and a subsequent yearly membership of the same amount.[13] Until the 1920s, Harmonie's membership remained remarkably consistent, continuing to attract Leipzig's important commercial and professional families. A total of 2,640 men were members of the organization between 1776 and 1926. Until 1900, virtually all members of the city council were members, as were the organizing committees behind all of the major cultural associations.

As can be seen from Table 6.3, the members of the *Konzertdirektion* were particularly active in the Gesellschaft Harmonie, but they also had a strong presence in the Vertrauten and the Kunstverein. Moreover, there was significant overlap with the membership of the city council. In other words, the *Konzertdirektion's* membership consistently exercised influence at the core of both Leipzig's associational life and the city's municipal government. This put them in an excellent position to lobby the city for help when the resources of the group alone could no longer suffice.

CREATING THE PROPER SETTING:
A NEW CONCERT HALL

By 1780, interest in the orchestra had outstripped the capacity of the available public spaces in Leipzig. For the first time, the city became involved in discussions about a concert hall. The move to create this new space was led by the mayor, Carl Wilhelm Müller, himself of course a member of the *Konzertdirektion.* His letter to the council cited two reasons for renovating and then renting out the future concert space. He mentioned the income (by his calculations about 450–600 marks per year) that would accrue to the city council for currently unused space. He also suggested that the new space would eliminate "complaints of so many local residents and foreigners regarding the lack of a respectable concert hall in Leipzig." Müller further reported that only the previous week the Duke Carl-August of Sachsen-Weimar had commented unfavorably about the "narrow and dangerous" entrances to the concert spaces in use in the city and had suggested that Leipzig needed a better space.[14]

One would be justified in speculating about how much of the early reputation of the Gewandhaus was due to the actual space into which the orchestra moved in 1781. Located on the top floor of the city-owned warehouse, directly behind the university, the structure had originally been built by the cloth-workers' guild (*Gewand* = cloth, hence the name of the orchestra) in 1482 and was considered then the most magnificent building in the city.[15] When the top floor was renovated to accommodate the new concert hall, no new masonry was used for fear of overloading the foundation. The resulting wooden structure, essentially built like the inside of a stringed instrument, was blessed with acoustics famous throughout Europe.[16] The hall had an "orchestra" platform at one of the narrow ends of the room. Most of the seats on the parquet level faced each other rather than facing the stage. Initially, the space seated 500 persons. A narrower second-gallery level with two rows of seats was built above the first level and then expanded in 1842, which increased seating to somewhere between 800 and 1,000.[17] The audience for these concerts indicated the patrician nature of the enterprise. The orchestra's official historian Alfred Dörffel called them "the most respectable, richest and most educated inhabitants of the city."[18]

The period between 1781 and 1848 was undoubtedly the high point of the Gewandhaus Orchestra's musical existence. This was principally due to the conducting skills of Felix Mendelssohn-Bartholdy, who led the orchestra from 1835 to 1843 and continued to conduct occasionally until his death in 1847.[19] This marked the end of an era for Leipzig's musical community in general and for the Gewandhaus Orchestra in particular; the

1850s and 1860s were a fallow period. The orchestra and its conductors rapidly gained a reputation for musical conservatism and a stubborn allegiance to the works of the early nineteenth century.[20] To the *Konzertdirektion,* however, the time seemed ripe to change the orchestra's home to a concert hall more representative of the group's importance in order to revitalize it and keep its reputation alive.[21]

The orchestra had long been drawing a larger audience than its rented hall could hold. In recognition of the limited number of seats and tickets, it began to make dress rehearsals open to the public in 1875 (with paid admission). However, any new seats that were created, for instance in 1879 by knocking down a wall, were reserved for such dignitaries as the new members of the imperial law courts (although the sources don't tell us how these seats were apportioned).[22]

One of the earliest formal attempts to spell out the requirements for a new building was the 1865 pamphlet produced by banker Wilhelm Theodore Seyfferth (1807–1881), a member of the *Konzertdirektion* from 1852 to 1881. He was a second-generation member—his father, Wilhelm Gotthelf Ernst Seyfferth (1774–1832), also a banker, had been on the board from 1816 until his death. Besides continuing in his father's bank, the younger Seyfferth was a founder of the Leipzig-Dresden Railroad and served on its board of directors from 1869 to 1878.

Listing the shortcomings of the old hall—uncomfortable seats, bad heating and ventilation, and narrow halls—Seyfferth argued that the orchestra needed to double its available seating to 2,000. The *Konzertdirektion* decided to raise the money for construction from "artistically aware fellow citizens" (*kunstsinnige Mitbürger*) rather than through a loan, and the fund-raising campaign got under way in 1877. There were two ways to support this endeavor. One could give 500 marks to the *Konzertdirektion,* for which one received the right to buy a season ticket to the orchestra for the standard price (which had been raised to 100 marks).[23] Alternatively, one could purchase shares for 1,000 marks, which gave the same right to buy season tickets and pass the seats on as property. The *Leipziger Tageblatt* reported 677 donations of 500 marks and 451 purchases of 1,000-mark shares, which took approximately 1,200 of 1,500 seats permanently out of circulation. Many of the remaining 300 seats were reserved for members of the university, the law courts, or the garrisons, leaving very few if any available tickets, even for those with the money to pay for them.[24]

Satisfied that it would not have to pay for construction, the city entered into the final stage of discussions with the *Konzertdirektion* about land.[25] In the end, the city *gave* them a plot of land, which it had received from merchant Friedrich August Adolf Voigt (1817–1885). The city was aware of the costs involved in developing a new area of town, and the proposal was made to the *Konzertdirektion* that, should Voigt and the municipal parliament agree to the gift of the site, the directors would be responsible for all associated costs affecting land abutting the property.[26] Voigt also benefited from this arrangement. The area where Voigt held property was near to the Pleiße River and had been swamp land. If it was to be made habitable, that is to say salable for Voigt, he would have to have water, gas, and drainage lines laid on his property. The city essentially received the site, which it passed on to the Gewandhaus-Directorate in exchange for providing Voigt with the needed infrastructure free of charge. That, of course, greatly increased the value of his other vacant lots, as did their future proximity to such an important building as the Gewandhaus Concert Hall.[27] This agreement underscores the point that cultural philanthropy could benefit the giver as well as the recipient.

The money raised by the shares was not enough to cover all the costs in the end, and the board eventually received a loan taken from the monies left to the city by Franz Dominic Grassi. Grassi's 1880 bequest to the city of Leipzig of 2.3 million marks stands as a pivotal point in cultural philanthropy. It was unusual because the city inherited the balance of his estate to be used for "amenities and beautification" and not for projects where funds already existed.[28]

The bequest contained no demands about specific projects or time limits; the city leadership was left to choose. The open-ended instructions in Grassi's will demonstrated his confidence in the city government to create and/or support institutions for the good of Leipzig without conditions. It further showed how much more trust was being placed in the city government to "do the right thing" with money it received from individual philanthropists. A comparison with the 1853 bequest of silk merchant Heinrich Adolf Schletter demonstrates this point. Not only was the latter sum significantly less (99,150 marks), but the instructions on how the money was to be used were much more restrictive. The bequest was intended specifically for an art museum that was to be built within five years of Schletter's death.[29] By 1880, apparently, Grassi could be confident that Leipzig's municipal administration would nurture the cultural life of the city without prompting, in part, of course, because of the close relationships between the philanthropic and governmental circles in town.[30]

The city used some of the Grassi Foundation funds to grant the *Konzertdirektion* an interest-free loan of 400,000 marks. However, this element of municipal patronage did not take place without more serious discussion on the part of the city council and parliament; while the Gewandhaus project got significantly less money from the Grassi-Stiftung than other projects, and was committed to paying the money back, the loan created more vocal opposition than did the assignment of any of the funds.[31]

Initially alone in its new part of town, the new concert hall "anchored" the *Musikviertel,* as the development came to be called. This was a very important new urban development for Leipzig. The Concert House was merely the first in a group of large ceremonial buildings built in the same relatively small area.[32] The streets were rapidly built up with villas, and property costs rose to between 300 and 470 marks per square meter.[33] Street names made the linkage of the cultural and the commercial clear; streets running east to west were named after composers and those running north to south were named after those men who were among the most important cultural benefactors of the city, for example Seyfferth and Grassi.

The new Concert Hall did indeed serve as a showplace for an orchestra renowned as an important musical institution in Germany (although by that time it deserved its reputation rather less than it had previously). It also served to physically separate the Gewandhaus from the other musical groups in Leipzig, creating an "official" and an "unofficial" musical culture. This exclusivity went farther; not only was the concert hall for the exclusive use of the orchestra, but the board of directors also vetoed any tours by the orchestra, arguing that if one wanted to hear the orchestra, one must come to Leipzig.[34]

While there was some recognition of the possible dangers embedded in the exclusivity of the Gewandhaus, most in the city government did not see this as a problem at the time. In fact, this exclusivity suited many. Certainly the city did nothing to encourage the board to provide concerts for the broader masses, and the board's reluctance to consider this issue was never challenged.[35] It seems fairly certain that, despite some lip service to the idea of broadening attendance, the orchestra actually became more exclusive and remained so to the end of the nineteenth century.

TONES OF DISCONTENT:
CHALLENGING AND DEFENDING EXCLUSIVITY

Nonetheless, by the 1880s and 1890s there were those who had begun to wonder if the Gewandhaus Orchestra's representation of itself as Leipzig's orchestra could in fact be squared with its exclusive audience and high prices. Gustav Wustmann, the director of the municipal archives, wrote in 1898 complaining that the high prices (100 marks per person per season) made it impossible for music lovers to enjoy the city's premier orchestra.[36]

Access to classical music for the less wealthy in Leipzig was provided primarily by the orchestra founded by Hans Winderstein in 1896.[37] Admission fees to the Sunday concerts ranged from 25 pfennig to 1.50 marks, and subscription costs for the concert series (8 concerts) ranged from 6 to 20 marks. Winderstein made a point of programming important but accessible classical music and booking important soloists, including giving concerts with these soloists at the *Städtisches Kaufhaus,* the new building built on the site of the original Gewandhaus on Universitätsstraße.[38] The orchestra and its conductor received very flattering attention from the local press as well as from important musical journals.[39]

Although not immune to financial difficulties, Winderstein's orchestra remained self-supporting until 1911. In that year, he began to petition the city for support for his orchestra, outlining the special functions he performed in the Leipzig cultural scene. Asking for a yearly grant of 10,000 marks, Winderstein argued that the Gewandhaus could not fulfill the symphonic music needs of Leipzig audiences and that a second orchestra that could "bring good music to a broad public" was sorely needed.[40]

The discussions of this subcommittee reveal divided loyalties. Of the seven members, one was also a member of the Gewandhaus *Konzertdirektion,* Councilor Dr. Göhring. While Vice-Mayor Roth (not a member of the directorate) supported the Winderstein case on the grounds of the orchestra's strong reputation and Leipzig's interest in a strong musical culture, Göhring was against the proposal on the grounds that it would open a door to demands from other musical organizations in the city. This seems a curious objection, however, since the city had just given the Bach-Verein choir 5,000 marks.[41] Ultimately the city council agreed to a grant of 10,000 marks per year for three years, although the reasons for their change of heart are unclear from the surviving record. Winderstein wrote frequently to members of the council and sent them clippings that put him in the best possible light, but other factors may well have been involved. Whatever the reason, the full council (with 9 nay votes, an unusually high number) agreed to the funding on June 7, 1911, subject to the approval of the city representatives and with three conditions attached. Winderstein was to maintain the quality of the orchestra, continue to give at least twelve concerts a year that were accessible to the broader public, and give additional concerts for Leipzig's young people and schoolchildren.[42] In its letter to the city representatives, the city council argued for supporting Winderstein on the grounds that since neither the Gewandhaus Orchestra nor the city orchestra could give additional concerts outside their schedule, many in the "Musikstadt Leipzig" would be deprived of concerts should no second concert orchestra be supported.[43]

In their meeting on June 28, 1911, the municipal parliament refused to support Winderstein in the long term, although they did agree to a onetime gift of 8,000 marks. The main voices against the proposal cited the danger of getting into a cycle of funding a "private concern" and skepticism that Winderstein would really leave Leipzig as he had threatened he would if funding fell through. Proposals for lesser grants were also denied. The nays were 37 of 64 votes.[44] Although records of the individual votes on this matter are unavailable, the subject of this vote was again debated in the press in 1925 on the occasion of Winderstein's death. At that time, the *Leipziger Volkszeitung*, the Social Democratic newspaper, spent most of the space given over to Winderstein's obituary arguing that he had always been rejected by the city fathers, who were intent on "maintaining the exclusivity of the Gewandhaus."[45] The city responded in a letter to the paper, pointing out that efforts to fund Winderstein had foundered in 1911. At that time, the letter continued, the Social Democratic faction made up a third of the body, all of whom voted against the measure.[46] The paper responded by arguing that this was irrelevant since the Social Democratic Party could not have carried the measure alone anyway and that its failure was proof of the council's indifference to the lack of "musical equity" in Leipzig.[47]

Whatever the motivations of the city council, the *Konzertdirektion* continued to jealously guard access to use of the Concert Hall. This reluctance to open its doors to a wider audience can be seen in their behavior toward the Arbeiter-Bildungs-Institut (ABI). The ABI was founded in 1907 and promoted the cultural education of Leipzig's workers.[48] This, of course, was much the same audience that Winderstein was trying to reach. The ABI tried for years with no success to get the Gewandhaus board to allow the orchestra to present a concert for workers. They finally did this in March 1915, when two "concerts" were given. Even in contemporary histories of the orchestra, these two concerts are trumpeted as a new opening of the concert hall to a more democratic audience. The reality, however, was quite different. For a ticket costing 60 pfennig (at a time when the average monthly salary was 15–20 marks), workers were allowed to hear two rehearsals (and not dress rehearsals) in a hall where the carpets had been rolled up, the seats had been covered, and only half the usual lighting was used. Despite this, both performances, each an all-Beethoven program, sold out.[49] The next significant combination of the Gewandhaus and the ABI did not take place until after the end of World War I, when the *Konzertdirektion* reluctantly agreed to lend the orchestral musicians (and Arthur Nikisch to conduct) for a midnight performance of Beethoven's Ninth Symphony on New Year's Eve 1918. The performance was staged at the Krystallpalast in Leipzig with an audience of over 2,800.[50] Indeed, it was with this concert that the nationwide tradition of playing Beethoven on December 31st was established.

Despite, or perhaps because of, this successful concert, the *Konzertdirektion* continued to complain bitterly about the "misuse" of their players by the city for other popular concerts well into the 1920s and 1930s.[51] In fact, the continued participation of the orchestra in the annual New Year's Eve concert was sometimes only effected by a bit of blackmail on the part of the ABI; in 1920, it was only after they had hired another orchestra that they received the reluctant accession of the board.[52] They also continued to oppose the use of the hall on Beethovenstraße for any other purpose, even charitable causes for survivors of the war.[53]

In the 1920s, several orchestras were founded and proposed to the city government as alternative "city orchestras." Winderstein continued his efforts to found a "city philharmonic," and Hans L'hermet went so far as to found an orchestra that performed on Thursdays, the traditional Gewandhaus concert date. By 1925, a third orchestra, the Leipzig Symphony Orchestra (Leipziger Sinfonieorchester) was up and running (it later became the founding center of the radio symphony for Middle German radio [MDR, or Mitteldeutscher Rundfunk]).[54]

The attention to a greater concertgoing public was not unusual in Germany—Leipzig's city government was in correspondence with musical associations in Frankfurt am Main and Hamburg (among others) about city-owned and -operated orchestras.[55] This was not, however, a move supported by the Gewandhaus directors. They and their supporters (not the least of whom was Karl Straube, the musical director of Leipzig's other claim to fame, the St. Thomas Church Choir) argued that to add orchestras would be to dilute the city's reputation. In other words, while it might be permissible to increase the number of musicians hired to fill the pit orchestra at the theater, one could not add a second symphonic group without debasing Leipzig's cultural coin.[56] The board had some justification for their stubbornness—the orchestra had regained its international reputation under Nikisch and retained it under Wilhelm Furtwängler, his successor until 1928, and Bruno Walter, who was hired in 1929. Not to put too fine a point on it—there was no other comparable orchestra in Germany outside the Berlin Philharmonic.[57]

The *Konzertdirektion* maintained its conservative stance toward use of the concert hall and retention of its players. The economic vicissitudes of the 1920s did much to disrupt their efforts to maintain relatively limited access to the concerts; in 1923, during the hyperinflation, short-term changes were made to the rights of shareholders to seats and again in 1931 ticket prices were lowered, although this was coupled with a downsizing of the orchestra itself.[58] What is important to emphasize here is that this was a complete contradiction to the actions of all of Leipzig's other institutions of high culture. While they continually broadened public access, the *Konzertdirektion* stubbornly refused to open their gates any wider.

As National Socialism grew in strength, the board of directors did little to oppose the new political and cultural climate. In 1931, Bruno Walter was asked to write the foreword to the latest history of the Gewandhaus published by the board of directors.[59] By March 1933, however, rather than allow Walter to continue in his post, the board of directors followed the new laws and allowed an open dress rehearsal and a concert to be canceled. By 1935, the orchestra was performing at Nazi Party rallies.[60] Only after the defeat of the Germans and the establishment of the German Democratic Republic did the Gewandhaus Orchestra become a wholly owned and operated part of Leipzig's government.

Full control of the orchestra's personnel and eventual administration of their concert space fell to the city of Leipzig after 1945. The concert hall in the *Musikviertel* was badly damaged by Allied bombs on December 3–4, 1943, and the decision was made not to rebuild it (against vehement local protest).[61] In 1981 a new concert hall was completed, prominently situated on the south side of Karl-Marx-Platz (now Augustusplatz). In October 1989, it was in the lobby of this newest concert hall that the New Forum in Leipzig first held open discussions on the future of the German Democratic Republic, led by the conductor of the Gewandhaus Orchestra, Kurt Masur. In the end, the Gewandhaus did fulfill its early promise of becoming a central element of modern civil society.

CONCLUSION

The development of the Gewandhaus Orchestra and its *Konzertdirektion* exemplifies the Janus face of cultural philanthropy in the long nineteenth century. The orchestra itself and its Concert Hall contributed an invaluable example of cultural excellence for the city of Bach and Mendelssohn. Their status as a premier modern orchestra contributed tremendously to local pride even as it also functioned as a "selling point" for a growing city, a fact acknowledged by the municipal government in its willingness to help the orchestra's board build its house on the Beethovenstraße. Yet the *Konzertdirektion*'s jealous retention of their "territorial rights" to that space hearkened back in many ways to the original Großes-Concert, a musical group who, after all, played "on command" for its wealthy patrons.

The key to seeing both of these faces is to look at the continued influence of the men who served on the board. Between 1781 and 1918, they helped to develop a small musical group into a modern professional orchestra and moved from renting concert space to designing a purpose-built concert hall (using municipal funds). That building and its inhabitants became a touchstone for Leipzigers' pride in their city. Yet access to board membership, use of the hall, and, indeed, to tickets remained tightly controlled. Neither efforts on the part of the city nor pressure from other cultural organizations was able to shake the *Konzertdirektion* from its position. The aphorism *"Res severa est verum Gaudium"* (It is hard work to bring joy), which appeared on the frieze of each of the concert halls used by the orchestra, while it embodied the bourgeois nature of the institution, did not by any means suggest that the business of spreading that joy should be taken seriously.[62]

NOTES

This chapter is part of a larger manuscript based on my 1998 doctoral dissertation, "Art and Civic Patronage in Leipzig, 1848–1914" (Harvard University, 1998).

1. Ekkehard Mai and Peter Paret, eds., *Sammler, Stifter und Museen: Kunstförderung in Deutschland im 19. und 20. Jahrhundert* (Cologne: Böhlau Verlag, 1993). English-language works on Germany's museums and art market have also tended to use the more traditional term "patronage." See, for example, Robin Lenman, *Artists and Society in Germany 1850–1914* (Manchester: Manchester University Press, 1997); and James J. Sheehan, *Museums in the German Art World: From the End of the Old Regime to the Rise of Modernism* (Oxford: Oxford University Press, 2000).

2. Manfred Frey, *Macht und Moral des Schenkens: Staat und bürgerliche Mäzene vom späten 18. Jahrhundert bis zur Gegenwart* (Zwickau: Fannei & Walz Verlag, 1999); Jürgen Kocka and Manuel Frey, eds., *Bürgerkultur und Mäzenatentum im 19. Jahrhundert* (Zwickau: Fannei & Walz Verlag, 1998); and Thomas W. Gaehtgens and Martin Schieder, eds., *Mäzenatisches Handeln: Studien zur Kultur des Bürgersinns in der Gesellschaft* (Zwickau: Fannei & Walz Verlag, 1998).

3. The yearly fee for the directors in the 1860s was 60 marks. Wilhelm Seyfferth, *Die Gewandhaus-Concerte in Leipzig* (Leipzig, 1865), 6.

4. Johann Salomon Riemer, *Andere Fortsetzung des Leipzigischen Jahr-Buchs so ehemals von Herr Mag. Vogel,* MSS 1771, Stadtgeschichtliches Museum Leipzig.

5. Andreas Herzog, ed., *Das Literarische Leipzig: Kulturhistorisches Mosaik einer Buchstadt* (Leipzig: Edition Leipzig, 1995), 67–69; Sigfrid Henry Steinberg, *Five Hundred Years of Printing,* 4th ed. (New York: Criterion Books, 1959), 140; and Friedrich Schmidt, *Das Musikleben der bürgerlichen Gesellschaft Leipzigs* (Lagensalza: Hermann Beyer & Söhne, 1912), 42. The Schwabe family immigrated to Saxony in the sixteenth century. Gerhard Fischer, *Aus Zwei Jahrhunderten Leipziger Handelsgeschichte 1470–1650* (Leipzig: Kommissionsverlag von Felix Meiner, 1929), 50.

6. Alfred Dörffel, *Geschichte der Gewandhausconcerte zu Leipzig* (Leipzig, 1884), 230.

7. Material for this and following tables was compiled from my prosopographical database.

8. Herbert Helbig and Joachim Gontard, *Die Vertrauten 1680–1980: Eine Vereinigung Leipziger Kaufleute* (Stuttgart: Anton Hiersemann Verlag, 1980), 7–22ff.

9. Helbig and Gontard, *Die Vertrauten 1680–1980,* 26, 68, and 74–75.

10. Gustav Wustmann, *Die Vertraute Gesellschaft* (Leipzig, 1880), and my prosopographical database.

11. Helbig and Gontard, *Die Vertrauten 1680–1980,* 43 and 56.

12. Ernst Kroker, *Die Gesellschaft Harmonie in Leipzig 1776 bis 1926* (Leipzig: B. G. Teubner, 1926). For a list of the original membership, see Friedrich August Eckstein, *Die Harmonie in dem ersten Jahrhundert ihres Bestehens* (Leipzig: B. G. Teubner, 1876), 1–8.

13. Kroker, *Die Gesellschaft Harmonie,* 38 and 67.

14. Quoted in Dörffel, *Geschichte der Gewandhausconcerte,* 15.

15. Wolfgang Hocquél, *Leipzig Baumeister und Bauten* (Berlin: Tourist Verlag, 1990), 20–21.

16. "Die Akustik des alten Gewandhaussaales in Leipzig," *Centralblatt der Bauverwaltung* (1895): 7; "Über die Akustik des abgebrochenen alten Gewandhaussaales in Leipzig wurde Bericht erstattet," *Zeitschrift für Instrumentenbau* 17 (1896): 889; and Hermann Kuhn, "Der alte Gewandhauskonzertsaal zu Leipzig," *Deutsche Baugewerbe-Zeitung* 25 (1927): 221–224.

17. Rudolf Skoda, *Neues Gewandhaus Leipzig: Baugeschichte und Gegenwart eines Konzertgebäudes* (Berlin: Verlag für Bauwesen, 1985), 11–18.

18. Dörffel, *Geschichte der Gewandhausconcerte*, 14.

19. Ibid., 138.

20. Axel Frey and Bernd Weinkauf, eds., *Leipzig als ein Pleißathen: eine geistesgeschichtliche Ortsbestimmung* (Leipzig: Reclam Verlag, 1995), 197–230; and Johannes Forner, "150 Jahre Musikhochschule in Leipzig," in *Musikstadt Leipzig*, ed. Rat der Stadt Leipzig (Leipzig: Ed. Leipzig, 1993), 103–104. See also Katrin Seidel, *Carl Reinecke und das Leipziger Gewandhaus* (Hamburg: von Bockel Verlag, 1998).

21. *Handbuch der Gewandhaus-Konzertdirektion* (Leipzig: C. G. Röder, GmbH, 1905), 30.

22. Eberhard Creuzburg, *Die Gewandhaus-Konzerte zu Leipzig: 1781–1931* (Leipzig: Breitkopf und Härtel, 1931), 113–114.

23. Gewandhaus-Concertdirection, "Aufforderung zur Betheiligung bei dem Bau eines neuen Concerthauses in Leipzig," November 1877, Kap. 32, no. 12, fol. 1–3 and Gewandhausdir. 4.2, Stadtarchiv Leipzig.

24. *Leipziger Tageblatt*, no. 501 (October 1, 1893); and Manfred Würzberger, "Die Entwicklung des Orchesterwesens in Leipzig ausserhalb des Stadt- und Gewandhausorchesters in den 2. Hälfte des 19. Jahrhunderts" (Ph.D. diss., Karl-Marx-Universität Leipzig, 1968), 77.

25. Letter from the Concert-Directorate to Stadt Leipzig dated March 1879 and Minutes of the City Council Meeting, March 29, 1878, Kap. 32, no. 12, fol. 5–8, Stadtarchiv Leipzig.

26. City Council Plenar Protocol, October 11, 1879.

27. Kap. 32, no. 12, fol. 24–29 and 43–54; and Kap. 31, no. 12, fol. 24–67, 144–154, both in Stadtarchiv Leipzig.

28. Kap. 36G, no. 10, fol. 4 and 9–10, Stadtarchiv Leipzig.

29. Heinrich Geffcken and H. Tykorinski, *Stiftungsbuch der Stadt Leipzig* (Leipzig: Bär und Hermann, 1905), 465.

30. Margaret Eleanor Menninger, "Städtische Kunstförderung, das sächsische Unternehmertum und der kaufmännische Geist Leipzigs am Beispiel des Grassi-Museums 1880–1900," in *Unternehmer in Sachsen. Aufstieg—Krise—Untergang—Neubeginn*, ed. Ulrich Heß, Petra Listewnik, and Michael Schäfer (Leipzig: Leipziger Universitätsverlag, 1998), 97–105.

31. Plenar Protocol Extract of July 13, 1881, Kap. 32, no. 12, fol. 103–104, Stadtarchiv Leipzig.

32. The other ceremonial buildings were the Music Conservatory, the university library, the art academy, the city trade school, and the Imperial Supreme Court.

33. Günter Eichler, "Die Entstehung und Entwicklung des Leipziger Musikviertels von 1884 bis zum Vorabend des Ersten Weltkrieges" (unpublished master's thesis, University of Leipzig, 1981), 10–11. See also Verein Musikviertel e. V., ed., *Das Leipziger Musikviertel* (Leipzig: Verlag im Wissenschaftszentrum, n.d.); and Peter Landau, "Reichsjustizgesetze und Justizpaläste," in *Kunstpolitik und Kunstförderung im Kaiserreich. Kunst im Wandel der Sozial und Wirtschaftsgeschichte*, ed. Ekkehard Mai, Hans Pohl, and Stephan Waetzoldt (Berlin: Gebr. Mann Verlag, 1982), 197–224.

34. The orchestra took its first international trip, to Switzerland, in 1916. Johannes Forner, *Die Gewandhauskonzerte zu Leipzig, 1781–1981* (Leipzig: VEB Deutscher Verlag für Musik, 1981), 131–132.

35. Kap. 32, no. 12, fol. 91–94, Stadtarchiv Leipzig.

36. Gustav Wustmann, *Aus Leipzigs Vergangenheit: gesammelte Aufsätze, neue Folge* (Leipzig: Fr. Wilh. Grunow, 1898), 463.

37. Quoted in Würzberger, "Die Entwicklung des Orchesterwesens in Leipzig," 131.

38. The older building was torn down in 1896. Kap. 32, no. 31, vol. I, fol. 47, Stadtarchiv Leipzig.

39. *Neue Zeitschrift für Musik* 93, no. 44 (1897) and 96, no. 14 (1900), Kap. 32, Stadtarchiv Leipzig; *Rheinische Musik und Theater Zeitung,* Jg. XII, no. 8 (Feb. 25, 1911); and *Leipziger Tageblatt,* no. 133, May 14, 1911.

40. Winderstein to City Council, February 17, 1911, Kap. 32, no. 31, vol. I, fol. 31–32, Stadtarchiv Leipzig.

41. Winderstein to Tröndlin, February 25, 1911, Kap. 32, no. 31, vol. I, fol. 33–35, Stadtarchiv Leipzig.

42. Minutes, City Council Meeting, June 7, 1911, Kap. 32, no. 31, vol. I, fol. 41–43, Stadtarchiv Leipzig.

43. City Council to City Parliament, June 10, 1911, Kap. 32, no. 31, vol. I, fol. 47, Stadtarchiv Leipzig.

44. Minutes, Meeting of the Municipal Parliament, June 28, 1911, Kap. 32, no. 31, vol. I, fol. 59–60, Stadtarchiv Leipzig.

45. *Leipziger Volkszeitung,* June 26, 1925, Kap. 32, no. 31, vol. I, fol. 69, Stadtarchiv Leipzig.

46. City Council to *Leipziger Volkszeitung,* July 2, 1925, Kap. 32, no. 31, vol. I, fol. 69, Stadtarchiv Leipzig.

47. *Leipziger Volkszeitung,* July 9, 1925, Kap. 32, no. 31, vol. I, fol. 70, Stadtarchiv Leipzig.

48. Thomas Adam, *Arbeitermilieu und Arbeiterbewegung in Leipzig 1871–1933* (Köln and Weimar: Böhlau Verlag, 1999), 143–146; Gustav Hennig, *Zehn Jahre Arbeiterbildungsinstitut* (Leipzig, 1927); "Das Allgemeine Arbeiter-Bildungs Institut," *Kulturwille* 1 (1924): 8–9; and "25 Jahre Arbeiter-Bildungsinstitut," *Kulturwille* 9 (1932): 9.

49. Forner, *Gewandhauskonzerte,* 178; C. Böhm and S.-W. Staps, *Das Leipziger Stadt- und Gewandhausorchester: Dokumente einer 250jährigen Geschichte* (Leipzig: Verlag Kunst und Touristik, 1993), 177–179; A. Malige, "Von den Anfängen des Rundfunk-Sinfonieorchester," *Jahrbuch zur Geschichte der Stadt Leipzig* (1980): 96–109.

50. After 1945, the *Sylvesterkonzert* became a staple of the Gewandhaus season. Böhm, *Stadt- und Gewandhausorchester,* 179. In 1919, workers were able to attend the dress rehearsal of the *St. Matthew's Passion* in the Thomaskirche. Forner, *Gewandhauskonzerte,* 183.

51. Frank Heidenreich, *Arbeiterkulturbewegung und Sozialdemokratie in Sachsen vor 1933* (Köln and Weimar: Böhlau Verlag, 1995), 315–318; Akten, die Überlassung des Stadtorchesters an das ABI zur Veranstaltung der Sylvesterkonzerte betr. (1919), Kap. 32, no. 34, Stadtarchiv Leipzig; and Barnet Licht, "Wem fällt die Erhaltung des Gewandhauses zu?" *Leipzig. E. Monatsschrift* (1930): 7.

52. Kap. 32, no. 34, fol. 12, Stadtarchiv Leipzig.

53. Rat der Stadt Leipzig to the Verband der Verein Ehemaliger Realschueler Deutschlands e. V. Ortsgruppe Leipzig, June 27, 1919, read into Minutes of the City Council, July 2, 1919, Kap. 32, no. 1, vol. II, fol. 37–38, Stadtarchiv Leipzig.

54. Forner, *Gewandhauskonzerte zu Leipzig,* 183; and Böhm, *Stadt- und Gewandhausorchester,* 187.

55. Kap. 32, no. 28, fol. 28–97 ff., Stadtarchiv Leipzig.

56. Karl Straube to Rat der Stadt Leipzig, June 29, 1919, Kap. 32, no. 28, fol. 136–137, Stadtarchiv Leipzig.

57. Claus-Christian W. Szejnmann, *Von Traum zum Alptraum: Sachsen in der Weimarer Republik* (Leipzig: Gustav Kiepenheuer Verlag, 2000), 81–84.

58. Böhm, *Stadt- und Gewandhausorchester,* 187 and 196.

59. Thomas Schinkröth, *Jüdische Musiker in Leipzig 1855–1945* (Altenburg: Verlag Klaus-Jürgen Kamprad, 1994), 91.

60. Böhm, *Stadt- und Gewandhausorchester,* 198–200; and Forner, *Gewandhauskonzerte,* 222–223.

61. See Christoph Kaufmann, *Von einem Abriß wird abgeraten* (Beucha: Sax-Verlag, 1996); and Johannes Frackowiak, "Kulturorganisation und -finanzierung in Leipzig zwischen 1945 und 1949," *Mitteldeutsches Jahrbuch für Kultur und Geschichte* 8 (2001): 141–155.

62. "True joy is a serious matter" was taken from the twenty-third letter of Seneca the Younger and adopted as the motto of the Großes-Concert in the 1770s.

SEVEN

Changing Perceptions of Philanthropy in the Voluntary Housing Field in Nineteenth- and Early-Twentieth-Century London

SUSANNAH MORRIS

INTRODUCTION

The role of historians in comparing the experiences of philanthropy of different countries is becoming increasingly important. As governments seek alternatives to state and market mechanisms for meeting their social welfare goals, social scientists are keen to advance understanding of the position and role of the variously called voluntary, nonprofit, or civil society sectors. Based on the findings of the most extensive comparative nonprofit sector project to date, Lester Salamon and Helmut K. Anheier have argued that what they call the "social origins" of a nation's nonprofit or civil society sectors is a crucial determinant of cross-national variation.[1] Thus the social, economic, and political relations which surrounded the historical development of the sector explain variations in the scale and scope of civil society between groups of nations today. This volume contributes to these debates by examining what lessons can be drawn from a number of historical studies of "philanthropy" as understood within a variety of national contexts and functional fields.

I argue in this chapter that historians need to explicitly articulate their understandings of the key characteristics by which they are defining their subject matter if we are to make meaningful comparisons about the scale and scope of voluntary activity in different historical periods and locations. The examination of voluntary housing provision in London over a 75-year period demonstrates important shifts in contemporary perceptions of the properties of voluntary activity, differences which had far-reaching implications for relations among the state, the market, and the voluntary sector in the twentieth-century social housing field. The findings suggest that we should be wary of drawing conclusions about distinct national models of philanthropy without taking into consideration how understandings of philanthropy may be subject to variation within nations over time.

HISTORIOGRAPHICAL PERSPECTIVES ON VOLUNTARY ACTION

Historians writing about voluntary activity in the social welfare field have variously described their subject matter as charitable, philanthropic, or voluntary in a variety of overlapping and interlocking ways which are often only implicitly defined.[2] Despite this plethora of terms, there is a degree of consensus that voluntary activity is located somewhere between the state and the market in the mixed economy of welfare, yet establishing the salient features of that activity is more problematic. Even if we focus on one term, "philanthropy," we could use motivation, action, or outcome as the variables by which we delineate our subject matter. Historians who want to chart and explain geographic and temporal variations in the mixed economy of welfare lack a clear analytical framework within which to do so: The historiography does not provide a common set of definitions which categorize welfare provision by voluntary agencies. Each choice of distinguishing variable embodies an alternative position and scale of activity for the voluntary sector in the welfare mix.

Wilbur K. Jordan and David E. Owen wrote at great length about the history of English philanthropy, which they defined as the voluntary donation of money. Jordan defined his purpose as being to "record every gift and bequest made to charities."[3] Owen built on Jordan's work and took a consciously "limited view of philanthropy" by applying a "pecuniary" test to define his subject.[4] His study had "little to do with good works, personal service, or labors in the public interest, save as these were accompanied by substantial contributions of money from individuals and groups."[5] Thus the histories written by both Jordan and Owen rest upon the definition of philanthropy as the donation of money, the input of financial resources to the voluntary sector. In terms of comparison over time, framing philanthropy as pecuniary donation understates the scale and scope of nonstatutory welfare provision in the English past. It is thus unsurprising that Owen emphasized English philanthropy's ultimate inadequacy when measured against the requirements of industrial-urban society: "It became only a matter of time until the State moved cautiously or decisively into areas previously occupied by voluntary agencies."[6]

Teleological accounts of welfare history, which considered voluntary solutions to social problems as inferior staging posts along the road to an all-encompassing welfare state, however, have been challenged. In this what we might call voluntaristic renaissance, Frank K. Prochaska has made what is probably the most extensive contribution to our historical knowledge of the breadth and vitality of the voluntary sector in the United Kingdom.[7] Rather than defining philanthropy as simply the donation of money, Prochaska argues that "it is suggestive to think of the history of philanthropy as the history of kindness."[8] Using this definition, Prochaska argues that if you "cast widely to include the informal, domestic expression of kindness, the philanthropic net catches virtually everyone at one time or another."[9] Brian Harrison adopts a similar definition of philanthropy as kindness, arguing that "philanthropy extends through a wide range of social behavior—from the informal expression of kindness to a dependent at one end to legislative campaigning for social justice at the other."[10] When one focuses on actors' motives, the definition of philanthropy as kindness encompasses various actions that include the voluntary donation of time, labor, or money, whether that donation be made in the context of mutual self-help between neighbors and kin or in the formal structure of a voluntary organization. This catchall definition is, however, problematic. Defining philanthropy as kindness presupposes that voluntary actors were motivated by regard for others. It encompasses the donation of labor or funds within the household or between friends and the provision of services by agencies, yet the relationship between the giver and receiver is very different in these cases. The range of motives for and rewards of voluntary action are likely to differ according to the institutional framework through which they are deployed. Both Prochaska and Harrison, however, are less concerned with trying to chart and explain geographic and temporal variations in the mix of welfare provision in the past and more intent on asserting the strength and vitality of the voluntary sector despite the development of state provision. In this sense, their approach is still rather state-centered.

The more recent historiography on welfare no longer considers the voluntary sector as simply a precursor to the welfare state, nor does it take for granted that other-regarding individuals will form voluntary organizations in response to social need. Thus we read about a mixed economy of welfare in which the state is only one provider among many.[11] For Geoffrey B. A. M. Finlayson, the other agencies in this arena may be broadly categorized under the term "voluntarism." His definition of voluntary activity is, however, rather confusing. The uncontroversial aspect of his definition is that voluntary activity must be the result of individual choice to partake in self-governing activity.[12] The confusion sets in, however, when one becomes aware of the self-contradictory nature of the other assertions which he makes.

Finlayson states that voluntary activity is "concerned with the advancement of others, rather than the self," yet "the word [voluntarism] does not necessarily mean doing things without material reward."[13] This activity takes place in a sector which is "not concerned with distributing a profit" yet for which there exists "a distinction between non-profit-distributing and profit-distributing voluntarism."[14] Finlayson's confusion over the relationship between other- and self-regarding interests, profit, and the voluntary sector is a common difficulty encountered when one tries to identify the salient properties of that area of activity that lies between the state and the market in the mixed economy of welfare. The implication of Michael B. Katz and Christoph Sachsse's volume on the mixed economy of welfare is that the boundary between the public (implying the local or national state) and the private (denoting provision by the individual, the family, or the voluntary association) is at best very fluid and permeable when applied in a historical context.[15]

Other historians have questioned the utility of the public/private divide as a way of delineating sectors in the mixed economy of welfare.[16] By looking at welfare outcomes rather than focusing on the institutional form of the agency providing the service, Paul Johnson provides an account of "how a variety of welfare instruments were used to reduce the incidence of social risk."[17] Martin J. Daunton argues that Johnson suggests that "most social risks, most of the time, have been met in a variety of ways which are obscured by simple dichotomies between private and public, individualistic and collectivist approaches."[18] By looking at outcomes rather than motives or forms of action, we are provided with yet another way of subdividing provision in the mixed economy of welfare.

For any individual with a given array of capabilities, it may not matter what institutional mix of provision meets their needs. However, this does not obviate the need for systematization and classification of the different institutions providing welfare services. It is only through the subdivision of the mixed economy of welfare into sectoral components that we can capture the dimensions and directions of geographic and temporal variation in the welfare arrangements through which individuals may meet their needs. Historians face the challenge of developing a language and method which can identify and describe the salient properties of voluntary activity if we are to chart historical changes in the mixed economy of welfare. This historical shifting of institutional boundaries, and hence in the meaning attached to these boundaries by contemporaries, raises a difficult but important methodological issue: How should historians of welfare or charity or giving or philanthropy define the scope of their study? Should they use late-twentieth-century definitions or should historians delimit their subject by reference to the historically specific conceptions of social need and public purpose which are subject to change over time? How can they establish the scale and scope of those organizations operating between the state and the market in the mixed economy of welfare?

Within the social sciences, the Johns Hopkins Comparative Nonprofit Sector Project represents the most comprehensive attempt to establish a universal definition of the "third sector occupying a distinctive social space outside of both the market and the state."[19] The project was launched in 1990 to inquire "into the scope, structure, history, legal position, and role of the nonprofit sector in a broad cross-section of nations."[20] In order to facilitate comparative analysis, the project developed what Anheier and Salamon term the structural-operational definition of the nonprofit sector.[21] This five-point definition is used to identify organizations that operate in the nonprofit or voluntary sector on their own terms rather than negatively as entities which belong to neither the market nor the state sectors.[22] While the structural-operational definition has merits as a metric for comparing nonprofit sectors between countries today, my work has demonstrated the difficulties of applying this definition historically.[23] Organizations which were considered to be social welfare agencies in nineteenth-century Britain appear to be indistinguishable from for-profit companies according to the structural-operational definition, which conflates organizational form with purpose so that organizations which can distribute surpluses to their members, such as friendly societies or model dwellings companies, are assumed by definition to be unable to operate in the public interest.[24] Surveying the mixed economy of welfare using this definition produces a map with boundaries that the Victorians would have found difficult to recognize.

Historians are therefore faced with the challenge of developing a language and mode of analysis of their own with which they can identify and describe changes in historical understandings of the nature and role of voluntary activity and its position in the mixed economy of welfare. This is necessary both for examining changes in the way in which societies have met their social welfare needs over time and for making meaningful comparisons between the historical experiences of different countries.

Our brief historiographical survey has shown that various authors on English philanthropy have considered boundaries in the mixed economy of welfare by focusing on actors' motives, the inputs they provided, or the outcomes of their actions. This chapter will examine the voluntary response to the problem of housing the working classes in nineteenth- and early-twentieth-century London as a case study that explores the implications of these various approaches for our understanding of philanthropy. It will do so in three ways: first by considering housing organizations on their own terms —by examining their goals, outputs, and relationship with the market; second, by considering how they fit with some of the common historiographical definitions of philanthropy; and finally, by examining the relationship between voluntary housing organizations and the state. By examining one functional field, namely housing, in one location, we can examine how historical perceptions of what constituted philanthropy may have changed over time. Differences in understandings of philanthropy that may be associated with the functional field or national context in which the activity is deployed are therefore held constant by using this method of analysis.

THE CASE OF VOLUNTARY ACTION AND THE HOUSING OF THE WORKING CLASSES

The Victorian housing problem concerned working-class lifestyles and living conditions in the private rental sector. Contemporaries considered that the slums and their inhabitants generated a number of socially unacceptable manifestations which were at odds with the public interest as they conceived it; this conflict was considered to be particularly acute in Victorian London.[25] The housing problem was therefore considered to be one of the most major public problems of its day, which threatened to harm the physical, moral, social, and even economic health of society.

The state responded by introducing legislation to try to force recalcitrant landlords to improve their properties.[26] However, the effectiveness of the national and local state's attempts to regulate the slums was limited due to both problems of self-interest among local politicians and insufficient administrative capacity. In addition, the housing legislation itself contributed to the problem. The law prevented the very change in behavior on the part of landlords which had been envisaged. The landlord was more likely to gain than to lose from not improving his property. If his property was not condemned but others were, available housing was reduced and the housing that remained was even more overcrowded. If he was caught and his property was compulsorily purchased, the system of compensation, which was based on rental income, rewarded the worst conditions of overcrowding and provided an incentive for landlords to make conditions still worse.[27] Overall, the system of fines and compensation seems to have made things better for the landlord of slum property and even worse for society.

Addressing this problem of external conditions required a system of housing provision which generated collective benefits to be enjoyed by the wider society, not just those who financed and consumed more salubrious working-class accommodation. From the 1840s onward, voluntary action led to the formation of a group of new institutions which attempted to find a practical way to combine the public and private interest in improving the housing of the working classes. There were essentially three organizational forms which were adopted by voluntary organizations formed in response to the housing problem: endowed trusts, subscription charities, and limited-liability companies. The defining characteristic of these different institutions was the way in which they raised capital. The endowed trusts did not have to raise capital at all in the sense that they were established as the result of the benefaction or bequest of one individual. Several large charitable trusts were established in the housing field between the years of 1860 and 1910, including those founded by George Peabody, Edward Cecil Guinness, Samuel Lewis, and William Sutton.[28] Subscription charities raised capital through the donations of their multiple patrons; the most widely known example in London was the Society for Improving the Condition of the Laboring Classes (SICLC).[29] The third type of organization was the model dwellings company (MDC), which was registered as a limited-liability joint-stock company and raised capital from investors in return for the payment of a dividend. "Five per cent philanthropy" is a term repeatedly used in the housing historiography, yet the term was not widely used at the time to describe the concept of providing dwellings in such a way as to do social good and earn a return on the investment made.[30] Thus, this chapter will refer to MDCs, a term more in sympathy with the terminology of the time and without the misleading suggestion that investment in these companies was associated with an empirically verifiable return of 5 percent.[31]

Aims

Despite the different forms which they adopted, all of the institutions that developed in response to the housing problem shared a common objective to provide a more salubrious standard of accommodation for the working classes at an affordable cost, thereby changing their lifestyles and living conditions to benefit the wider society as a whole. In 1841, the Metropolitan Association for Improving the Dwellings of the Industrious Classes (MAIDIC) became the first organization to be founded in response to the London housing problem.[32] The charter of incorporation states that "several persons came together" for the purpose of "the purchase and construction of dwelling houses, to be let to the poorer classes of person, so as to remove the evils arising from the construction and arrangement of such dwellings, more especially in densely populated districts."[33] In reviewing the achievements of MAIDIC, Dr. Southwood Smith, the public health campaigner, argued that the outcomes of this organization's activities demonstrated that its aims had been fulfilled. The mortality rates of their tenants had become lower than for the poorer London boroughs and "moral pestilence has, at the same time, been checked. The intemperate have become sober, and the disorderly well conducted, since taking up their abode in these healthful and peaceful dwellings."[34]

The SICLC, founded in 1844, also aimed to improve both the physical and moral condition of the working classes. The organization claimed that "we *have* a remedy against all diseases be they physical or moral. . . . The simple, single aim of the Society has always been to teach the poor man to help and respect himself, to improve him physically and morally, and thus indirectly to check immorality, to counteract crime, to diminish intemperance, to encourage virtue."[35]

If the behavior of the poor man could be changed in the way in which the SICLC, MAIDIC, and other housing organizations claimed, then the results of their activities would be beneficial to both the poor man himself and the wider society. To be moral, law-abiding, temperate, and virtuous was to conform to the norms of social behavior of this time, and these characteristics were therefore the required prerequisites of the full social and economic integration of the poor in society.

In order to fulfill their aims, voluntary housing organizations had to direct their activities toward the attention of the more typical for-profit private landlords. They had to demonstrate that it was possible to profit from following their example in order to provide an incentive for commercial landlords to do so. Those that responded to the housing problem were all committed to establishing themselves on self-supporting principles, which entailed earning some sort of return. The charitable trusts such as the Peabody Trust, despite the absence of shareholders to satisfy, also chose to set aside a portion of their revenue each year so they were self-perpetuating in their activities.[36] Both the Local Government Board and the London County Council suggested to the trustees of the Sutton estate that they should aim to make a return of around 2.5 per cent, a suggestion which the Trust adopted.[37] Even Octavia Hill shared this commitment to generating a surplus. Hill repeatedly stressed that she must conduct her affairs on a sound financial footing, following the advice of Ruskin, who believed that for her system to succeed it must demonstrate that it could be profitable.[38] This commitment to generating a return on investment, however, was most obvious in MDCs. The Central London Dwellings Improvement Company (CLDIC) was established in 1861 "by some gentlemen, chiefly belonging to Lincoln's Inn, who wished to help on the [housing] movement in the West Central Postal District, and try for themselves whether a company might not get a fair return out of weekly house property, and yet deal considerately with the tenants."[39]

Following the establishment of the CLDIC in West London, Sydney Waterlow commenced his experimentation in housing provision by building a block of dwellings at Mark Street, Finsbury, to demonstrate the financial viability of his plan. Once he had demonstrated the financial viability of providing improved dwellings as an alternative to the slums, other businessmen joined Waterlow to form the Improved Industrial Dwellings Company in 1863.

Housing organizations had to use various types of campaigning activities to demonstrate their model. As first movers in this new field of housing provision, MAIDIC and the SICLC explicitly encouraged others to follow their example. The SICLC saw its primary role as providing models, plans, and information about its own experiences to enable others to follow its example.[40] Perhaps the best known, and therefore most successful, example of the campaigning activities of the SICLC were the model cottages which they exhibited in the Great Exhibition of 1851. After visiting one of the SICLC's buildings, the Prince of Wales declared that "it will show to those who possess capital, that they may invest it with great advantage and profit to themselves, in consulting the convenience and dispensing comfort to their poorer brethren."[41]

MAIDIC also sought to encourage others to emulate its example. The company told its shareholders that they were "pioneers in this great movement, . . . [and] . . . may reflect with satisfaction . . . upon the good effects which their example may be fairly considered to have produced. Considerable sums of money have been expended in London on the like objects by several other societies and individuals . . . in addition to which about 30 societies have been formed for the same object in various parts of England."[42]

Voluntary housing organizations in London thus had a demonstration effect on others that extended beyond the capital. After the close of the Great Exhibition the SICLC received a regular stream of letters from individuals in Britain and abroad claiming that they were going to build dwellings based on their designs.[43] During the 1860s, they exchanged information with many kindred associations and schemes, including one in Naples based on their model, another in Amsterdam, and numerous English schemes.[44] More generally, Thomas Adam has shown how the examples of London MDCs were followed in Germany, Canada, and the United States.[45]

Outputs

While we have demonstrated that the aims of these organizations were philanthropic, we also need to consider whether their outputs accorded with their aims. Figure 7.1 shows the number of housing organizations established in London between 1840 and 1914 by type and the number of dwellings they produced during this time.[46] At least forty-three organizations were established, thirty-one of which produced 35,864 dwellings, which was over two and a half times the combined contributions of the London City Council, the metropolitan boroughs, and the City Corporation during the same period.[47] These private or voluntary-sector housing

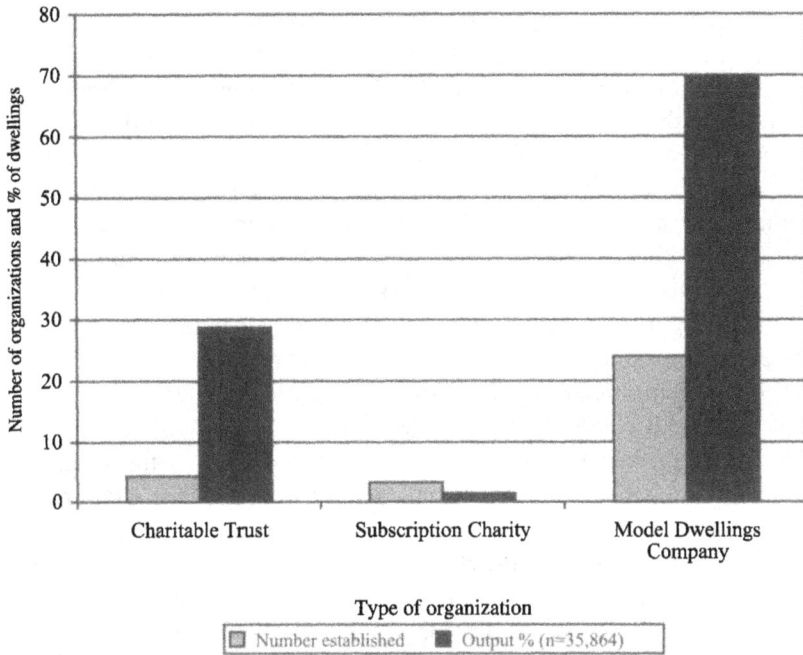

Figure 7.1. Number and Output of Housing Organizations Established in London, 1840–1914

organizations provided between 11 and 15 percent of all new working-class accommodation built in London between 1856 and 1914.[48]

If we consider the philanthropic contribution of these organizations in terms of quantity alone, this figure demonstrates that model dwellings companies, rather than more traditional forms of charity, represented the most significant contribution to the housing field in terms of both the number of organizations established and their output. As a demonstration effect, these numbers are significant, although of course we should bear in mind that the majority of the working classes remained housed by more traditional private landlords.[49] The continued dominance of private landlords, however, was in accordance with the aims of these organizations; they did not seek to usurp their role but to demonstrate an alternative model of housing provision for them to follow.

Some commercial builders of working-class housing followed the lead of MDCs in developing flats, which in the nineteenth century were an unusual form of housing in London. This began to change by the turn of the twentieth century; the census estimates that by 1911, although there were 478,024 inhabited ordinary dwelling houses, there were 15,600 blocks of flats with 121,047 separate flats.[50] However, not all of this housing was of a similar quality. The housing organizations under study here provided the highest standard of apartment buildings for the working classes in London. Ninety-eight percent of the block dwellings owned by "philanthropic and semi-philanthropic" associations (the category which included MDCs) were reported as being "'Fair', 'Good' or 'Very Good,' as to light and air or sanitation" by Booth's survey, while 81 percent of all apartment buildings fell into this category.[51] Thus, model dwellings companies can be differentiated from other market providers in part by the quality of their output.

MDCs also differed from other housing providers in terms of the price of their output; that is, the rents they charged their tenants. As one contemporary observer put it, "Here is a higher test of social economic utility [of these organizations]. . . . Such utility is disclosed by the well known fact that the rentals charged in model dwellings are almost universally lower than those exacted for fairly similar accommodation in the neighborhood."[52] Comparison of the rents charged for working-class accommodation owned and managed by various landlords who provided improved dwellings with those generally charged in the private market does, indeed, demonstrate that these organizations charged below-market rents.[53] Morris has shown that in terms of the quality of their dwellings, the rents they charged, and the characteristics of the tenants they housed, model dwellings companies performed better that the private market and at least as well as the more traditional subscription charities and trusts operating in the field.[54] Despite the achievements of voluntary housing organizations, however, MDCs would not be considered philanthropic according to some twentieth-century historical definitions.

LOCATING VOLUNTARY HOUSING ORGANIZATIONS IN THE WORLD OF PHILANTHROPY

So far we have seen that model dwellings companies and other voluntary housing organizations were distinct from the existing private housing market in terms of both their aims and their outputs. Despite this, they do not sit easily in the world of philanthropy as it has been defined by some historians. The activities of MDCs would clearly lie outside the scope of Jordan and Owen's studies of philanthropy in that they were financed by the input of invested rather than donated funds. This leaves us with only the subscription charities and trusts located firmly in the philanthropic sphere. As shown by Figure 7.1 above, however, the exclusion of MDCs dramatically reduces the scale and scope of voluntary-sector activity in the housing field. Initially, subscription charities and trusts, such as the SICLC and the Peabody Trust, do not appear to present any problems for the pecuniary definition of philanthropy in that they were organizations founded because of the actions of individuals who voluntarily donated money. However, when one looks in more detail at the issue of voluntary monetary donation, the validity of this distinction becomes less clear. Consideration of philanthropy as simply the donation of money is also problematic as it fails to appreciate the distinctions that some contemporaries drew between individuals' monetary donations, as shown by the response to George Peabody's philanthropic activities in London.

In 1862, the wealthy U.S. banker donated £150,000 to "ameliorate the condition of the poor and needy of this great metropolis, and to promote their comfort and happiness."[55] The resultant Peabody Trust is perhaps the most well-known example of the nineteenth-century housing trusts both because of the scale of the donation and the characteristics of the donative action. In terms of scale, Peabody gave another £100,000 in 1862, £100,000 in 1868, and a bequest of £150,000 in his will.[56] In terms of the action itself, Peabody's donation was perceived by contemporaries to have been a great and unparalleled sacrifice for the public good: "We all understand how much a gift exceeds a legacy . . . but charitable donations made in a person's lifetime are comparatively rare."[57] Following Peabody's first London benefaction, the *Times* commented:

> There have been many among us who, from various motives, have bequeathed large sums, and even their whole fortunes, to charitable purposes, or for the promotion of literature or art, or to carry out some scheme which was their fancy during life. But this posthumous liberality has little in it that resembles the personal sacrifice of Mr. Peabody. The testator deprives himself of nothing; he only diverts the destination of that which he must necessarily leave behind. He cannot carry with him to the grave the wealth which was his enjoyment during life; and he may, without any impulse of exalted virtue be willing to enrich an institution rather than an heir.[58]

The *Times* thus suggested a hierarchy of voluntary action in Victorian England in which lifetime benefaction counted for more than bequests. This view was echoed by the city chamberlain at the ceremony of presentation of the freedom of the city of London to Peabody, when he stated that the "aspects in which that gift . . . may be regarded as enhancing very greatly its value" included the fact that Peabody "relinquished during his life the possession and enjoyment of the large sum" which he donated.[59] According to this contemporary viewpoint, the Peabody and Guinness Trusts, founded by lifetime benefactions, would have been clearly distinct from the subsequent Samuel Lewis and Sutton housing trusts which were established as the result of bequests. This distinction is based not only on the characteristics of their action and the nature of the inputs they provided but also on whether their motives were considered to be self-interested or other-regarding.

The issue of motive is central to some other definitions of philanthropy. Prochaska defined philanthropy as kindness toward others, thereby presupposing that it is an action that expresses other-regarding motives; an action that does not seek a personal reward. Defining philanthropy according to actors' motives, however, is also problematic. The general problem is that motives are notoriously difficult to establish and even when identified are often found to be mixed. Donating money during one's lifetime presents more problems of interpretation. Taking the example of George Peabody, although his lifetime benefaction was thought to enhance its value, it also had a potentially contradictory effect on the perceived generosity of the gift. Peabody could bask in the glory of his action in a way that someone who was dead could not, and he certainly chose to act in a very public manner. First, Peabody chose to disregard the advice of Lord Shaftesbury that he should address the housing problem by investing £75,000 in an existing housing charity, the SICLC, of which Shaftesbury was the chairman.[60] By choosing instead to pursue his own brand of voluntary action and establish a trust fund bearing his name, Peabody raised his own profile in a way he could not have done by giving money to an existing organization. Second, he announced the founding of his trust by way of a letter addressed to the *Times*, which was subsequently reproduced and commented upon in countless newspapers around Britain and across the Atlantic in Peabody's native homeland of the United States.[61] As another illustration of Peabody's personal interests, Robert Winthrop made the following comment in his eulogy at Peabody's funeral:

> Our lamented friend was not, indeed, without ambition. He not only liked to do grand things, but he liked to do them in a grand way. . . . He was not without a decided taste for occasional display,—call it even ostentation, if you will. We certainly may not ascribe to him a pre-eminent measure of that sort of charity which shuns publicity, which shrinks from observation, and which, according to one of our Saviour's well-remembered injunctions, "doeth its alms in secret."[62]

Thus Peabody not only sought to benefit the poor; he also appeared to seek public acclaim for himself, thus suggesting that his motives were mixed.[63]

There is another specific problem relating to motive in the case of Victorian social housing: Despite the payment of a direct return to patrons in the form of a dividend payment, contemporaries still regarded investment in model dwellings companies to be philanthropic. Rather than expecting patrons to be purely other-regarding, it was argued that "he who helps the poor man to obtain a better home at the same price he pays for his present wretched accommodation, and at the same time obtains a fair return for the capital invested, is a greater philanthropist than he who maintains him in idleness, or lodges him in charity."[64]

There appears to be an inherent paradox in the suggestion that by letting accommodation for a fair return, a landlord is more philanthropic than the Good Samaritan who grants a poor man shelter for nothing. Nevertheless, this was a central tenet of MDCs. At a public meeting held by MAIDIC in 1854, one of its members pointed out the differences between it and other forms of voluntarism: "The association was not charitable in the ordinary sense of the word, where all was given on the one side and all was received on the other. (Hear hear.) It was, however, a philanthropic institution and the benefits that it conferred were only limited by the powers and resources at its command."[65]

This system was described by Lord Stanley as a "fair and equal bargain between man and man," for "there was no sacrifice of independence on either side. They [the investors] got a fair return for their capital, and the workman got a better quality of lodging."[66] Patrons were encouraged to buy shares in the company and then received dividends in return for their investment. The institution was philanthropic insofar as its primary aim was not profit maximization per se but the development of a system of provision which could solve the housing problem. The reason they were not charitable was that they did not reduce independence and self-reliance among the working classes, since working men were charged rent for their dwellings. Thus, distinctions were made in the housing field between charity and philanthropy. Charity simply entailed the donation of money and was considered to be a one-sided action which actually harmed its recipients, while philanthropy was considered to work for the mutual benefit of the parties involved.[67] Motive alone was therefore an insufficient criterion for establishing whether an action was philanthropic.

As we have seen, adopting a definition of voluntary activity that restricts itself to those organizations founded as the result of the donative actions of their members drastically reduces the scale and scope of voluntary activity in the mixed economy of housing provision in nineteenth-century London. In addition, if we turn to consider the voluntary housing sector in terms of the motives of those who became involved we find that this definition has a similarly restrictive effect on the scope of the field. Looking for examples of kindness by philanthropists or examining the act of donating money to the cause cannot capture the contemporary meanings of charity and philanthropy in the housing field. We also need to take account of the aims and outputs of MDCs and contemporary understandings of how these related to the public interest. By using this approach we can differentiate MDCs from both the market and the state and therefore place them where contemporaries would have put them: as part of the voluntary response to the housing problem. Thus the action, the input, and the output of the activity in question all had important roles to play in distinguishing philanthropy from market or state activity in the housing field in Victorian London.

VOLUNTARY ACTION AND THE STATE

Although we have demonstrated that simple definitions of voluntary activity based on actors' motives or the provision of particular forms of input do not adequately capture the scale and scope of voluntary action as it was perceived in nineteenth-century London, we have not considered contemporary concerns regarding the boundary and relationships between the voluntary sector and the state in the housing field and how these contributed toward understandings of philanthropy.

The state helped to shape the role and position of voluntary organizations through particular areas of legislation designed to enforce sanitary standards for housing.[68] The Cross Act of 1875 was particularly important for state and voluntary-sector relations. Under the terms of this legislation, the Metropolitan Board of Works was empowered to compulsorily purchase large areas of slum housing in London, clear it, and then sell the sites for the provision of new housing for the working classes.[69] The combined effect of the rehousing clauses and the terms of compensation for the owners of properties purchased in this way meant that the land was sold at a lower price than the Metropolitan Board of Works paid for it; this embodied an implicit subsidy from the public purse to the voluntary sector.

The activities of voluntary housing organizations under the terms of the Artisans' and Labourers' Dwellings Acts became a subject of intense scrutiny for the Select Committee on Artisans' and Labourers' Dwellings Improvement in 1881.[70] The reports concluded that the Peabody Trust, the only organization to make extensive use of the scheme, "may fairly be considered a *quasi* public body."[71] Thus, in this respect the boundaries between the state and at least the Peabody Trust were blurred; a charitable trust acting in what was considered to be the public interest was officially considered to be an adjunct to the state.

The clearest example of the importance of the state in implicitly defining the boundaries of voluntary activity, however, are the subsidized loans which central government had been offering for the provision of working-class housing since the Labouring Classes Dwelling Houses Act of 1866. The 1866 act provided for the public works loan commissioners to advance funds for the "erection, altering and adapting of Dwellings for the Labouring Classes." These funds were made available to "any . . . company . . . established for the purposes of this Act or for trading or manufacturing purposes" as well as local authorities and any private person with a title to land for a period of not less than fifty years.[72] Thus, no distinction was made between the institutional form of the agency seeking funds: The qualifying condition was based upon the object of the loan, not whether the applicant could profit from this provision or was publicly accountable in any way.

Public works loans were offered for the provision of dwellings suitable for the working classes at an interest rate of not less than 4 percent with repayment over a period of forty years.[73] These terms were subsequently altered to vary both the rate of interest and the repayment period. By 1914 the Public Works Loans Board, which had been established in 1875 to administer public works loans, reported that they had advanced nearly two and a half million pounds for the housing of the working classes to a total of seventy-eight societies, associations, companies, and individuals providing working-class housing throughout England and Wales.[74] Another £64,218 had been lent for the same purpose in Scotland. These sums do not include the advances made to organizations and individuals which had repaid their loans in full by this date. They are therefore an underestimate of the total public funds loaned to private organizations for the purposes of providing working-class housing.

It would appear that the Public Works Loan Board was indifferent about the institutional forms of those receiving public funds. The Board made funds available to institutions which pursued approved objectives. Thus, whether an institution was a for-profit company, a not-for-profit association, a private individual, or the local state, it was eligible to receive publicly financed capital to assist in its operations. By the end of the First World War, however, when government was considering the introduction of a mass program of public subsidies, public-utility societies had come to be regarded as the only private agencies to which the Housing (Financial Assistance) Committee could recommend the provision of subsidies. The committee came to the conclusion that they could not recommend subsidies for employers, landowners, or "companies or bodies . . . formed for the purpose of building improved dwellings for the working classes."[75] Clearly, something had changed.

When public loans for housing were first introduced in 1866, the primary concern of the state was the object of the loan—the stated purpose of MDCs and other housing organizations to provide more salubrious accommodation for the working classes. The public interest in this case was conceived in terms of the housing output alone, and analysis of the output of these organizations suggests that they acted in accordance with their aims.[76] Interwar housing policy, however, was a vehicle for pursuing other goals. The political expediencies of providing "homes fit for heroes" have already been discussed elsewhere.[77] What I would like to draw attention to are the preferential terms extended to public-utility societies which, given their institutional form, demonstrate an interesting change in the attitudes of the state toward voluntary housing organizations and the public interest.

Public-utility societies had started to develop in the late nineteenth century. According to Keith J. Skilleter, they "combined a unique mixture of both co-operative and business characteristics. This made them ideologically acceptable to a range of housing reformers and early town planners, including the co-operative and labour movement and the British Liberal Party."[78] They differed from MDCs in that their members were entitled to rent their houses at market rents and the share of profits distributed to these shareholding tenants was credited in capital against the value of the house until they became owner-occupiers.[79] In their operations before the war, public-utility societies had been financially unsuccessful, had produced little, and had only succeeded in housing the middle and upper working classes.[80] However, by 1918, both the designs of dwellings they provided and the institutional form they adopted were considered more politically acceptable than those of the MDCs.

As far as the report of the Housing (Financial Assistance) Committee was concerned, public-utility societies were considered desirable not simply for the housing they could provide but because they offered "an opportunity for securing the social advantage of the tenant, and, in the case of Societies in which employers have a share, make for better relations between employer and employed."[81] The advisory housing panel of the Ministry of Construction stated with respect to public-utility societies that "we recognise the extension of their activities is in the highest degree worthy of encouragement in the interests of the community."[82] Model dwellings companies with their stock-exchange quotations and non-shareholding tenants could claim none of these advantages. The interests of capital and labor in public-utility societies were, theoretically at least, much more closely aligned. Thus, as far as the state was concerned, it was not only the output of housing organizations that mattered; it was their mode of operation and the positive outcomes which certain forms of action were perceived to provide for society.

This changing attitude toward the joint public-private provision of working-class housing was to have lasting effects on the social housing sector in Britain. It represented a fundamental shift in the boundaries in the mixed economy of welfare as the then government conceived of them. An alternative notion of the voluntary sector and the public interest was introduced which diminished the role of what had previously been considered as voluntary agencies in the field of housing provision. The chosen system of housing-market intervention in twentieth-century Britain was, internationally speaking, atypical, and in many other European countries private landlords and voluntary organizations have remained the major providers of rented accommodation operating in various public regulatory frameworks and subsidy systems.[83] It was not until the 1970s and 1980s, when public-housing estates were shown to have become plagued by problems of their own, that the government again seriously turned to encouraging the voluntary sector to assist in the provision of low-cost social housing in Britain.[84] This period represents the second most obvious shift in the mixed economy of housing provision in the United Kingdom, again occasioned, in part, by changing contemporary perceptions about the relative roles and merits of voluntary provision.

Examination of the history of social housing provision in nineteenth-century London suggests that in order to take account of changing understandings of the role and position of voluntary action in the mixed economy of welfare, we not only need to consider the characteristics of the action, the input, and the output; we should also be alert to changing contemporary perceptions of the significance of the form of organization through which these resources were deployed.

CONCLUSION

In this chapter, we have examined a variety of different approaches to identifying that area of activity between the state and the market in the field of housing provision in Victorian and Edwardian London. We have seen that contemporary meanings of charity and philanthropy in the housing field cannot be captured by looking for examples of kindness by philanthropists or by examining the donation of money to the cause. By focusing on the relationship between voluntary activity and the state, we have detected important differences in contemporary perceptions regarding the properties of voluntary activity. During the second half of the nineteenth century, the state was prepared to recognize and subsidize the activities of any organization that provided working-class dwellings. Equal terms were offered to all organizations pursuing the same goals. By 1918, however, the state had become concerned with the form of action which organizations adopted to pursue their goals. Preferential terms were therefore offered to particular types of organization in the housing field—most notably public-utility societies. Thus, MDCs, the organizations which had done the most in response to the housing problem, became less-preferred providers. This change of attitude represents an important shift in relations between the state and other providers in the mixed economy of welfare. Whereas previously boundaries had been drawn according to output—in this case, the housing service being provided—the state was now seeking to differentiate between providers in terms of the form of action they adopted to provide these services. It was seeking to redefine the salient characteristics of those organizations operating between the market and the state in the housing field and to encourage its own preferred type of voluntary activity. Thus, organizations which appeared philanthropic in one time period do not do so in the next.

This historical case study suggests that in examining the history of philanthropy and its place within the mixed economy of welfare we need to take account of the aims, inputs, outputs, and form of organization associated with the area under study. This study has shown that even when we restrict our analysis to one field of philanthropic activity in one place, not all of these characteristics will hold equal importance at all times. Historians need to explicitly examine which of these characteristics may be important for their own understandings of philanthropy and which are most appropriate for the period and location in question. By making our positions on each of these criteria clear we may then have a metric which can be used to assist us in comparing and contrasting philanthropy in different historical periods and locations.

NOTES

1. Lester Salamon and Helmut K. Anheier, "Social Origins of Civil Society: Explaining the Nonprofit Sector Cross-Nationally," *Voluntas* 9 (1998): 213–248.

2. For the U.K. literature, see Olive Checkland, *Philanthropy in Victorian Scotland: Social Welfare and the Voluntary Principle* (Edinburgh: Donald, 1980); Martin J. Daunton, ed., *Charity, Self-Interest, and Welfare in the English Past* (London: UCL Press, 1996); Geoffrey B. A. M. Finlayson, *Citizen, State and Social Welfare in Britain 1830–1990* (Oxford: Clarendon Press, 1994); Wilbur Kitchener Jordan, *Philanthropy in England 1480–1660: A Study of the Changing Pattern of English Aspirations* (London: George Allen & Unwin, 1959); Jane Lewis, *The Voluntary Sector, the State and Social Work in Britain: The Charity Organisation Society/Family Welfare Association Since 1869* (Aldershot: Edward Elgar, 1995); David Edward Owen, *English Philanthropy 1660–1960* (Cambridge, Mass.: Belknap Press of Harvard University Press, 1965); and Frank K. Prochaska, *The Voluntary Impulse: Philanthropy in Modern Britain* (London: Faber, 1988).

3. Jordan, *Philanthropy in England*, 15.

4. Owen, *English Philanthropy*, 1.

5. Ibid.

6. Ibid., 6.

7. Frank K. Prochaska, *Women and Philanthropy in Nineteenth-Century England* (Oxford: Clarendon Press, 1980); Prochaska, *The Voluntary Impulse*; Frank K. Prochaska, "Philanthropy," in *The Cambridge Social History of Britain, 1750–1950*, ed. F. M. L. Thompson

(Cambridge: Cambridge University Press, 1990), 3: 357–393; Frank K. Prochaska, *Philanthropy and the Hospitals of London: The King's Fund, 1897–1990* (Oxford: Clarendon Press, 1992); Frank K. Prochaska, *Royal Bounty: The Making of the Welfare Monarchy* (New Haven, Conn., and London: Yale University Press, 1995).

    8. Prochaska, "Philanthropy," 360.

    9. Ibid., 60.

    10. Brian Harrison, *Peaceable Kingdom: Stability and Change in Modern Britain* (Oxford: Clarendon Press, 1982), 220. His chapter entitled "Philanthropy and the Victorians" is a reworking of a similarly entitled article he published in 1966. Although in the earlier working of this piece he called for more systemization in the study of philanthropy, in the latter publication he considered the subject immeasurable and too broad to warrant closer definition: Brian Harrison, "Philanthropy and the Victorians," *Victorian Studies* 9 (1966): 353–374.

    11. Finlayson, *Citizen, State and Social Welfare in Britain*, 6.

    12. Ibid., 8.

    13. Ibid., 7–8.

    14. Ibid., 6–7.

    15. Michael B. Katz and Christoph Sachsse, eds., *The Mixed Economy of Social Welfare: Public/Private Relations in England, Germany and the United States, the 1870s to the 1930s* (Baden-Baden: Nomos, 1996).

    16. Daunton, *Charity, Self-Interest, and Welfare*, 1.

    17. Paul Johnson, "Risk, Redistribution and Social Welfare in Britain from the Poor Law to Beveridge," in Daunton, *Charity, Self-Interest, and Welfare*, 244.

    18. Daunton, *Charity, Self-Interest, and Welfare*, 17.

    19. Lester Salamon and Helmut K. Anheier, *Defining the Nonprofit Sector: A Cross-National Analysis* (Manchester: Manchester University Press, 1997), 1.

    20. Ibid., xi.

    21. Lester Salamon and Helmut K. Anheier, "In Search of the Nonprofit Sector. I: The Question of Definitions," *Voluntas* 3 (1992): 125–151.

    22. Salamon and Anheier, *Defining the Nonprofit Sector*, 33–34.

    23. Susannah Morris, "Defining the Nonprofit Sector: Some Lessons from History," *Voluntas* 11 (2000): 25–43.

    24. Ibid., 39.

    25. Although slumlike conditions were not an exclusively metropolitan problem, contemporary comment was focused on the capital, and inquiries such as Mearns's *Bitter Cry of Outcast London* were an impetus behind the 1884–1885 Royal Commission on the Housing of the Working Classes, which itself was predominantly focused on London. Anthony S. Wohl, ed., *The Bitter Cry of Outcast London* (Leicester: Leicester University Press, 1970).

    26. For a discussion of the main housing legislation, see J. A. Yelling, *Slums and Slum Clearance in Victorian London* (London: Allen & Unwin, 1986).

    27. Joseph Chamberlain, "Labourers and Artisans Dwellings," in Wohl, *The Bitter Cry of Outcast London*, 145.

    28. The resultant trusts and their years of founding are as follows: the Peabody Dwellings Fund, later known as the Peabody Trust (1862); the Guinness Trust (1889); the Sutton Dwellings Trust (1900); and the Samuel Lewis Trust (1909).

    29. Other subscription charities included the Lever Street Buildings, the Onslow Model Dwellings, the Parochial Association for Improving the Dwellings of the Industrious Classes, and the Wells & Campden Charity.

    30. The only contemporary reference I have found to the phrase is in a prospectus produced by the National Dwellings Society to accompany a particular share issue. National Dwellings Society, *Homes of the London Working Classes: Philanthropy and Five Per Cent*

(London, 1877). The phrase is too prevalent in the secondary literature to reference all its uses here, although it is particularly associated with John Nelson Tarn, *Five Per Cent Philanthropy: An Account of Housing in Urban Areas between 1840 and 1914* (London: Cambridge University Press, 1973).

31. For analysis of the rates of return actually earned by model dwellings companies in London, see Susannah Morris, "Market Solutions for Social Problems: The Case of Working-Class Housing in Nineteenth-Century London," *Economic History Review* 54 (2001): 535–540.

32. John Nelson Tarn, "Housing in Urban Areas 1840–1914" (Ph.D. thesis, University of Cambridge, 1962), 67.

33. Metropolitan Association for Improving the Dwellings of the Industrious Classes (MAIDIC), *Charter of Incorporation* (London, 1845).

34. Southwood Smith, "Results of the Sanitary Improvement, Illustrated by the Operation of the Metropolitan Societies for Improving the Dwellings of the Industrious Classes, the Working of the Common Lodging-Houses Act, Etc.," reprinted in MAIDIC, *Healthy Homes* (London, 1854), 4, 9–12, 16.

35. Society for Improving the Condition of the Labouring Classes, *Eighteenth Annual Report of the Society for Improving the Condition of the Labouring Classes* (London, 1862), 4–5.

36. Select Committee on Artisans and Labourers Dwellings Improvement, PP 1881, VII (c.358) q.4497.

37. "'William Sutton Trust," Acc. 2983/008/1–13, London Metropolitan Archive.

38. Charles Edmund Maurice, *Life of Octavia Hill as Told in Her Letters* (London: Macmillan & Co, 1913), 189–190; Emily Southwood Maurice, ed., *Octavia Hill: Early Ideals* (London: Allen & Unwin, 1928), 162–163.

39. Charles B. P. Bosanquet, *London: Some Account of Its Growth, Charitable Agencies and Wants* (London: Hatchard & Co., 1868), 273.

40. Archives of the SICLC are kept by the London Metropolitan Archive, Acc. 3445. As this accession is being recataloged, items will be referred to by their title: SICLC, *Prospectus*, 1.

41. MAIDIC, *Fourth Report of the Directors* (1848).

42. MAIDIC, *Nineteenth Report of the Directors* (1863).

43. SICLC, Minute Book 2.

44. SICLC, Minute Book 4.

45. Thomas Adam, "Transatlantic Trading: The Transfer of Philanthropic Models between European and North American Cities during the Nineteenth and Early Twentieth Centuries," *Journal of Urban History* 28 (2002): 328–351.

46. For the data from which this table is derived, see Table 3.1 and Appendix 1 in Susannah Morris, "Private Profit and Public Interest: Model Dwellings Companies and the Housing of the Working Classes in London, 1840–1914" (D.Phil., University of Oxford, 1998).

47. Ibid., 60–64, 259–260.

48. Ibid., 64–69.

49. Martin J. Daunton, *House and Home in the Victorian City: Working-Class Housing 1850–1914* (London: Edward Arnold, 1983).

50. "Census Returns of England and Wales 1911, VI (c.6577)," p. 146.

51. Charles Booth, *Life and Labour of the People in London*, first series, vol. 3 (London: Macmillan & Co., 1902), 13–17. In blocks rated "fair," four tenants shared a water tap and closet and sunlight did not reach the lower tenements. Tenements belonging to MDCs were seldom rated "fair"; they were usually "good" or "very good."

52. Carroll D. Wright, *Eighth Special Report of the Commissioner of Labor: The Housing of the Working Classes* (Washington, D.C.: Government Printing Office, 1895), 432.

53. Morris, "Market Solutions for Social Problems," 533–534.

54. Ibid., 531–532.

55. George Peabody, letter to his trustees, reproduced in full in J. S. Bryant, *The Life of the Late George Peabody Merchant and Philanthropist with a Short Account of his Gift to the People of London* (London, 1914), 10–12.

56. Bryant, *The Life of the Late George Peabody,* 12–13; Royal Commission on the Housing of the Working Classes, 1884–85, XXX (c.4402) qq. 11, 536.

57. *Saturday Review,* March 29, 1862.

58. *Times,* March 26, 1862.

59. "The Peabody Donation," MSS 181: B212, 16, James Duncan Philips Library (hereafter JDPL), Peabody Essex Museum, Salem, Mass.

60. C. P. McIlvaine to Peabody, Southampton, February 9, 1862, MSS 181 B196 F5, JDPL.

61. *Times,* March 26, 1862. The papers that subsequently covered the story included the *Daily News, Star and Dial, Daily Telegraph, Morning Post, Morning Herald, Standard, Sun, Morning Advertiser, Examiner, Saturday Review, London Review, Illustrated London News, City Press, Liverpool Mail, Manchester Examiner and Gazette,* and *Leeds Mercury.*

62. R. C. Winthrop, *Eulogy Pronounced at the Funeral of George Peabody, at Peabody, Massachusetts* (Boston, 1870), 8.

63. For a discussion of Peabody and his motives and the issue of motives in general, see Morris, "Private Profit and Public Interest," 133–180.

64. National Dwellings Society, *Homes of the London Working Classes,* 12.

65. MAIDIC, *Charter of Incorporation,* 3. Similar claims were made about the Artisans' and Labourers' General Dwellings Company in the 1870s. W. Martin, *Unhealthy Houses, "The Terror of Europe and the Disgrace of Britain." The Remedy. A Letter Addressed by Permission to the Right Honourable the Earl of Derby* (1871), 16.

66. "Report of a Public Meeting Held at the London Tavern, on Saturday, the 18th February, 1854," *Times,* February 20, 1854, reproduced as part of MAIDIC, *Charter of Incorporation,* 6.

67. This view has commonalities with the doctrines of C. S. Loch and the Charity Organisation Society.

68. Yelling, *Slums and Slum Clearance in Victorian London,* 9–30.

69. Ibid., 10–12.

70. Select Committee on Artisans' and Labourers' Dwellings, "Report," PP 1882, VII (c.235), ii.

71. Select Committee on Artisans' and Labourers' Dwellings, "Report," with the Proceedings of the Committee, Minutes of Evidence, Appendix, and Index, PP 1882 VOL VII 235, x.

72. "First Annual Report of the Public Works Loan Board, 1876," PP 1876, XXI, 29 Vict. C.28, 3, 6.

73. Ibid., 6–7.

74. "Thirty-Ninth Annual Report of the Public Works Loan Board, 1913–1914," 93–95. The exact sum was £2,480,694 in England and Wales.

75. Housing (Financial Assistance) Committee, "Interim Report on Public Utility Societies," PP1918, X, Cd. 9223, 15.

76. Morris, "Market Solutions for Social Problems."

77. Mark Swenarton, *Homes Fit for Heroes: The Politics and Architecture of Early State Housing in Britain* (London: Heinemann Educational, 1981).

78. Keith John Skilleter, "The Role of Public Utility Societies in Early British Town Planning and Housing Reform, 1901–36," *Planning Perspectives* 8 (1993): 126.

79. Ibid., 129, 132.

80. Ibid., 143–145, 147.

81. Housing (Financial Assistance) Committee, "Interim Report on Public Utility Societies," PP 1918, X, Cd. 9223, 5.

82. Ibid.

83. Anne Power, *Hovels to High Rise: State Housing in Europe Since 1850* (London and New York: Routledge, 1993).

84. J. B. Cullingworth, *Essays on Housing Policy: The British Scene* (London: Allen and Unwin, 1979), Chapter 7, "Alternative Tenures," 116–132.

PART THREE

Jewish Philanthropy and Embourgeoisement

EIGHT

Rabbinic Study, Self-Improvement, and Philanthropy: Gender and the Refashioning of Jewish Voluntary Associations in Germany, 1750–1870

MARIA BENJAMIN BAADER

The research on Jewish associational life presented in this chapter is part of a larger project on gender, Jewish culture, and middle-class formation in Germany from 1800 to 1870.[1] In these decades, the social profile of German Jewry changed dramatically. Having formed a mostly impoverished and culturally isolated population in the second half of the eighteenth century, by 1870, the majority of Jews in Germany had risen into the middle classes and had adopted bourgeois lifestyles and value systems. In the history of the gendered patterns of middle-class formation, the gendered division of public and private realms constitutes the dominant paradigm, and scholars of women and gender history have argued that women were excluded from the bourgeois public arena as it was in the making.[2] But in accounts on the emergence of modern civil society, going back to Jürgen Habermas's model, voluntary societies played a central role in the formation of the bourgeois public sphere.

I thus began to inquire into women's access to nineteenth-century Jewish associations and found that, surprisingly, a world of independent Jewish women's voluntary societies began to flourish in the last decades of the eighteenth century. This development ran counter to the exclusion of women from a public arena that was conceived of as male both in its symbolic construction and in its social realization. In fact, non-Jewish women in Germany established female voluntary associations only hesitantly. Not until the 1830s did non-Jewish women create lasting networks of organized female benevolence. Non-Jewish female benevolent societies first emerged in the period between 1812 and 1814, when the German states fought the Napoleonic occupation. However, these *Vaterländische Frauen-vereine* (patriotic women's associations) typically dissolved again after the wars of liberation.[3]

The female mutual aid and charity associations founded by Jewish women in the late eighteenth and early nineteenth centuries, conversely, tended to operate for decades. In 1810, Jewish women in at least sixteen Jewish communities—in small towns such as Gunzenhausen in Bavaria and Aurich in northern Germany as well as in urban centers such as Frankfurt, Hamburg, Berlin, and Breslau—ran female benevolent associations that did not have non-Jewish counterparts.[4] Jewish women's voluntary societies, however, by no means constituted a common feature of Jewish communal life in early modern Germany. Rather, it appears that the emergence of Jewish women's associations was a modern phenomenon. This proliferation of female voluntary societies was not in line with the gendered division of public and private spheres in bourgeois culture and society. Nevertheless, I argue, it resulted from the embourgeoisement of German Jewry and from the transformation and modernization of Jewish associational life in the late eighteenth and in the nineteenth centuries.

I shall describe this shift in the character of Jewish associations during the transition from premodern *hevrot* (confraternities) to bourgeois voluntary associations. Starting by discussing the world of religiously motivated *hevrot* in early modern Europe, I shall lay out how the religious character of Jewish voluntary societies resulted in women's marginal position in the associational life of Jewish communities at the time. In the late eighteenth century, however, a new type of Jewish association emerged. In youth *hevrot* and other bourgeois voluntary associations, the importance of male prayer and study diminished and mutual aid features gained prominence. Jewish women began to found and direct independent female voluntary societies after the model of male mutual aid societies to care for the sick. Frequently, women also established charitable associations with no or little religious content, while men's associations often held on to religious practices. But overall, contemporaries came to conceive of benevolence as an expression of enlightened humanity rather than as the fulfillment of a religious commandment.

I shall also analyze what Jewish men and women understood by organized benevolence in early and mid-nineteenth-century Germany. In the documents of their associations, contemporaries declared *Menschenliebe* (love of mankind) to be the founding of their philanthropic enterprise. *"Menschenliebe"* is the German equivalent of the Greek-derived term "philanthropy," and German Jews indeed asserted that their benevolent deeds, inspired by tender feelings for the sick and the needy, aimed to serve the welfare of humankind. However, the benevolence which Jewish men and women practiced in voluntary associations was not a philanthropy in which the wealthy supported the poor. Many of the members of Jewish benevolent societies themselves had barely attained an income level which allowed them to join the associations. Mutual aid figured prominently in Jewish voluntary associations at the time and, for contemporaries, acting for the welfare of mankind included self-help. German Jews, indeed, did not distinguish sharply between mutual aid societies and other benevolent associations. For them, benevolence motivated by *Menschenliebe* encompassed both improving their own situation and aiding others as a way to raise the Jewish community as a whole out of poverty. In the last decades of the eighteenth and the first part of the nineteenth century, philanthropy formed part of the project of social upward mobility of German Jewry and their purposefully pursued acculturation into German middle-class society. During this process of social and cultural embourgeoisement, the values of civil society came to shape a Jewish associational life which previously had been defined within a religious framework.

THE MALE CULTURE OF
PREMODERN JEWISH ASSOCIATIONAL LIFE

With its roots in Talmudic times, the burial society, called *hevra kaddisha* (holy confraternity), forms the prototype of the Jewish voluntary association. When they established the first *hevrah* in Central Europe in 1564, Jewish men in Prague founded a burial society. Only a few decades later, they established a Talmud Torah society, an association in which the members primarily dedicated themselves to religious learning. Originally founded for the study of mystical texts, these groups had spread from Palestine to Italy and had finally reached Central Europe and Western Europe. Soon, every significant Jewish community in Ashkenaz (the area of Jewish settlement and Jewish culture in Europe north of Italy) possessed such study circles as well as Talmud Torah societies which ran schools and educated the poor.[5] From the late seventeenth century on, Jews in larger German communities founded *hevrot* specializing in one or the other charitable purpose, and some of these associations may have stopped performing burials. As a rule, no matter what the name of an association was and no matter what its statutes claimed to be the function for which the club was founded, a *hevrah* always fulfilled more than one purpose.[6]

Hevrot cared for the dead and the needy of the whole community. Their members were greatly esteemed in Jewish society, had particular responsibilities, and enjoyed certain privileges. When a member of a *hevrah* died, his fellows had the honor and the duty to study Mishnah (a part of the Talmud) in the house of the deceased during the first seven days of mourning, the period of *shivah*. Members were also required to participate in performing funeral rites, visit the sick, or whatever else the activities of their association included, and they had to attend the *hevrah's* study sessions and worship services. The members of a *hevrah* indeed usually prayed together and learned religious texts together, and they often employed a rabbi or a teacher. Or to put it differently: A *hevrah* was a prayer circle whose members aspired to fulfill the *mitzvot* (religious commandments) of studying Torah, giving charity (*zedakah*), and performing "acts of loving-kindness," called *gemilut hesed*. As the historian Jacob Katz explains, among the "acts of loving-kindness, the value of providing proper burial for the dead, referred to as *hesed shel emet* (literally: act of true loving-kindness) was the first to take on separate, institutionalized form."[7]

In their core prayer and study circles, *hevrot* formed a male domain. In rabbinic Judaism, the duty of studying Torah (meaning primarily rabbinic literature, including the Mishnah) and of reciting Hebrew prayers fell exclusively upon men. Throughout the centuries, women had only very limited access to these highly valued religious practices. While women were not forbidden to study religious texts in Hebrew and to recite standardized prayers in the sacred tongue, many, if not most, of them lacked the language skills to do so. Moreover, women were excluded from being counted in a halakhically (by Jewish law) defined prayer quorum, a *minyan*, and they could not form a *minyan* of their own. In the religious economy of premodern Judaism, if women ever gathered to study a text such as the Mishnah, their act possessed significantly less weight than when men fulfilled the religious obligations for which they were held responsible. By definition, then, full membership in a *hevrah* that constituted a *minyan* and whose members dedicated themselves to the communal study of Torah was a male prerogative.

Accordingly, evidence of women's associations in early modern Ashkenaz remains scarce. In the seventeenth century, female Jewish voluntary associations existed sporadically.[8] In Prague, for instance, Jewish women formed a female burial society more than a century after the founding of Central Europe's first *hevra kaddisha* in the city. Yet it is uncertain whether this female *hevrah* was an auxiliary of the men's burial society or an independent organization.[9] Male burial societies had undoubtedly always delegated the ritual ablutions of female corpses and the dressing and guarding of these bodies to women. Independent women's societies, however, appear to have formed exceptions. Because of their marginal position in the religious world of premodern Jewish society, women remained on the periphery of the associational life of German-Jewish communities. This began to change in the last decades of the eighteenth century, when the study and worship functions of *hevrot* diminished in importance and the charitable, social, educational, and mutual aid aspects of Jewish voluntary associations gained new meaning.

Toward the end of the eighteenth century, influenced by the ideas of the German Enlightenment and its Jewish equivalent, the Haskalah, young Jewish men founded a new generation of Jewish associations that included the Gesellschaft der Freunde (Society of Friends) in Berlin and Königsberg and the Gesellschaft der Brüder (Society of Brothers) in Breslau.[10] In Dresden, Heidelberg, Prague, and other German and Central European towns, unmarried Jewish men established similar mutual aid *hevrot*, most commonly associations to care for the sick. Most of these youth *hevrot* of the eighteenth century did not break with established customs such as personal visits to the sick, the performance of burial rites, and poor relief. In fact, in many of the young men's societies, the members still engaged in communal study and prayed together.[11] The youth *hevrot* of the late eighteenth century as well as a significant part of the Jewish voluntary associations which sprang up in the following decades continued to fulfill religious functions. Some of these societies, however, introduced a practice that marked a significant shift in the character of the associations and in the orientation and outlook of its constituency: Members now received standardized medical care and monetary benefits when sick, convalescent, or otherwise in need.[12] In the new generation of Jewish voluntary associations, mutual aid aspects gained prominence. The needs of the living began to take priority, while the concern for the afterlife diminished in importance. In the old-style Jewish associations to care for the sick, called *hevrot bikkur holim* (societies for visiting the sick), the spiritual dimension of support in illness and death had constituted the framework in which the association operated. In the nineteenth century, Enlightenment and bourgeois values began to form the frame of reference for Jewish voluntary societies. Spiritual welfare and the care of the dead, prayer, and religious study ceased to define a Jewish voluntary society.

THE PROLIFERATION OF
JEWISH WOMEN'S ASSOCIATIONS

Women occupied a marginal position in the *hevrot* of the early modern period because the religious practices of Talmud Torah and communal Hebrew prayer which stood at the center of Jewish associations primarily addressed the male population. As prayer, study, and the fulfillment of religious commandments ceased to define the realm of activity and the character of Jewish voluntary societies, women began to play a more prominent role in Jewish associational life. In communities in which Jewish men established modern bourgeois self-help associations, Jewish women often followed the example of their male contemporaries. In Frankfurt, for instance, men founded two Jewish mutual aid associations to care for the sick in 1738 and 1756. In 1761, five Jewish women established the Israelitische Frauenkrankenkasse (Israelite Women's Sick Fund), which was to become one of the largest female Jewish associations of the era.[13] This women's sick-benefit association was not much more than health insurance. Regular members neither visited the sick nor cared for them and, as in most Jewish women's associations of the period, the Israelitische Frauenkrankenkasse did not expect its members to perform burial rites for their deceased colleagues.[14] In the eighteenth century, similar women's associations emerged in communities such as Mainz, Dresden, Mannheim, and Offenbach.[15]

The pattern of Jewish women founding female societies to care for the sick after the model of male self-help associations in their communities persisted into the second half of the nineteenth century. In 1851, Jewish men in Grünstadt, Rhineland-Palatine, created a mutual aid society to care for the sick called Wohltätigkeitsverein (Benevolence Association). Nine years later no fewer than forty Jewish women in the small community of Grünstadt erected the Israelitische Frauen-Verein (Israelite Women's Association), apparently the first female Jewish voluntary association in town.[16] The Wohltätigkeitsverein and the Israelitische Frauen-Verein provided sick benefits for their members and dispensed charity to the needy of the entire Jewish community. Yet only the members of the male association also performed the halakhically prescribed burial rites for their deceased colleagues, held prayer services in the house of the deceased during the seven-day period of mourning, and gathered on Jewish holidays such as the evening of Shavuot and Hoshana Rabba, the seventh day of Sukkot, when study meetings were customary. In Grünstadt, as in other Jewish communities throughout Germany, male Jewish voluntary societies held on to some of the practices which had stood at the core of early modern *hevrot*. However, the transformation of Jewish associational life overall, during which religious values and practices moved into the background, opened the door to the founding of Jewish women's associations. Jewish women established parallel female associations on the model of male mutual aid societies to care for the sick.

Jewish women also began to establish female benevolent associations without mutual aid features. In Hamburg, Jewish men founded a burial society in 1670.[17] In the eighteenth century, male Talmud Torah and *bikkur holim* associations followed, death-benefit chests and sick-care societies appeared, and existing associations expanded their realm of activities or shifted it from religious to mutual aid functions.[18] In the second decade of the nineteenth century, Jewish women created at least three female voluntary societies: a society for the support of poor Jewish women in childbed, an association that aided Jewish widows in need, and a society that provided clothing for pupils of the Jewish Free School.[19] These Jewish women's associations pursued their philanthropic enterprises throughout the nineteenth century; in contrast, Hamburg's only non-Jewish women's association of the period, the Hamburgische Frauen-Verein, disbanded after the Napoleonic Wars during which it was founded.[20]

Women's marginal position in Jewish associational life had been predicated on their exclusion from religious practices central to Jewish voluntary societies. In the late eighteenth and early nineteenth centuries, when these practices no longer defined Jewish associational life as a whole, the mechanism that had held women at the periphery of Jewish voluntary societies ceased to exercise its normative function. Between 1745 and 1870, Jewish women in German lands founded more than 150 sick-care, charitable, and other benevolent societies and directed most of them for decades. This proliferation of female Jewish voluntary societies did not follow a trend in non-Jewish society; non-Jewish women created similar associations later than Jewish women did. The entry of women into Jewish associational life resulted from the process of embourgeoisement of Jewish culture, during which middle-class ideas of self-improvement, civic responsibility, and philanthropy superseded the ideological framework of premodern religiosity.

EMBOURGEOISEMENT, *MENSCHENLIEBE,* AND PHILANTHROPY

An investigation into women's position in Jewish associational life and the emergence of female voluntary societies thus reveals larger patterns of cultural and social change. The transformation of Jewish culture which comes into focus in an analysis of the period through the lens of gender formed part of the project of upward social mobility of German Jewry. The youth *hevrot* of the late eighteenth century, such as the Gesellschaft der Freunde in Berlin, offered their members the opportunity to put novel ideas such as delayed burials into practice and they allowed unmarried men to assume leadership positions from which they were barred in the old-style *hevrot*.[21] But as mutual aid societies, these associations also fulfilled an economic function. Many of their members had arrived in urban centers recently and, without family support, found themselves in a precarious situation when they fell ill. Communal charity boards hesitated to aid foreigners and individuals without established residence rights.[22] Founding or joining a mutual aid society constituted a way to achieve economic stability and professional success. German Jews who joined such associations expressed an aspiration to improve their economic situation and to raise their social status. In this project of upward mobility, material considerations and the desire to embrace contemporary German notions of respectability and civil virtues were closely connected. Thus, the benevolence that German Jews practiced in voluntary associations gained new meaning.

In the religiously motivated *hevrot* of early modern society, Jewish men had fulfilled the *mitzvot* of *zedakah* (charity) and *gemilut hesed* (loving-kindness) in order to acquire spiritual benefits. Whether or not a pious benevolent act benefited a deceased, sick, or poor person, the philanthropic deed aimed ultimately at honoring God and his commandments. Statutes of Jewish associations commonly cited the reward in the *olam ha-ba* (world to come) as a motivation for establishing a holy confraternity. In the nineteenth century, however, self-help, friendship, *Menschenliebe* (love of mankind), enlightened morality, civic responsibility, patriotic commitment, and bourgeois respectability moved into the center of attention in Jewish associational life. Giving a member of a sick-care association a standardized monetary sick benefit no longer provided the donor with the opportunity to fulfill a religious commandment. Rather, the donor was a self-respecting individual who aspired to contribute to the welfare of humanity in the hopeful spirit of the rising German middle classes. In its annual report of 1832, the Hamburg Verein für Krankenpflege (Association for Sick Care) expressed these ideas clearly:

> The light of a better enlightenment and nobler civilization has spread since [the founding of older institutions of benevolence]; in the place of a welfare that seeks retribution is the higher love of mankind and only foundations which owe their inception to the latter can now render to the educated and refined individual [*Gebildeter*] what was formerly rendered by compassion alone.[23]

The members of the Verein für Krankenpflege apparently repudiated a welfare that was driven by a concept of heavenly reward. Hailing the progress of their age, they understood themselves as neither disbursing nor receiving charity in the old sense. Rather, these Hamburg Jews of the era before emancipation aimed at becoming honorable and respectable citizens, claimed to be *gebildet*, and declared "the higher love of mankind," or *Menschenliebe*, to be the motive and the goal of benevolence.

The ideal of *Menschenliebe* held a central position in the Jewish associational life of this period. The Hevrat Ezrat Nashim (Association for the Help of Women) of the small community in Emmendingen in Baden, like the Verein für Krankenpflege in Hamburg, professed its commitment to *Menschenliebe*. When they established the voluntary society in 1823, the women of Emmendingen opened the preamble of the founding statutes of their association by announcing: "Among all the duties incumbent on humanity, *Menschenliebe* stands out as the first and holiest duty."[24] They declared: "Only a good and feeling heart is capable of true *Menschenliebe,* and a good heart encompasses all other virtues, too. . . . Rightly thus, that famous rabbi considered *Nächstenliebe* [the love for our fellow] as the fundamental law from which all sacred religious laws derive." These statements are remarkable. With them, the Jewish women of Emmendingen reversed the value system of premodern *hevrot* and of rabbinic Judaism. According to the founding document of the Hevrat Ezrat Nashim, *Menschenliebe,* this enlightened concept of brotherly love, formed the highest of all duties rather than the performance of *mitzvot,* divine commandments. Here, the loving relationship among humans took precedence over the relationship of the community to God. This train of thought was pursued in the statement that "a good heart" formed the foundation of all virtues. In rabbinic Judaism, Talmud Torah and the fulfillment of ritual obligations represented the key to and constituted virtue. The women of Emmendingen, however, embraced a more universal concept of morality, in which emotional receptivity and tender sentiments led to virtue. Indeed, the preamble of Hevrat Ezrat Nashim's statutes stated unmistakably that "the love for our fellow" constituted the very basis of modern Judaism, "the fundamental law from which all sacred religious laws derive."

In this text, the Jewish women of Emmendingen expressed some of the fundamental tenets of the Haskalah, the Jewish Enlightenment, according to which human relationships and emotional sensitivity ranked higher than religious dogma.[25] Moreover, the preamble of the founding document of the Hevrat Ezrat Nashim explicated how the ideal of *Menschenliebe* was to be put into practice. *Menschenliebe,* the document held, not only found expression in feelings of compassion but it also needed to result in "benevolent deeds" (*wohltätige Handlungen*) and "tender acts" (*Mildtätigkeit*). The preamble thereupon described in vivid colors the unfortunate situation of a sick person lacking economic resources and declared that the newly founded benevolent association aimed "at assisting the poor sick, in order to lessen the pitiful plight of these unhappy people." In the document, the women of Emmendingen emphasized the sacred character of their enterprise and asserted that "nothing can be sweeter and more magnificent for the loving benefactor than the consciousness of having contributed to the convalescence of a sick person, of having recovered him for humanity." *Menschenliebe* thus connoted a compassionate humanity which led to acts of benevolence. The text of the preamble seems to suggest that the women of Emmendingen understood acts of *Menschenliebe* as disinterested deeds of generosity for the benefit of compatriots in need in the sense in which "philanthropy" came to stand for welfare to the poor.

A look at the statutes of the Hevrat Ezrat Nashim of Emmendingen which follow the preamble, however, reveals that this voluntary society was not a philanthropic association primarily dedicated to assisting others. Hevrat Ezrat Nashim was a mutual aid society which restricted its benefits to its members. While paragraph twelve of the statutes conceded that in exceptional cases of great distress the association might provide support to someone who was not a member, only members appear to have been entitled to financial support and to personal care. When a member of Hevrat Ezrat Nashim fell ill, the director of the society was to appoint another member to watch over the sick woman. Despite the rhetoric of compassion and disinterested generosity, *Menschenliebe,* as conceived of by the women who founded the Hevrat Ezrat Nashim, meant most of all self-help in an organized form. For the women in Emmendingen and in other Jewish communities in nineteenth-century Germany, being raised by tender sentiments and seeking the welfare of humanity at large included ameliorating their own situation.

At the time, in fact, the boundaries between mutual aid associations and other benevolent societies were fluid. Hevrat Ezrat Nashim declared itself committed to helping those who suffered, while it focused on its own members. Other Jewish voluntary societies, such as the women's sick-care association of Grünstadt, understood themselves explicitly as mutual aid associations, yet they disbursed a considerable portion of their funds to non-members in need.[26] Likewise, the men's sick-care society of Grünstadt carried the name Wohltätigkeitsverein (Benevolence Association) even though it was a mutual aid association.[27] Thus, the notions of *Menschenliebe* and benevolence which members of Jewish associations embraced encompassed assisting each other in voluntary societies as well as aiding members of the larger Jewish community through donations and personal support. Nineteenth-century German Jews regarded all of these activities as acts of virtue and civic morality.

In the statutes and reports of their voluntary societies, the German Jews of the early and mid-nineteenth century used a language informed by Enlightenment or early bourgeois ideas of philanthropy. This model of philanthropy has often been understood to mean that individuals, families, and organizations selflessly and nobly promoted the welfare of mankind by donating money and resources for social welfare purposes. Many Jewish voluntary associations disbursed charity and gave support to poorer Jews in their communities. The philanthropy that German Jews in this period practiced, however, included the members of voluntary associations themselves as beneficiaries. Often, members of mutual aid and other benevolent associations had just recently escaped outright poverty and had founded or joined a voluntary society in order to mark as well as to secure their social and economic advancement. The prestige of belonging to a bourgeois voluntary association and material interests were interconnected. In this respect, the philanthropic enterprise of organized German-Jewish benevolence of the late eighteenth and early and mid-nineteenth centuries resembled the culture of philanthropy as patronage of the late nineteenth and twentieth centuries, when philanthropy constituted a strategy by which social groups such as urban elites funded welfare, cultural, educational, scholarly, and scientific projects and thereby gained influence in politics and culture. These later philanthropists, however, usually did not profit directly from their donations. In the Jewish voluntary associations of the late eighteenth and early and mid-nineteenth centuries, self-help figured prominently, and membership in a mutual aid society could have a direct impact on the economic failure or success of Jewish women and men.

The introduction of mutual aid features into Jewish associational life, most commonly in the form of sick-care benefits, indeed constituted an important and often the first step in the transformation from religiously oriented *hevrot* to bourgeois Jewish voluntary associations. Instead of practicing a charity defined by a spiritual economy of prayer, study, religious virtue, and reward in the afterlife, German Jews turned toward concepts of *Menschenliebe* and began to understand benevolence as a means of raising their own position, of improving the condition of their co-religionists, and of working toward the welfare of humankind at large. For Jewish women, furthermore, the transformation of Jewish associations from prayer and study circles to bourgeois voluntary societies resulted in ending their exclusion from Jewish associational life. Even though nineteenth-century ideologues and today's scholars have conceived of the middle-class public sphere as a male domain, Jewish women created their own independent voluntary associations as Jewish associational life turned bourgeois.

STATUTES OF THE JEWISH WOMEN'S ASSOCIATION OF EMMENDINGEN, BADEN, 1823

Hevrat Ezrat Nashim (Association for the Help of Women)

Original document in Judeo-German in the Central Archives for the History of the Jewish People, Jerusalem, file Ga/S 222.5. Translated into English by M. B. Baader.

PARTIAL TRANSLATION OF THE PREAMBLE

p. 1

Among all the duties incumbent on humanity, *Menschenliebe* [love of mankind] stands out as the first and holiest duty. Only a good and feeling heart is capable of true *Menschenliebe,* and a good heart encompasses all other virtues, too. . . . Rightly, thus, that famous rabbi considered *Nächstenliebe* [the love for our fellow] as the fundamental law from which all sacred religious laws derive.

Yet we would not be significantly superior to those who neglect this law, be it due to their natural callousness or because of base motives, if we did not move beyond feelings, if we offered only compassion and tears rather than support. By means of benevolent deeds, we are expected to set forth how much we are devoted to the sanctity of this duty. Helping those who suffer and assisting those in need by tender acts is the entire and weighty content of these statutes.

p. 2

If it is our holiest duty to assist a person in need with all our might, how much more are we called to give as much support as possible to a sick person in distress?

This person who by cruel misfortune is thrown into bitter misery, how must he feel, . . . thrown down to his sick-bed, due to financial and physical weakness not able to lift his weak head?[28] . . . Oh, which feeling heart would not be moved . . . where everything cries for help!

p. 3

. . . Nothing can be sweeter and more magnificent for the loving benefactor than the consciousness of having contributed to the convalescence of a sick person, of having recovered him for humanity.

Having recognized this as true, for a considerable time already, associations have been founded in all civilized towns of Europe but especially among the Israelite communities, whose purpose it is to establish—by means of charitable contributions—benevolent funds with the help of which it is possible to assist the poor class in general, but in particular to care for the needy sick.

Our Israelite community, being not less inspired with *Menschenliebe,* has had the wish to create a similar fund. And only because of the small number of its members and of their not entirely brilliant financial circumstances has this wish not been fulfilled yet.

p. 4

Considering these circumstances, the Israelite women of our community—the sex which is endowed by nature with the capacity for tender and mild feelings—are eager to put an end to this lack . . . and to bring aid through charitable contributions, when help is needed. The benevolent women's association Hevrat Ezrat Nashim aims at assisting the poor sick in order to lessen the pitiful plight of these unhappy people, where possible. . . .

CONTENT DESCRIPTION OF THE STATUTES

p. 5

§ 1. Every member has to pay a monthly fee that needs to be paid weekly.

§ 2. Penalties for late payments and exclusion from the association after 3 months of outstanding payments.

§ 3. Every member has to pay an admission fee.

§ 4. Every member who takes part in a festive meal is required to collect charitable contributions from the other participants.

§ 5. Every member has to pay a fee when leaving the association.

§ 6. The association is led by four women.

§ 7. On election procedures.

§ 8. The money collected by the association will only be used for the support of the needy sick. The directors are required to verify the plight of the applicants and they decide on the amount and the kind of support given.

§ 9. The association has a charity box and, on fast days, collects money in the synagogue.

§ 10. The directors are required to keep records of the incoming and outgoing money.

§ 11. The association employs a secretary. He helps the directors with the bookkeeping.

§ 12. Nonmembers are not entitled to receive any money from the association. However, in exceptional cases of great distress the directors can decide to support a nonmember.

§ 13. Members are required to keep watch over sick women. The directors keep a special list on these sick watches. Sick nonmembers who are financially able to pay for such services are not entitled to sick watches.

§ 14. If a member gets sick, the *Vereinsdienerin,* a woman employed by the association, has to report the sickness to the director in charge. The director then designates a member to go and watch for the sick woman. Regulations on exemptions from the duty of performing sick watches.

§ 15. Every 3 years, on Rosh Hodesh Tevet, the association holds a dairy banquet.

§ 16. Changes of these statutes need to be agreed upon by the entire membership. The association has the right to exclude a member who committed an offense or who leads "an immoral lifestyle."

NOTES

1. Maria Baader, "Inventing Bourgeois Judaism: Jewish Culture, Gender, and Religion in Germany, 1800–1870" (Ph.D. diss., Columbia University, 2002). See also Maria Benjamin Baader, "When Judaism Turned Bourgeois: Gender in Jewish Associational Life and in the Synagogue, 1750–1850," *Leo Baeck Institute Year Book* 46 (2001): 113–123 and 164–170.

2. See for instance Leonore Davidoff and Catherine Hall, *Family Fortunes: Men and Women of the English Middle Class, 1780–1850* (Chicago: University of Chicago Press, 1987); and Mary P. Ryan, *Cradle of the Middle Class: The Family in Oneida County, New York, 1790–1865* (Cambridge and New York: Cambridge University Press, 1981).

3. This, at least, is the picture that emerges from the available literature. See for instance Alfred Kall, *Katholische Frauenbewegung in Deutschland: Eine Untersuchung zur Gründung katholischer Frauenvereine im 19. Jahrhundert* (Paderborn, Munich, Vienna, and

Zurich: Ferdinand Schöningh, 1983); Elisabeth Meyer-Renschhausen, *Weibliche Kultur und soziale Arbeit: Eine Geschichte der Frauenbewegung am Beispiel Bremens 1810–1927* (Cologne and Vienna: Böhlau, 1989), 44–56; Catherine Prelinger, *Charity, Challenge, and Change: Religious Dimensions of the Mid-Nineteenth-Century Women's Movement in Germany* (New York, Westport, Conn., and London: Greenwood Press, 1987); Jean H. Quataert, *Staging Philanthropy: Patriotic Women and the National Imagination in Dynastic Germany, 1813–1916* (Ann Arbor: University of Michigan Press, 2001), 21–53; and Dirk Reder, *Frauenbewegung und Nation: Patriotische Frauenvereine in Deutschland im frühen 19. Jahrhundert (1813–1830)* (Cologne: SH-Verlag, 1998), 19–20.

4. Community Collection Breslau, microfilm HM 2 6084, Central Archives for the History of the Jewish People, Jerusalem; Rechtsanwalt Dr. Guggenheim, "Die Entwicklung des Krankenkassenwesens in der israelitischen Gemeinde zu Offenbach am Main," in *Die Entwicklung der Krankenversicherung in Offenbach a.m.,* ed. Streb (Offenbach and Main: Gerstung, 1910), 4; Arthur Ruppin, *Die Juden im Großherzogtum Hessen,* Veröffentlichungen des Bureaus für Statistik der Juden, no. 6 (Berlin, 1909), 123; Josef Unna, "Die israelitische Männer- und Frauen-Krankenkasse ("Kippestub") in Frankfurt a. M.," *Bulletin des Leo Baeck Instituts* 8, no. 29–32 (1965): 230; Zentralwohlfahrtsstelle der deutschen Juden, ed., *Führer durch die jüdische Wohlfahrtspflege in Deutschland* (Berlin: Dr. Fritz Scheibel, 1928), 46, 54, 60, 74, 79, 82, 118, 129, 144, and 163; *Zur Geschichte der Krankenpflege in der jüdischen Gemeinde zu Berlin* (Berlin: J. S. Preuß, 1887), 5

5. Networks of Jewish voluntary societies in Western Europe predated their counterparts in Central Europe: Historians have documented them in medieval Spain, early modern Italy, and the Ottoman Empire. Adolf Kober, "Armenwesen, " in *Jüdisches Lexikon,* ed. Georg Herlitz and Bruno Kirschner (Berlin: Jüdischer Verlag, 1927), 1: 476; Salo W. Baron, *The Jewish Community: Its History and Structure to the American Revolution* (Philadelphia: The Jewish Publication Society of America, 1942), 1: 348–350; Sylvie-Anne Goldberg, *Crossing the Jabbok: Illness and Death in Ashkenazi Judaism in Sixteenth- through Nineteenth-Century Prague* (Berkeley, Los Angeles, and London: University of California Press, 1996), 75–98; Jacob R. Marcus, *Communal Sick-Care in the German Ghetto* (Cincinnati: Hebrew Union College Press, 1947), 67–68; Andreas Reinke, *Judentum und Wohlfahrtspflege in Deutschland: Das Jüdische Krankenhaus in Breslau, 1726–1944* (Hanover: Hahnsche Buchhandlung, 1999), 32–33.

6. Yitzhak (Fritz) Baer, "Der Ursprung der Chewra," in *Wissenschaft des Judentums im deutschen Sprachbereich,* ed. Kurt Wilhelm (Tübingen: J. C. B. Mohr, Paul Siebeck, 1967), 1: 304 (originally published in *Zeitschrift für jüdische Wohlfahrtspflege* 1 [1929]: 241–247); Goldberg, *Crossing the Jabbok,* 193–194; Jacob Katz, *Tradition and Crisis: Jewish Society at the End of the Middle Ages* (New York: Schocken Books, 1993), 134–136; Erika Hirsch, *Jüdisches Vereinsleben in Hamburg bis zum Ersten Weltkrieg: Jüdisches Selbstverständnis Zwischen Antisemitismus und Assimilation* (Frankfurt am Main: Peter Lang, 1996), 28; Marcus, *Communal Sick-Care,* 142–143; Reinke, *Judentum und Wohlfahrtspflege in Deutschland,* 33.

7. Katz, *Tradition and Crisis,* 134; Marcus, *Communal Sick-Care,* 116–119; Jacob Rader Marcus, "The Triesch Hebra Kaddisha," *Hebrew Union College Annual* 19 (1945–1946): 189; Reinke, *Judentum und Wohlfahrtspflege in Deutschland,* 37–40.

8. Goldberg, *Crossing the Jabbok,* 194; Hirsch, *Jüdisches Vereinsleben,* 28; Andreas Reinke, "Wohltätige Hilfe im Verein: Das soziale Vereinswesen der deutsch-jüdischen Gemeinden im 19. und beginnenden 20. Jahrhundert," in *Juden und Armut in Mittel- und Osteuropa,* ed. Stefi Jersch-Wenzel (Cologne, Weimar, and Vienna: Böhlau, 2000), 225.

9. Marcus, *Communal Sick-Care,* 136. A picture of the Prague *hevra kaddisha* from 1783/1784 depicts a group of women below a funeral cortège of men. Anne Alter, "Armut und Wohltätigkeit in der Kunst der Aschkenasim," in *Zedaka: Jüdische Sozialarbeit im Wandel der Zeit: Ausstellung im Berlin Museum,* ed. Jüdisches Museum der Stadt Frankfurt am

Main (Frankfurt am Main: Jüdisches Museum der Stadt Frankfurt am Main und Zentralwohlfahrtsstelle der Juden in Deutschland, 1992), 47. In Italy, a women's association was listed as early as 1617 as one of the eight *hevrot* in Rome, and, a century earlier, a burial society in Northern Italy had admitted female members. The social and religious character of Jewish voluntary associations in Italy, however, significantly differed from that of their northern counterparts, and women seem to have been more integrated into Jewish associational life in Italy. Avigdor Farine, "Charity, and Study Societies in Europe of the Sixteenth–Eighteenth Centuries," *Jewish Quarterly Review* 64 (1973): 16–47 and 164–175; Reinke, *Judentum und Wohlfahrtspflege in Deutschland*, 33; David Ruderman, "The Founding of a *Gemilut Hasadim* Society in Ferrara in 1515," *Association for Jewish Studies Review* 1 (1976): 236.

10. David Sorkin, *The Transformation of German Jewry, 1780–1840* (New York and Oxford: Oxford University Press, 1987), 116–120.

11. The members of the Gesellschaft der Freunde, probably the most modern and secular of these "youth *hevrot*," did not congregate for study and prayer. Yet they visited each other in case of sickness and the association provided burials for its members. Ludwig Lesser, *Chronik der Gesellschaft der Freunde in Berlin* (Berlin, 1842), 10–12, 15, 25–27, 40, 47–48, 66, and 71.

12. Marcus, *Communal Sick-Care*, 143–159.

13. Paul Arnsberg, *Die Geschichte der Frankfurter Juden seit der Französischen Revolution*, vol. 2, *Struktur und Aktivitäten der Frankfurter Juden von 1789 bis zu deren Vernichtung in der nationalsozialistischen Ära* (Darmstadt: Eduard Roether Verlag, 1983), 122–123; *Gesellschaftsvertrag der Krankenkasse für Frauen zu Frankfurt am Main* (Frankfurt, 1820), iii–iv; Arno Lustiger, ed., *Jüdische Stiftungen in Frankfurt am Main: Stiftungen, Schenkungen, Organisationen und Vereine mit Kurzbiographien jüdischer Bürger dargestellt von Gerhard Schiebler* (Frankfurt am Main: Kramer, 1988), 139–140; Josef Unna, "Israelitische Männer- und Frauen-Krankenkasse," 227–230.

14. *Gesellschaftsvertrag der Krankenkasse*, 4.

15. Guggenheim, "Entwicklung des Krankenkassenwesens"; Marcus, *Communal Sick-Care*, 141–142.

16. Community Collection Grünstadt, PF IV, folders 47 and 71, Central Archives for the History of the Jewish People, Jerusalem.

17. Salomon Goldschmidt, *Geschichte der Beerdigungs-Brüderschaft der deutsch-israelitischen Gemeinde in Hamburg: Zur Jahrhundertfeier der Neugründung 1812* (Hamburg: Siegmund Nissensohn, 1912).

18. Hirsch, *Jüdisches Vereinsleben*, 25–35 and 364–365.

19. Ibid., 44 and 260n168; Rainer Liedtke, *Jewish Welfare in Hamburg and Manchester, c. 1850–1914* (Oxford: Clarendon Press, 1998), 164.

20. Schul- und Kultuswesen, Israelitische Freischule, 362-6/8, I D 6, Staatsarchiv Hamburg; Herbert Freudenthal, *Vereine in Hamburg: Ein Beitrag zur Geschichte und Volkskunde der Geselligkeit* (Hamburg: Museum für Hamburgische Geschichte, 1968), 98–99; Moses Michael Haarbleicher, *Aus der Geschichte der Deutsch-Israelitischen Gemeinde in Hamburg*, 2nd ed. (Hamburg: Otto Meissner, 1886), 304–305; Hirsch, *Jüdisches Vereinsleben*, 39 and 43–44; Liedtke, *Jewish Welfare*, 164–165.

21. Marcus, *Communal Sick-Care*, 153. In the last decades of the eighteenth century, German Jewry was divided by a conflict about burial practices: traditionalists insisted on burying the dead immediately as was customary while modernizers advocated delaying funerals for three days. Michael Meyer, *German-Jewish History in Modern Times* (New York: Columbia University Press, 1996), 1: 347–348; Sorkin, *Transformation of German Jewry*, 116–120.

22. Lesser, *Chronik der Gesellschaft der Freunde*, 6–7; Marcus, *Communal Sick-Care*, 153.

23. Quoted in Liedtke, *Jewish Welfare*, 193.

24. Community Collection Emmendingen, Ga/S 222.5, Central Archives for the History of the Jewish People, Jerusalem. An English translation of the founding statutes of Hevrat Ezrat Nashim can be found at the end of this chapter. See there also for all further quotations from this document.

25. Sorkin, *Transformation of German Jewry,* 41–73.

26. Community Collection Grünstadt, PF IV, folders 71 and 74, Central Archives for the History of the Jewish People, Jerusalem.

27. Ibid., folder 47.

28. This association clearly aims, at least primarily, to support sick women. However, in the preamble, the sick person in need of assistance is consistently referred to as "he."

NINE

Ethnic Difference and Civic Unity: A Comparison of Jewish Communal Philanthropy in Nineteenth-Century German and U.S. Cities

TOBIAS BRINKMANN

Philanthropy both connects and divides people. It connects giver and recipient but it can also connect recipients with each other and one giver with other givers. The distinction between giver and recipient also creates hierarchical divisions between givers with means and recipients with less means and between givers with more means and givers with less means. Philanthropy entails obligations for the recipient and confers honor to the giver. The concepts of social status, of separation and integration, of difference and unity, therefore, are intrinsic to the theme of philanthropy. For Jews, at the beginning of the nineteenth century a socially marginal group, the possibility of becoming "connected" by engaging in philanthropy for the common good was enticing. At the same time, Jews could look back on a strong tradition of community-oriented "philanthropy"—in a period when Jewish assimilation increasingly raised the possibility of the disintegration of Jewish *Gemeinschaft*.

This chapter focuses on the role of philanthropy in the process of transformation from traditional to modern Jewish communities in Germany and the United States in the nineteenth century. It compares recent studies on the history of Jewish philanthropy in Breslau and Hamburg with a study of community-oriented Jewish philanthropy in Chicago in the second half of the nineteenth century. Aside from the problem of how to define Jewish philanthropy, the following basic questions need to be addressed: When and under which circumstances did modern forms of community-oriented Jewish philanthropy evolve? Was the transition from traditional Jewish poor relief to modern concepts of social work primarily a process of passive adaptation to non-Jewish philanthropic models? And did this transformation initiate an integration of hitherto separate Jewish philanthropic systems? But I am more concerned with the metalevel; that is, how community-oriented Jewish philanthropy functioned throughout the assimilation process in the nineteenth century for Jews as a group. What impact did traditional community-oriented Jewish philanthropy have on the process of assimilation of Jews and their relationship with non-Jews?

Until recently, the function of philanthropy for Jews on their way "out of the Ghetto" (in the words of Jacob Katz) has been neglected by most scholars who deal with the modern Jewish experience. One obvious reason is that few historians have looked at the social transformation of Jewish communities and Jewish associational life in Germany between 1780 and 1933.[1] Only recently have specific studies on Jewish philanthropy in Germany and Europe been published.[2] The history of Jewish philanthropy in the United States is better researched, yet most authors have focused on the post-1880 period, when Jewish immigration to the United States increased significantly. However, even for this period, few studies are devoted to the differences in the way Jewish philanthropy functioned in traditional Jewish culture and in the New World.[3] The rise of the new urban history in the late 1960s produced a few analytical social histories of Jewish communities, but few of these studies dealt with the function of Jewish philanthropy.[4]

How should the term "Jewish philanthropy" be defined? The studies mentioned use the terms "charity," "social work," "welfare," "Wohltätigkeit," and "Wohlfahrtspflege." In the field of American Jewish history, the term "Jewish philanthropy" is quite common. This confusion of terms points to the complexities of defining Jewish philanthropy in the specific context of the transformation from traditional to modern Jewish communities in the nineteenth and early twentieth centuries, a process that went hand in hand with Jewish assimilation and integration into transforming societies. Studies by Rainer Liedtke, Derek J. Penslar and Andreas Reinke show that community-oriented Jewish philanthropy during the nineteenth century exerted a major impact on the formation of a modern supra-religious Jewish identity.[5]

The themes of modern Jewish history and philanthropy intersected during the nineteenth and early twentieth centuries in two major fields:

Jewish Individuals and Philanthropy: Several authors have recently examined individual Jewish philanthropists or a thin strata of wealthy Jews who promoted social and civic institutions such as homes for orphans, hospitals, philharmonic orchestras, and museums, among other reasons to gain entry into a status group—in Imperial Germany in particular into the upper bourgeoisie.[6] Although the exact motives of Jewish philanthropists are still debated, the study of individual Jewish philanthropists, especially in comparison with non-Jews, can provide important information on the status, identities, and visions of Jews as a group in a crucial period of transition. "Cultural philanthropy," as opposed to "charity" or "welfare," will not be analyzed in this chapter.

Jews as a Group and Philanthropy: Another approach is to analyze the function of philanthropy for Jews as a group, especially during the crucial transformation period after the opening of the ghetto between the late eighteenth century and the early twentieth century. Penslar and Liedtke have recently emphasized the impact Jewish philanthropy, or rather the development of modern forms of philanthropy, had on the transformation of Jewish identities and vice versa.[7] In the rapidly changing world of the nineteenth century, Jewish philanthropy provided a strong link to Jewish tradition. Yet Jewish philanthropy served as the common ground for Jews with increasingly differing concepts of Jewishness in the modern context.

The Hebrew term "*zedakah*" describes the traditional Jewish community-oriented practice of philanthropy; the exact translation is "righteousness" or "justice." *Zedakah* obliges observant Jews not only to give alms to poor Jews; it obliges every Jew to enable Jews who are poorer to become self-sustaining. Therefore, even poor Jews are required to give to more indigent Jews.[8] It is often overlooked that the beneficiaries of *zedakah* are not limited to Jewish recipients; the poor and the stranger are included in its purview, including non-Jews.[9] *Zedakah* ennobles the giver and provides support for the recipient, whose dignity must be honored. *Zedakah* is a sustained approach to the prevention of poverty on a long-term basis rather than simply alleviating poverty in the short term. The Talmud and Rabbinic literature emphasize the importance ascribed to *zedakah* in the Jewish tradition.[10] These traditions, however, did not remain unchanged or unchallenged throughout the centuries. Outside influences on Jewish philanthropic practices were more important than has hitherto been realized. It still needs to be studied how Jews supported non-Jews in the premodern era and how they were influenced by Christian and Islamic models. In this context, Penslar has argued for a "comparative" rather than an "essentialist" approach to the history of modern Jewish philanthropy by reminding scholars to read sources within their specific historical context.[11]

Zedakah was central to the premodern Jewish experience in the ghetto. In early modern Europe, Jews were forced to live separately from the rest of the population. They had a lower civil status, and their movement was restricted. Jews could not own land, and they could not participate in many occupations. Many cities did not allow Jews to settle within their walls. By the end of the eighteenth century, most Ashkenazic Jews in Central and Eastern Europe were poor. From the middle of the seventeenth century, Jewish communities in Western and Central Europe had to deal with growing numbers of indigent Ashkenazic migrants from East Central Europe. Many of these itinerant Jews were refugees fleeing not only war and persecution but also economic and social crisis in the East.

In Central Europe, the authorities forced Jewish *Gemeinden* (communities) to take care of their own poor. All Jews at a given village or town belonged to the local *Gemeinde,* which had a semi-autonomous status. The *Gemeinde* collected taxes, had limited jurisdiction, and supervised many social tasks such as education, care of the sick, and (not least) charity for poor Jews, not all of whom were members of the local *Gemeinde.* A large number of Jewish males worked as itinerant peddlers. While on the road, they relied on the support of Jewish communities other than their own. Throughout the early modern period, Jewish *Gemeinden* cared for a large variety of traveling Jews.[12] *Zedakah* was not only carried on by the *Gemeinde* but also by the so-called *hevrot kaddishot* (sacred associations). These voluntary associations were formed by Jews in early modern Europe to support the communal welfare of Jewish communities. Some *hevrot* specialized in caring for sick Jews; others were burial societies or financed dowries for the daughters of poor parents. Membership, while voluntary, was coveted, it was often difficult to obtain, and it carried social prestige in the community.[13]

The Sephardic diaspora communities in Western Europe, which were less isolated than their Central European counterparts but not as autonomous, took a different approach in the seventeenth century. These small communities were often formed by wealthy Sephardic merchants who played an important part in the emerging transatlantic economic system of the sixteenth and seventeenth centuries. They adhered to the Jewish tradition by caring for poor Jews, but they also devised more rational methods. The Sephardim of seventeenth-century Amsterdam provided only limited aid to the growing Ashkenazic group, allegedly because of their moral degradation. While prejudice played a part, the Amsterdam Sephardim also discussed plans to teach useful trades to poor Ashkenazim. In Bordeaux, Jews devised a poor register and controlled the recipients of aid, even finding employment for them. This early rationalization of Jewish care of the poor was influenced by economic considerations and fears about loss of social status. Earlier than Jews in Central Europe, the relatively prosperous merchants in the Sephardic diaspora were influenced by non-Jewish values of efficiency and rationalization with regard to labor and charity.[14]

The opening of the ghetto by the end of the eighteenth century in Western and Central Europe initiated a process of increasing erosion of the traditional Jewish community. In France, all Jews were fully emancipated as individuals in 1790/1791. Yet the French state formally dissolved traditional Jewish communities completely during this same period. Later, Napoleon regulated Jewish communities through the centralized *consistoire* system.[15] In the German states, the emancipation was a long and uneven process. Jews were not fully emancipated until 1871. However, the traditional Jewish community was not completely dismantled. The *Gemeinde* lost much of its autonomy but remained intact as a semi-autonomous, state-regulated body that served the religious and social needs of its members. The erosion of traditional Jewish communities that accompanied state regulation in Central and Western Europe differed significantly from the situation in the United States. There, Jews were never formally emancipated. Even before the Revolution the few hundred Jews who lived in the British colonies enjoyed far-reaching social rights. With the Revolution, they, like all other free colonists, became free and equal citizens of the new republic.[16] Initially, these unique conditions mattered little for the small Jewish minority in the United States, but they had great consequences for potential and actual Jewish emigrants in Europe.

I will use these two rather different cases—Germany, which had state regulation and a prolonged emancipation of its Jews, and the United States, where emancipation was not an issue and where the state did not supervise Jewish communities—to examine the function of philanthropy in the period of transformation from traditional to modern Jewish communities. In the nineteenth century, American Jews, most of them first-generation immigrants from Europe, observed Jewish traditions, in particular *zedakah*, but they employed community-oriented Jewish philanthropy to further their integration into the unique American society of immigrants. Several authors have shown, in contrast, that the preservation of community-oriented Jewish philanthropy in Germany slowed down the process of integration of Jews into German society.

This chapter focuses on urban Jewish communities. Long before 1800, modern Jewish history developed in the urban context. In Amsterdam, Bordeaux, Marseille, Trieste, Charleston, Philadelphia, and other trade and port cities, Jews, most of them of Sephardic background, overcame their outsider status, participating freely as insiders in the economic and, to a limited degree, social spheres. In these often cosmopolitan cities, Jews established relatively open communities, constantly renegotiating the boundaries between tradition and modernity.[17] After the opening of the ghetto, Jews in central Europe moved in large numbers from rural and traditional Jewish *Gemeinden* to growing cities such as Berlin, Breslau, Cologne, Frankfurt, Vienna, Łodz, Lemberg, and Warsaw. In 1871, most Jews in Imperial Germany lived in cities. Jewish migrants from Central and Eastern Europe in the United States also moved disproportionately (compared with other immigrants) to expanding cities such as New York, Chicago, Cincinnati, Baltimore, and Philadelphia. The exact reasons for this rapid urbanization of Jews as a group, a process that was closely related to upward social mobility, are still not entirely clear. New markets, the lifting of restrictions in the field of commerce, and the free choice of residence pulled many rural Jews into expanding cities where they could emancipate themselves from their hitherto marginal social status.[18] Most of these Jewish migrants to cities had grown up in close-knit rural Jewish communities (in Europe) and were quite familiar with *zedakah* and Jewish poverty. Thanks to the existence of the *hevrot*, which had spread in the eighteenth century to many rural *Gemeinden*, Jewish migrants to urban areas in Europe and the United States brought with them voluntary forms of organizing philanthropy.

GERMANY

Modern European Jewish history and American-Jewish history are still very separate fields on a historiographic level. A transatlantic comparison reveals significant differences but also unexpected similarities, even parallel developments. A summary of the recent studies on the German context shows that in particular the main hypothesis—that Jewish philanthropy was a stumbling block to full-fledged integration—differs significantly from historiographic analysis of Jewish philanthropy in the United States.[19]

The rather swift and broad social rise of Jews as a group into the middle and higher income groups resulted in a rapid decrease in the number of poor and indigent Jews in Germany. Yet beginning in the 1860s, and particularly after 1880, the number of indigent Jewish migrants from Eastern Europe increased, although to a much lesser degree than in the United States, where Jewish immigrants from Eastern Europe outnumbered earlier arrivals from Central and Eastern Europe as early as 1900.[20]

During the first half of the nineteenth century, the semi-autonomous status of the Jewish *Gemeinden* was dismantled, but state authorities still forced Jews to belong to the one local and state-regulated Jewish *Gemeinde*, even after full emancipation in 1871. Once fully emancipated, Jews were legally entitled to communal welfare. Consequently, maintaining separate Jewish philanthropic institutions was no longer required. But the Jewish *Gemeinden* in the German states, and later in Imperial Germany, kept their philanthropic systems. Jews even organized a large variety of additional philanthropic associations—for Jews. The persistence of Jewish welfare networks after the emancipation is the starting point for Liedtke's comparative study of Jewish welfare in Hamburg and Manchester between 1860 and 1914. He looks at Jewish welfare, among other reasons, to examine the process of the integration of the Jewish minority into the larger society.[21]

Liedtke's approach is informed by David Sorkin's concept of the development of a German-Jewish "subculture." On their way "out of the Ghetto" during the first half of the nineteenth century, Jews in the German states came up with increasingly differing concepts of Jewishness, especially on the religious level. Thus, traditional Judaism, which until then had united Jews in the ghetto, could no longer sustain Jewish *Gemeinschaft*. But Jewish *Gemeinschaft* did not disintegrate. Sorkin argues that most Jews in Germany identified with the supra-religious, inclusive, and universal ideal of *Bildung*, which can be defined as constant spiritual self-education with a strong emphasis on universal principles such as freedom, equality, and openness. German Jews, especially in their professional lives, spent much time outside Jewish circles, but after 1800 they organized hundreds of secular Jewish associations, which adhered to *Bildung* and were devoted to music, literature, and education. Often, these associations had a philanthropic purpose. The existence of this strong network of Jewish *Vereine* (associations), united by the identification with *Bildung*, leads Sorkin to the term "subculture." Jewish assimilation, he argues, led to the transformation and secularization of Jewish *Gemeinschaft* rather than to its disintegration.[22]

Sorkin examined intellectual and cultural life in Jewish communities before 1840. By looking at Jewish welfare, Liedtke has emphasized the social dimension of the German-Jewish subculture after 1860. He gives a number of reasons why Jews in Hamburg (and Manchester) kept separate Jewish welfare systems after the emancipation:

- Jewish leaders worked for the preservation of separate Jewish welfare networks to defend their position in the community.

- Jewish leaders constantly emphasized that poor Jews would not become a public charge. This point forms an integral part of what Sorkin has called the "ideology of emancipation." In return for the act of emancipation, according to an unwritten contract, Jews felt obliged not be a burden on the state which had given them legal equality.

- The preservation of separate Jewish welfare systems was a response to anti-Jewish and anti-Semitic stereotypes or, rather, was informed by the fear of anti-Semitism and the perceived threat of a reversal of the emancipation.

- Jewish welfare systems strengthened the cohesion of Jewish communities and thus the German-Jewish subculture, serving as a basis for a secular Jewish identity.[23]

Reinke's study on Breslau supports the argument that Jewish communities were increasingly defined by their social and philanthropic networks. In the 1840s, the famous Breslau *Rabbinerstreit* (conflict between rabbis) almost split the Jewish *Gemeinde*. The philanthropic *hevrah*, which among other tasks maintained the Breslau Jewish Hospital, became the substitute *Gemeinde* for the Jews in Breslau until a compromise was reached within the *Gemeinde* in 1847 that averted a split.[24] The Breslau *hevrah* is also an example of a traditionally exclusive premodern Jewish association that became modern by reorganizing itself into a supra-religious *Verein* that included all Jews. Its philanthropic nature put it increasingly at the center of organized Jewish life in Breslau. Like Liedtke, Reinke describes in detail how Jewish *Wohltätigkeit* (welfare) became modern. The Jewish hospital in Breslau was one of the most advanced hospitals in the city. Before 1914, however, most of its patients and staff were Jewish.[25]

Jewish welfare systems in Germany (and even in Britain) formed an integral part of the German-Jewish (and of the Anglo-Jewish) subculture. Liedtke even speaks of a "separate Jewish culture of welfare, which, voluntarily or involuntarily, consciously or unconsciously, contributed significantly to the pronounced and durable social separation of Jews and non-Jews."[26] In Hamburg and in Manchester, Jewish philanthropic organizations and their work resembled general philanthropic institutions in terms of organization and even in their value systems. The distinguishing feature was that Jewish welfare early on tended to prevent poverty in the long run rather than to alleviate it on a short-term basis. Nevertheless, in Breslau, Hamburg, and Manchester, Jews adopted existing models instead of pioneering new forms of sick care and social work themselves. One reason for this adaptation may be that Jews did not want to open up their philanthropic networks to outsiders, preferring to remain separate. This point requires more research, especially because Jews in the United States employed a different strategy.[27]

For the most part, Liedtke's thesis applies to the German *Gemeinde*. Closer research into other *Gemeinden* is necessary to confirm his findings. National and local Jewish philanthropic organizations also have not yet been sufficiently researched. Marion Kaplan has shown that individual Jewish women played a crucial role in the German women's movement and in the transition from charity to professional social work. After the outbreak of World War I, Jewish women's associations shifted their focus far beyond the Jewish group.[28]

THE UNITED STATES

In the United States the conditions for Jewish life and thus for the function of Jewish philanthropy differed significantly from those in Germany (and Britain). Several factors determined Jewish community-building in the nineteenth-century United States:

- The state does not interfere in religious affairs and the state and religion are completely separate; membership in religious bodies was (and is) voluntary.[29]

- Jewish emancipation was not an issue in the United States. Although anti-Jewish stereotypes were widespread, a debate over a "Jewish question" did not take place.[30]
- Jewish traditions were not present on an institutional level.[31]
- Americans could not rely on publicly funded welfare in the nineteenth century. Existing poorhouses and hospitals were privately financed by individual donors, foundations, or by religious (usually Christian) bodies.
- In Europe in the second half of the nineteenth century, Jews were visible minority groups, even in urban areas. In the United States, Jews were just one among many different ethnic, religious, and social groups, most of whose members were immigrants.

In 1820, very few Jews lived in the United States. After 1820, thousands of Jewish immigrants left Central and Eastern Europe for the United States. Many of the new immigrants settled in cities with existing Jewish communities on the East Coast, soon outnumbering the established Jews. Others established new communities in young cities such as Cincinnati, St. Louis, Chicago, San Francisco, and in smaller towns.[32]

Until about 1820, Jewish communities in the United States were small; congregation and community were identical. Few Jews intermarried or lived outside these communities. With the great increase in the number of immigrants from Europe after 1815, the weak tradition of the close-knit Jewish "synagogue-communities" was literally swept away.[33] "Synagogue-communities" were replaced, as Jonathan Sarna has argued, with "communities of synagogues."[34] But the impact of the migration went beyond the synagogue: As in Germany, Jewish immigrants in the United States founded secular Jewish associations, of which some, notably burial societies, collective relief societies, and sewing associations, had roots in the traditional *Gemeinde*, while others, such as fraternal lodges and literary societies, were new. Even before the middle of the nineteenth century, it was apparent that especially in large cities with sizeable Jewish populations, new ways to organize most Jews under one rubric had to be devised.[35] In Central Europe, especially in large cities, Jewish *Gemeinden* also faced tremendous social change, in particular rapid growth through increased immigration from rural areas, but the institutional framework remained intact and was even protected by the state. In the United States, Jewish elites, hierarchies, or traditional institutions did not exist and the state did not regulate religious bodies. Therefore, grassroots community-building on the local level in the second half of the nineteenth century had to provide the basis for national Jewish organizations and thus for the emergence of a Jewish-American ethnicity.

In Chicago, Jews were among the early settlers. In 1846, the pioneers organized the Jewish Burial Ground Association, the first Jewish association in Chicago.[36] The Jewish burial society and a number of collective relief societies that were formed shortly afterward resembled the *hevrot kaddishot*. For Jewish immigrants the tradition of the *hevrot* eased the transition from the European *Gemeinde* to American-style communities. The voluntary character of the *hevrot* was well suited to American conditions, and it explains why burial societies and collective relief associations were quickly established, especially since they provided a social network for recent immigrants in a new environment. Collective relief societies offered aid to members who became sick or lost their property, provided a decent burial, and supported the families of deceased members. But Jewish tradition alone does not explain why collective relief associations were formed. Non-Jewish immigrants also organized similar associations. They were necessary because communal or state-financed welfare was not present in the United States. In addition, many privately organized philanthropic institutions in the antebellum period were influenced by Protestant theological concepts and thus did not appeal to Jews.[37]

The early organization of social networks, however, went hand in hand with increasing divisions. As they were in other cities, Jewish immigrants in Chicago were divided by different regions of origin, social mobility, religious orientation, and even political affiliation.[38] Especially on the religious level, differences ran deep, resulting in the organization of several separate congregations.[39] But what could bring Jews in the United States together other than their common religion? In Chicago and many other American cities, a new Jewish association emerged in the 1840s which assumed a central role in building and sustaining Jewish communities on the basis of philanthropy, the Independent Order B'nai B'rith (Sons of the Covenant). This fraternal order, loosely modeled after Masonic organizations, was founded in 1843 in New York to overcome the cultural, social, and religious differences which increasingly divided Jewish immigrants.[40]

In Chicago and other cities, lodges of the B'nai B'rith promoted Jewish *Gemeinschaft* on the local level through philanthropy. In a period of intense religious conflict among Jews, the leaders of Chicago's first B'nai B'rith lodge organized the institutional platform for Chicago's Jewish community in 1859, the United Hebrew Relief Association (UHRA). The immediate cause for founding the UHRA was the need for a more efficient organization to distribute relief to poor Jews "by systemizing charity, examining each case, and not throw[ing] money away upon undeserving vagabonds."[41] By making this distinction between "deserving" and "undeserving" applicants for relief, UHRA leaders acknowledged the influence of non-Jewish welfare institutions in Chicago which took a similar approach.

According to such approaches, the poor, rather than social and economic circumstances, were responsible for their own misfortune. "Able-bodied" men in particular were regarded as "unworthy." "Worthy" applicants were widows with children, orphans, and old people.[42]

The main task of the UHRA was to coordinate relief for poor (and deserving) Jews. In 1865, the UHRA board declared in a typical statement: "The Israelites of this city and Cook County do not permit any of their coreligionists to become the charge of public charity. This Association claims the privilege of taking care of our own poor." The UHRA intended to protect the good social standing of Jewish immigrants in Chicago. And indeed, while Jews participated in upper echelons of Chicago politics as early as the 1850s (much earlier than in many other American cities), anti-Jewish prejudice was latent and widespread. Coordinated Jewish philanthropy was a genuine attempt to care for poor and needy Jews, but it also reflected fears that anti-Jewish prejudice could damage the unique social status that Jewish immigrants enjoyed in Chicago. Fear of anti-Jewish stereotypes and the emphasis that Jews took care of "their own" poor paralleled the way Jews in Germany and Britain responded to Jewish poverty.[43]

Another obvious reason for organizing the UHRA was the absence of a public welfare institution. The Chicago Relief and Aid Society, which was led and organized by private businessmen, was mobilized only in times of crisis—during the recession of 1857 or immediately after the disastrous fire of 1871, for example. Other immigrant groups also founded inclusive philanthropic organizations, notably immigrants from Scandinavia, Eastern Europe, and Germany. Jewish immigrants were among the founders and, until the 1880s, among the leaders of the Deutsche Gesellschaft (German Aid Society). But the UHRA was more than an organization devoted to the coordination of relief for poor Jews; it also represented the Jewish community of Chicago. All Jewish congregations, the B'nai B'rith lodge, and the collective relief societies became corporate members of the UHRA. The member societies sent representatives to the annual council, which elected the board. The UHRA was supra-religious and included all Jews.[44] The professional organization and structure of the UHRA was unique in Chicago. The organization and structure of other immigrant philanthropic associations did not resemble the corporate membership model of the UHRA.[45]

From the beginning, Jewish leaders emphasized that the UHRA was more than a philanthropic organization—it was the common platform for most Jews in Chicago. In a telling article for the *Allgemeine Zeitung des Judenthums* on the situation of Chicago Jewry in 1864, merchant Raphael Guthmann did not want to focus on "differences." Guthmann devoted his remarks, which clearly echoed the B'nai B'rith rhetoric, to the UHRA, "a product of unity and peace"; it would exist "as long as Jehudim will live in

Chicago, be they orthodox or reform, German or Polish or whatever else. Here is the platform where they can unite as brothers."[46] Jewish communities in other American cities were also organized on the basis of philanthropy. The founding of a central benevolence association usually indicates the origins of an inclusive community, often expressed by the word "United." Jews in Boston established their United Hebrew Benevolent Society in 1864, and the United Hebrew Relief Association of St. Louis was formed in 1871.[47]

The UHRA and similar Jewish bodies in other cities were a Jewish response to unique conditions in the United States. These philanthropic networks resembled a supra-religious *Gemeinde*, which under American circumstances had to be built and sustained from the bottom up and had to be neutral about religious issues. Rabbis played a minor role in the UHRA. The power rested with community-oriented businessmen, many of whom were B'nai B'rith members. The UHRA and similar organizations were rooted in the premodern Jewish tradition, but they also served as institutional anchor for loose (compared with the state-regulated framework of the German-Jewish *Gemeinde*) Jewish community networks in the dynamic American urban context.[48]

Philanthropy played a crucial role on the local level in Imperial Germany and Britain by connecting Jews with different backgrounds, poor Jews with rich Jews, religious Jews with secular Jews, Jews from different countries, modern Jews with traditional Jews. Participating in Jewish philanthropy provided an opportunity to identify with Jewishness without shedding one's religious or other beliefs.[49] In the United States, where conditions for Jewish life were unique, where most Jews from different parts of Europe were newcomers, where state-regulated Jewish communities did not exist, and where Jews had sustained common institutions, *zedakah* became even more important.

In one crucial respect, American Jews opted for a different strategy than Jews in Germany. In the unique setting of the American society of immigrants, Jews constituted a relatively small group before the 1890s. In the urban context, where immigrants and their American-born children made up more than half of the population, Jewish migrants did not face a homogeneous and dominant "majority society." Rather, in the United States, the processes of mutual adaptation, ethnicization, and the creation of overarching ethnic communities were intertwined.[50] Unlike their co-religionists in Hamburg and Breslau, leading Jews in Chicago and other American cities were committed to openness and inclusiveness toward non-Jews when building community-oriented philanthropic institutions. For these leaders, strengthening Jewish *Gemeinschaft* meant strengthening the urban and even national *Gemeinschaft*. For them, Jewish philanthropy served to further the integration of Jews into the American society of immigrants. The construction of an ethnic Jewish group identity in the unique setting of the United States was not considered to conflict with the process of integration.[51]

Jewish leaders in Chicago made sure that the large philanthropic projects were based on openness to everyone regardless of his or her background. In 1867, the Jews of Chicago put philanthropy literally on parade, celebrating the beginning of construction of the Jewish hospital which, although financed by the Jewish community, would be open to everyone. For Jewish leaders, the hospital was a powerful statement of civic unity and duty that transcended all religious, social, ethnic, and racial boundaries. Yet the hospital also supported the cohesion of the Jewish community. A UHRA representative claimed that Jews in Chicago were divided into many groups, but one force continued to unite Jews "from the North-Sea, the Baltic, from the Rhine and Danube" as "true brothers and sisters": Philanthropy (*Wohlthätigkeit*) was the true source of unity for Jews in Chicago and, he concluded, "unity makes us strong."[52]

Jews in Chicago and other American cities invested much time and energy in charitable efforts that reached beyond their own group. In relation to other immigrants from Germany, Jews were disproportionately active in Chicago's Deutsche Gesellschaft, which was founded and led by Jews in the early 1850s.[53] In 1871, Jewish lawyer Julius Rosenthal became the first immigrant board member of the Chicago Relief and Aid Society, which was directed by the leading businessmen of the city.[54] The Jewish engagement with philanthropic causes in Chicago was strong. Therefore, the hospital was not an isolated case; it became an important public symbol of Jewish civic engagement for Chicago. It simultaneously strengthened the acceptance of Jews and the cohesion of the Jewish community.

The Chicago Jewish hospital differed significantly from its Breslau counterpart. These differences symbolize the larger difference between the function of philanthropy for Jewish communities in Germany and the United States. The Chicago hospital was open to non-Jewish patients, most of its staff was not Jewish, and kosher food was not available.[55] How can these differences be explained? In the United States, every individual Jew determined his or her relationship to Judaism, to other Jews, and to a Jewish community; neither the state nor the *Gemeinde* determined these roles. The noninvolvement of the state in religious affairs and religious pluralism in the United States reinforced the secularization of Jewish communities. Jewish institutions with a long-term perspective that wished to include the maximum number of Jews in a larger city could function only on a supra-religious level. Thus, Jewish philanthropy served as the foundation for overarching ethnic Jewish communities. The Jewish hospital had to be supra-religious, otherwise most Jewish associations and congregations would not have supported it. This rather unique set of circumstances led to an unusual degree of openness with regard to non-Jewish philanthropy, making cooperation between Jews and non-Jews easier.

The growth of Chicago, the dispersal of Jews in the expanding city, economic recessions, and increasing Jewish immigration brought the work of the UHRA almost to a standstill in the late 1870s. These developments weakened the cohesion of the Chicago Jewish community. Because of the increase in Jewish immigration from Eastern Europe after 1880, more and more Jews were in urgent need of support, while the UHRA held firm to its commitment to take care exclusively of all needy Jews in the city. By the mid-1880s, Jewish leaders in Chicago (and in other American cities) began to discuss the long-term consequences of the increasing numbers of Jewish immigrants. Several philanthropic projects were conceived to "Americanize" Jewish immigrants as swiftly as possible. Jewish leaders were motivated—as they were in Britain in this period—by fears of anti-Jewish stereotypes, by genuine belief of their own superiority as civilized Jews, and also by genuine pity. Around the turn of the twentieth century, when the new immigrants outnumbered earlier arrivals, leading Jews realized that they could not dictate the conditions of assimilation to the new arrivals. In Chicago, this awareness opened the way to build a new community which would mediate between newcomers and established Jews.[56]

The Americanization projects for Jewish immigrants, which were begun in the late 1880s and early 1890s, reinforced the process of opening Jewish philanthropy to non-Jews. Not only did Jews closely collaborate with non-Jewish institutions and individuals such as Chicago's Hull House Settlement, Jewish leaders emerged as leading social reformers in this period. Many Jewish-sponsored Americanization projects for Jewish immigrants adopted progressive and scientific methods of social work. In New York and Chicago, Jewish schools for immigrant children from Eastern Europe served as models for the reform of the public school.[57] Jewish participation in non-Jewish associations during the transition from traditional charity to modern concepts of social work in the United States has parallels with the Jewish experience in Germany which require more research, as the findings of Marion Kaplan in her study on Jewish women in Imperial Germany indicate. In particular, the question of whether national philanthropic Jewish organizations devoted funds or projects for non-Jews is of interest here.[58]

CONCLUSION

A comparison of Jewish philanthropy in Germany and the United States shows a number of parallels. As in German cities, Jewish philanthropy in

Chicago defined Jewish *Gemeinschaft.* Jews made sure that no Jew became a public charge. They were clearly influenced by the fear of anti-Jewish stereotypes which, although pervasive, coexisted in Chicago with an unusually high degree of acceptance of Jews on an official and public level, in politics, in the field of cultural philanthropy, and among progressive social reformers after 1890.

In Germany, religious divisions were contained in the *Gemeinde*; in the United States, religious conflicts led to separation into different communities. Jewish immigrants in the nineteenth-century United States built overarching and supra-religious communities. Community-oriented Jewish philanthropy, with its strong roots in the Jewish tradition, provided the basis. Given the specific circumstances in the United States, where the state did (and does) not interfere with religion, philanthropy played an even more important role in the organization of an overarching Jewish *Gemeinschaft* than it did in Imperial Germany.

The first philanthropic Jewish associations in Chicago and other American cities were based on the *hevrot.* The *hevrot* served as an obvious and familiar blueprint for the early immigrants, not least because they were based on voluntary membership. Other immigrant groups created similar associations which provided a social net for their members partly because public welfare was not available. The *hevrot* are an example of a transatlantic link between Jewish tradition and new voluntary American forms of organizing Jewish *Gemeinschaft.*

In the society of immigrants that was the United States, Jews were not a minority but rather one ethnic group among others. The conditions for integration there differed significantly from the German context. The comparison shows that the term "integration" in the context of Jewish emancipation and assimilation needs to be discussed more thoroughly. In the United States, where Jews built overarching and, compared with the German-Jewish *Gemeinde,* loose communities on an ethnic and supra-religious basis, Jewish philanthropy did not lead to separation but rather to increasing integration—on American terms.

After the Civil War, Jewish leaders in Chicago employed community-oriented Jewish philanthropy successfully as an instrument to promote the acceptance of Jews in the city. The Jewish hospital initiated this new vision, which (seemingly paradoxically) simultaneously strengthened ethnic and civic unity. Jewish institutions such as the hospital and later the Jewish school for immigrant children were open to non-Jews. In order to receive support from most Jews in the city, almost all Jewish philanthropy projects in Chicago were explicitly supra-religious and thus accessible to non-Jews.

In 1901, reform rabbi and social reformer Emil G. Hirsch emphasized that Jewish philanthropy as a principle was not exclusively Jewish and that it was setting new standards for charity work in Chicago: "In the domain of philanthropy the Jewish citizens of Illinois have not been laggards. While, as their co-religionists always and everywhere, contributing to the maintenance of public institutions, under whatever denominational auspices, they have never neglected to provide for the nearer needs of their dependent classes. In certain ways the Jews of Chicago may claim the credit of having been among the first to inaugurate the better methods according to the truer standard of the new philanthropy in the dispensation of relief or the provision for the education of the young. . . . The Jews of this city can proudly point to the fact that they were the first to bring about systematic co-operation among the various agencies for the administration of the charities."[59]

Early in the nineteenth century, Jewish immigrants adapted to the unique form of religious pluralism in the United States. Traditional forms of organizing Jewish *Gemeinschaft* on religious terms in the *Gemeinde* could not sustain Jewish communities. Religious pluralism in the United States thus became a strong impetus for Jews to define community outside the synagogue, a factor that eventually produced looser but also more open Jewish communities than in the German context. From a German-Jewish viewpoint it may have been ironic that Jewish philanthropic institutions were much more open in the American context; Jews could only come together and organize ambitious projects such as the hospital on a supra-religious level.

NOTES

1. Aharon Bornstein, "The Role of Social Institutions as Inhibitors of Assimilation: The Jewish Poor Relief System in Germany 1875–1925," *Jewish Social Studies* 50 (1988): 201–222; Jacob Toury, *Soziale und politische Geschichte der Juden in Deutschland, 1848–1871* (Düsseldorf: Droste, 1977); Marion Kaplan, *The Making of the Jewish Middle Class: Women, Family, and Identity in Imperial Germany* (New York and Oxford: Oxford University Press, 1991), 192–228; Derek J. Penslar, "Philanthropy, the 'Social Question' and Jewish Identity in Imperial Germany," *Leo Baeck Institute Year Book* 38 (1993): 51–73.

2. Andreas Reinke, *Judentum und Wohlfahrtspflege in Deutschland: Das Jüdische Krankenhaus in Breslau 1726–1944* (Hanover: Hahnsche Buchhandlung, 1999); Rainer Liedtke, *Jewish Welfare in Hamburg and Manchester, c. 1850–1914* (Oxford: Oxford University Press, 1998); Derek J. Penslar, *Shylock's Children: Economics and Jewish Identity in Modern Europe* (Berkeley and Los Angeles: University of California Press, 2001); Stefi Jersch-Wenzel, François Guesnet, et al., eds., *Juden und Armut* (Cologne and Vienna: Böhlau, 2000); Bornstein, "The Role of Social Institutions."

3. Arthur Goren, *New York Jews and the Quest for Community: The Kehillah Experiment 1908–1922* (New York: Columbia University Press, 1970); Susan Ebert, "Community and Philanthropy," in *The Jews of Boston,* ed. Jonathan Sarna and Ellen Smith (Boston: Northeastern University Press, 1995), 211–237; Tobias Brinkmann, "'Praise upon you: The

U.H.R.A.!': Jewish Philanthropy and the Origins of the First Jewish Community in Chicago 1859–1900," in *The Shaping of a Community: The Jewish Federation of Metropolitan Chicago*, ed. Rhoda Rosen (Chicago: Spertus Press, 1999), 24–39; Tobias Brinkmann, *Von der Gemeinde zur "Community": Jüdische Einwanderer in Chicago 1840–1900* (Osnabrück: Universitätsverlag Rasch, 2002).

4. Stephen Mostov, "A 'Jerusalem' on the Ohio: The Social and Economic History of Cincinnati's Jewish Community 1840–1875" (Ph.D. diss., Brandeis University, 1981); William Toll, *The Making of an Ethnic Middle Class: Portland Jewry over Four Generations* (Albany: State University of New York Press, 1982).

5. Reinke, *Judentum und Wohlfahrtspflege;* Liedtke, *Jewish Welfare in Hamburg and Manchester;* Penslar, *Shylock's Children.*

6. Kathleen D. McCarthy, *Noblesse Oblige: Charity and Cultural Philanthropy in Chicago, 1849–1929* (Chicago: University of Chicago Press, 1982); on individual Jewish philanthropists, see Elisabeth Kraus, *Die Familie Mosse: Deutsch-jüdisches Bürgertum im 19. und 20. Jahrhundert* (München: C. H. Beck, 1999), 400–452; Olaf Matthes, *James Simon, Mäzen im Wilhelminischen Zeitalter* (Berlin: Borstelmann und Siebenhaar, 1999), 9–19, 99–133; Erika Bucholtz, *Henri Hinrichsen und der Musikverlag C. F. Peters* (Tübingen and London: J. C. B. Mohr, 2001), 274–283.

7. Penslar, *Shylock's Children*, 96.

8. Gittin, Section 7a (see *Der Babylonische Talmud*, German translation by Lazarus Goldschmidt [Berlin: Jüdischer Verlag, 1930–1936], 6: 207). For a general overview, see Raphael Posner, Haim-Hillel Ben-Sasoon, and Isaac Levitats, "Charity," in *Encyclopaedia Judaica* (Jerusalem: Keter Publishing House, 1972), 5: 338–353; Jacob Neusner, *Tzedakah: Can Jewish Philanthropy Buy Jewish Survival?* (Atlanta: Scholars Press, 1990).

9. R. Moses Maimonides, *De Jure Pauperis et Peregrini Apud Judaeos*, Latine vertit & notis illustravit Humphridus Prideaux (Oxoni: Sheldon, 1679); Joseph Caro, *Shulhan Arukh Yoreh De'ah*, sections 247–259, esp. 251.

10. Posner, Ben-Sasoon, and Levitats, "Charity," *Encyclopaedia Judaica*, 5: 340; Rabbi Assi, for instance, stated that "*tzedakah* is as important as all the other commandments put together" (Talmud, *Bava Batra*, Section 9a. See *Der Babylonische Talmud*, 8: 32).

11. Kaplan, *The Making of the Jewish Middle Class*, 193; Posner, Ben-Sasoon, and Levitats, "Charity," *Encyclopaedia Judaica*, 5: 338–353; Penslar, *Shylock's Children*, 90–92.

12. Penslar, *Shylock's Children*, 92–96; Mordechai Breuer, "Frühe Neuzeit und Beginn der Moderne," in *Deutsch-jüdische Geschichte in der Neuzeit*, ed. Michael Meyer (München: C. H. Beck, 1996), 1: 166–170.

13. Reinke, *Judentum und Wohlfahrtspflege*, 31–42.

14. Penslar, *Shylock's Children*, 95–96; on Amsterdam, see Daniel M. Swetschinski, *Reluctant Cosmopolitans: The Portuguese Jews of Seventeenth-Century Amsterdam* (Amsterdam: Littman, 2000), 177–187; Miriam Bodian, *Hebrews of the Portuguese Nation: Conversos and Community in Early Modern Amsterdam* (Bloomington: Indiana University Press, 1997), 47–48, 131, 133; and Paolo Bernadini and Norman Fiering, eds., *The Jews and the Expansion of Europe to the West 1450 to 1800* (New York: Berghahn, 2001).

15. Michael Graetz, *The Jews in Nineteenth-Century France: From the French Revolution to the Alliance Israélite Universelle* (Stanford, Calif.: Stanford University Press, 1996), 17–40.

16. Ira Katznelson and Pierre Birnbaum, eds., *Paths of Emancipation: Jews, States, and Citizenship* (Princeton, N.J.: Princeton University Press, 1995).

17. Lois Dubin, *The Port Jews of Habsburg Trieste: Absolutist Politics and Enlightenment Culture* (Stanford, Calif.: Stanford University Press, 1999); Silvia Marzagallia, "Atlantic Trade and Sephardim Merchants in Eighteenth-Century France: The Case of Bordeaux," in Bernadini and Fiering, *Jews and the Expansion of Europe*, 268–286; Bodian, *Hebrews of the Portuguese Nation.*

18. Monika Richarz, ed., *Bürger auf Widerruf: Lebenszeugnisse deutscher Juden 1780–1945* (München: C. H. Beck, 1989), 19; David Sorkin, "The Impact of Emancipation on German Jewry: A Reconsideration," in *Assimilation and Community: The Jews in Nineteenth-Century Europe,* ed. Jonathan Frankel and Steven J. Zipperstein (Cambridge: Cambridge University Press, 1992), 180.

19. Michael A. Meyer, *Response to Modernity: A History of the Reform Movement in Judaism* (New York and Oxford: Oxford University Press, 1988) is an important study with a transatlantic focus.

20. Jack Wertheimer, *Unwelcome Strangers: East European Jews in Imperial Germany* (New York: Oxford University Press, 1987).

21. Rainer Liedtke, "Integration and Separation: Jewish Welfare in Hamburg and Manchester in the Nineteenth Century," in *Two Nations: British and German Jews in Comparative Perspective,* ed. Rainer Liedtke, Michael Brenner, and David Rechter (Tübingen: Mohr Siebeck, 1999), 248.

22. David Sorkin, *The Transformation of German Jewry, 1780–1840* (Oxford and New York: Oxford University Press, 1987); George L. Mosse, *German Jews Beyond Judaism* (Bloomington: Indiana University Press; Cincinnati: Hebrew Union College Press, 1985).

23. Liedtke, "Integration and Separation," 262–271; on Jewish immigration from Eastern Europe, see Steven Aschheim, *Brothers and Strangers: The East European Jew in German and German Jewish Consciousness 1800–1923* (Madison: University of Wisconsin Press, 1982); and Wertheimer, *Unwelcome Strangers.*

24. Reinke, *Judentum und Wohlfahrtspflege,* 118–131.

25. Liedtke, "Integration and Separation," 306ff.

26. Ibid., 270.

27. Ibid., 258ff.

28. Kaplan, *The Making of the Jewish Middle Class,* 192–227.

29. Seymour Martin Lipset, "A Unique People in an Exceptional Country," in *American Pluralism and the Jewish Community,* ed. Seymour Martin Lipset (New Brunswick, N.J.: Rutgers University Press, 1989), 7–8.

30. Ira Katznelson, "Between Separation and Disappearance: American Jews on the Margins of American Liberalism," in Katznelson and Birnbaum, *Paths of Emancipation,* 164–166.

31. Eli Faber, *A Time for Planting: The First Migration 1654–1820,* The Jewish People in America, vol. 1 (Baltimore: Johns Hopkins University Press, 1992); Meyer, *Response to Modernity,* 235–236.

32. Avraham Barkai, *Branching Out: German-Jewish Immigration to the United States, 1820–1914* (New York: Holmes & Meier, 1994); Hasia R. Diner, *A Time for Gathering: The Second Migration, 1820–1880,* The Jewish People in America, vol. 2 (Baltimore: Johns Hopkins University Press, 1992).

33. Barkai, *Branching Out,* 15–39.

34. Jonathan Sarna, "The Evolution of the American Synagogue," in *The Americanization of the Jews,* ed. Robert M. Selzer and Norman J. Cohen (New York: New York University Press, 1995), 218–219.

35. For a general overview, see Diner, *A Time for Gathering,* 86–89.

36. Herman Eliassof and Emil G. Hirsch, *The Jews of Illinois: Their Religious and Civic Life, Their Charity and Industry, Their Patriotism and Loyalty to American Institutions, from Their Earliest Settlement in the State unto Present Time,* supplement to *Reform Advocate* (Chicago), May 4, 1901, 287; Walter Ehrlich, *Zion in the Valley: The Jewish Community of St. Louis* (Columbia: University of Missouri Press, 1997), 51–52.

37. Eliassof and Hirsch, *Jews of Illinois,* 298 and 305.

38. Ibid., 299.

39. Ibid., 292–294, 303–305.

40. Deborah Dash Moore, *B'nai B'rith and the Challenge of Ethnic Leadership* (Albany: State University of New York Press, 1981).

41. *First Annual Report of the United Hebrew Relief Association* (Chicago, 1860).

42. *10th Annual Report of the United Hebrew Relief Association* (Chicago, 1869); Paul Boyer, *Urban Masses and Moral Order in America, 1820–1920* (Cambridge, Mass.: Harvard University Press, 1978), 143–161; for Chicago, see McCarthy, *Noblesse Oblige*.

43. *First Annual Report of the United Hebrew Relief Association;* on Jews in Chicago politics, see Edward Mazur, "Minyans for a Prairie City: The Politics of Chicago Jewry, 1850–1940" (Ph.D. diss., University of Chicago, 1974).

44. Brinkmann, "'Praise upon you,'" 29–31; Bessie Louise Pierce, *A History of Chicago* (New York and Chicago: Knopf and University of Chicago Press, 1937–57), 2: 20–23; 3: 30.

45. Eliassof and Hirsch, *Jews of Illinois,* 305–322.

46. *Allgemeine Zeitung des Judenthums* (Leipzig), January 12, 1864.

47. For Boston, see Ebert, "Community and Philanthropy," 212; for St. Louis, see Ehrlich, *Zion in the Valley,* 220–224.

48. Eliassof and Hirsch, *Jews of Illinois,* 315–322.

49. Liedtke, *Jewish Welfare in Hamburg and Manchester;* Reinke, *Judentum und Wohlfahrtspflege.*

50. Lawrence Fuchs, *The American Kaleidoscope: Race, Ethnicity, and the Civic Culture* (Hanover, N.H.: New England University Press, 1990), 22; Ewa Morawska, "In Defense of the Assimilation Model," *Journal of American Ethnic History* 13 (1994): 76–87.

51. Tobias Brinkmann, "Charity on Parade: Chicago's Jews and the Construction of Ethnic and Civic 'Gemeinschaft' in the 1860s," in *Celebrating Ethnicity and Nation: American Festive Culture from the Revolution to the Early Twentieth Century,* ed. Jürgen Heideking and Geneviève Fabre (New York: Berghahn 2001), 157–174.

52. *Illinois Staatszeitung* (Chicago), September 4, 1867; *Allgemeine Zeitung des Judenthums,* October 15, 1867; *American Israelite* (Cincinnati), September 13, 1867.

53. *D. B. Cooke & Co.'s Chicago City Directory for the Year 1860–61* (Chicago, 1860).

54. McCarthy, *Noblesse Oblige,* 66.

55. *Die Neuzeit* (Vienna), September 25, 1868, 463; *9th Annual Report of the United Hebrew Relief Association* (Chicago, 1869).

56. Brinkmann, "'Praise upon you,'" 38.

57. Ibid., 37; Eliassof and Hirsch, *Jews of Illinois,* 309, 353–357; Stephan F. Brumberg, *Going to America, Going to School: The Jewish Immigrant Public School Encounter in Turn-of-the-Century New York City* (New York: Praeger, 1986).

58. Kaplan, *The Making of the Jewish Middle Class,* 192–227.

59. *Reform Advocate,* May 4, 1901.

TEN

Bürgerlichkeit, *Patronage,* and Communal Liberalism in Germany, 1871–1914

SIMONE LÄSSIG

GERMAN-JEWISH PATRONAGE

Jews played a prominent role as patrons in the *Kaiserreich*. The proportion of Jews active in foundations clearly exceeded their proportion in the overall population in several municipalities. In Frankfurt am Main and Berlin, Jews were involved in up to a third of all foundations.[1] This fact has prompted a surge in research on Jewish patronage. However, historians have rarely asked about the causes of this activity. When the question has been asked, the answers typically center on specifically Jewish perspectives. The common argument suggests that as members of a minority, German Jews hoped that extensive involvement in charity activities would enable them to completely assimilate and would dispel anti-Semitic prejudices. This argument stresses the religious tradition of charity and the notion of a special Jewish social ethic—both of which are linked to the concept of *zedakah,* or the tradition of charity within the Jewish community.[2] The dominant explanations of German-Jewish patronage derive from discussions about "tradition," "minority status," "pressure to conform," "compensation," "integration," and even, occasionally, "overcompensation."[3] This framework, however, serves to confirm the myth of the selfless patron.

A more complex picture emerges when one adds social status and the resultant cultural and political behavioral patterns linked to patronage to ethno-religious interpretations. From this vantage point, the Jewish minority can be seen and understood primarily as a bourgeois (*bürgerlich*) social group. In 1870, 55 of the 133 most highly taxed citizens of Frankfurt were Jewish. In Breslau during the 1870s, between 40 and 60 percent of Jewish residents belonged to the bourgeoisie—a proportion three to four times higher than that of the Protestants of the city and ten times higher than that of the Catholics.[4] Even in Dresden, where the settlement of Jews became legally possible only in the 1860s and where the overall percentage of Jews in the city never rose above 1 percent of the total population, the Jewish community was a bourgeois society *en miniature* in terms of its organizational as well as its social structure. If we define "bourgeoisie," in accordance with the German term "*Bürgertum,*" as a group of individuals belonging to the upper and upper-middle classes, then even in the Saxon capital more than half of all Jews belonged to the bourgeoisie.[5]

According to research conducted on the composition of various cities in the *Kaiserreich,* on average 72 percent of the residents belonged to the lower classes. Only 11 percent can be considered bourgeois, including between 1 and 5 percent who clearly belonged to the upper class.[6] Jews achieved leading positions in areas that went beyond income or social class. The same level of accomplishment was apparent in terms of their economic independence, which was greatly valued and seen as a sign of success by the Jewish and non-Jewish bourgeoisie alike. In Dresden, for instance, more than two-thirds of all members of the Jewish community were self-employed in some fashion.

It should not come as a surprise that both contemporaries and historians have considered the German Jews to be the most bourgeois social group. There is no doubt that German Jews were a wealthier, overwhelmingly middle- and upper-middle-class, and, to a large extent, urbanized group.[7] However, it is important to consider Jewish patrons not simply as Jews but as members of the German bourgeoisie—in the political, cultural, and social senses of the term. It is essential to investigate the common bourgeois motivations for giving as well as the background of this cultural practice, including other dimensions of bourgeois life.

This chapter is concerned with the political and social dimensions of giving. This cultural practice was common to both groups in the *Kaiserreich,* which makes it easier to investigate the ways in which Jewish patronage differed from non-Jewish patronage and to determine if, in the end, these differences were due to ethno-religious or social, cultural, and political reasons. In other words, were the differences between Jewish and non-Jewish patronage due to the minority status of German Jews or to a distinctive *Bürgerlichkeit*?[8] To resolve this quandary, I will approach more general questions: What motivated patrons to use their own wealth to further the natural and social sciences and the arts? To what degree can patronage be understood as the cornerstone of liberal society and a living *Bürgerlichkeit*? And more important, were there intersections between the practice of patronage, on one hand, and the political, social, and cultural self-definition of the German bourgeoisie on the other?

Research on patronage is currently in vogue in Germany. This trend is the result of an ongoing discussion about the merits and disadvantages of private funding for education and the arts. It is also the result of a new trend in the academic world to study patronage, which the *Bürgertums-forschung* (research on the bourgeoisie) had almost completely ignored until the mid-1990s. While many historians intensively studied the nature of bourgeois associations and the development of a specific bourgeois value system, they paid very little attention to the varied forms of patronage. Yet the practice of donating must be seen as a constituent element of bourgeois life and culture. The provision of private means for public causes corresponded to the bourgeoisie's interests in the common good. This practice also demonstrated the firm establishment of bourgeois norms, moral customs, and visions of society as well as strongly antigovernmental tendencies. In this sense, patronage, as Jürgen Kocka has aptly suggested, is the "bourgeois behavior *par excellence.*"[9] The German *Bürgertum* was a specific grouping of the middle strata which expressed its distinctiveness through a particular mentality, lifestyle, and social and cultural vision. *Bürgerlichkeit*, according to Kocka, can be understood as the expression of the ideal bourgeois lifestyle.

In this chapter, I use the term "cultural patronage" (*Mäzenatentum*) as Jürgen Kocka and Manuel Frey have defined it. According to Kocka and Frey, patronage is the provision of private means for public causes intended for general use. I do not use "patronage" merely or primarily to indicate the support of art and culture; I use it to mean giving for the natural or social sciences, education, and social causes. I use the terms "patronage" and "charity" interchangeably. This might obscure the differences between both concepts in terms of the level of investment made. Charity is normally assumed to be the donation of smaller sums of money, whereas patronage is seen as crossing a particular monetary threshold. Nevertheless, for this chapter, the amounts of money given are of far less importance than the act of giving itself.

This chapter links several central theoretical considerations and findings which are rooted in the analysis of the nature of patronage in Dresden. The choice of that Saxon court city was appealing in that nearly all new work on patronage in Germany focuses on the capital city, Berlin, or on larger cities such as Hamburg or Frankfurt—thus, on cities which are representative of neither the German bourgeoisie as a whole nor of the German-Jewish bourgeoisie. Research which has considered these other "less important" cities in terms of both municipal Liberalism and the nature of bourgeois patronage is still rare.[10] Yet it is precisely these cities which provide us with a much deeper understanding of the "normality" of the everyday life of the bourgeoisie in the *Kaiserreich*, more so than the descriptions of the exceptional cases, such as Berlin or Frankfurt, which supposedly epitomize patronage and the German bourgeoisie.

LIBERALIZING PATRONAGE AND
PATRONIZING LIBERALISM AROUND 1900

In which instances do the concepts of patronage, *Bürgerlichkeit,* and Liberalism overlap? Clearly, these areas of intersection influenced the behavior and habits of the bourgeoisie on cultural as well as political levels. The first important connection between Liberalism and patronage consists of the will to actively structure and complete important tasks on one's own initiative. Individual self-responsibility and the rejection of state regulation are central Liberal axioms. Thus, the concept of economic autonomy holds a central place in Liberalism. For this reason, Liberals were very skeptical of democratization of the municipality. The right to vote and make decisions about the common good was considered applicable only to those whose intellectual abilities or material possessions allowed them to make independent decisions.[11] German Jews fulfilled these bourgeois criteria to a great extent. As such, they were predestined to act as members of the *Bürgertum* and, under the proper economic conditions, as patrons.

A second commonality between Liberalism and patronage lies in the fixation on the municipality as the central space for all individual action for the common good and as the model for the self-organization of a civil society. This was relevant to the majority of German Jews because of their unusually strong urban character and orientation. As a result of their predominantly bourgeois social profile, Jewish citizens, more than other inhabitants of the city, possessed the legal status of citizens with corresponding voting rights. This social and political status in turn provided a comparatively large percentage of Jews with an entrance into the political and cultural control apparatuses of the German bourgeoisie. Because of the level of social embourgeoisement of Jews and the specific political culture of municipalities, it should not come as a surprise that Jewish citizens were politically involved in many, though not all, German cities and were even more involved on the state and federal levels. German Jews actively participated in the city parliament, the electoral colleges, and honorary municipal offices.[12] The desire for independence or latitude in making decisions regarding city politics was a fundamental principle of municipal governance according to the Liberal *Weltanschauung.* Particular issues resulting from industrialization threatened to destroy the ability of the bourgeoisie to solve community problems. Patronage served to put pressure on the municipal government to deal with those issues which, despite private initiative, were unsolvable without the intervention of the municipality or the state. The state had to assume responsibility for these tasks.[13]

The deeds of the majority of patrons were guided by a strong interest in the good of the municipality—a fact demonstrated by the rapid secularization of charitable projects. Though Traugott Bienert, the wealthy owner of several mills, and his sons participated in the charitable activities of their church just as the Jewish banking family Arnhold did within their religious community, most charitable activities of the time benefited the general public. In scale and scope, charitable organizations that benefited religious, or even national, causes were significantly less important than similar organizations whose goal was the general good of the municipality.[14]

Another similarity between Liberalism and patronage is their focus on the individual. From a Jewish perspective, this focus was not always self-evident. Traditional Jewish life was oriented toward the collective and, in this sense, strongly aligned with the community, the family, and a general sense of togetherness. However, the long process of emancipation brought about a slow but profound change in this sense of collectivity. The institutional nature of the association was helpful in the process and had a strong influence on patronage in general.[15]

The distinctive orientation toward the independent and industrious individual corresponded to another political-cultural phenomenon—a system of privilege which Liberalism defended tooth and nail. In this context, the German *Bürgertum* defined "community" as a necessary extension of bourgeois individualism. Patrons, in their actions and attitudes, represented two Liberal poles: the freedom of autonomous individuals to make their own decisions and an interest in the common good. Charitable behavior was the result of this tension between bourgeois individualism and a fundamental sense of responsibility for the social structures of the city. This corresponded with the German bourgeoisie's desire to represent general interests rather than religious, political, or economic "special interests." Patrons presented themselves as competent defenders of the common good, which in turn allowed them to establish their own priorities and control their expenses and the amount of money they made on their investments. This control was a very important motivation for their charitable activities. The "ideal *Bürger*" had internalized the social obligation to give back to society but wanted to use his individual interests and tendencies to decide to use his money for causes which he, and not the state, felt to be deserving of aid. The use of ideal and material resources for specific charitable causes was connected to the desire for political control. This attitude could even border on arbitrariness.[16]

Even if one cannot always speak of arbitrariness, patronage was employed in all cases for cultural domination. This corresponded with the Liberal vision to, if possible, shape the entire society according to bourgeois values. Both the promotion of regular work for the poor and the encouragement toward self-help, rather than relying on help from outside sources, were accorded central places in this bourgeois value system. The beginnings of self-help were founded in the Jewish tradition of *zedaka*. Over time, the notion of self-help grew and developed into a genuinely bourgeois pattern which was visible in almost all, not just Jewish, charitable projects. In many statutes of charitable organizations, "industry," "education," "creativity," and "success" were important keywords and guiding principles. Each person who lived according to the "bourgeois code of virtue" was considered an appropriate recipient of aid regardless of his social position.[17] In almost all social and charitable foundations, the connection between bourgeois morality and the values of the patrons was clearly visible. Charity was not intended to merely provide help to those in need; rather, charity was used to exercise social control. At the heart of all charitable action was the desire to give help to a person down on his luck for a short amount of time so that he could again become active. According to the bourgeois work ethic, only those seen as industrious and hardworking were granted temporary help. Long-term support, such as old age pensions, was rare.[18] With this, a stark contrast between patronage and a concept proposed by Social Democracy becomes apparent. While patronage provided short-term solutions, Social Democracy saw poverty and unemployment as structural problems which could only be resolved through the reformation of the very foundation of society. Liberal politicians and patrons, by contrast, did not want to change the structures; they merely wanted to decrease the undesirable symptoms.

Despite the bourgeoisie's interest in art, culture, and education, patronage for the arts and education was of marginal importance in Dresden when one looks at the actual distribution of money for charitable causes. Even the studies of Berlin and Frankfurt have overestimated the importance of cultural patronage. The relatively small amount of patronage destined for cultural purposes is probably due to the fact that associations created in the early nineteenth century were responsible for the financial support of this prestigious field in smaller cities. The founding of the Dresden Museum Association and the Association of Dresden Gallery Friends (*Patronatsverein*) in 1911 and 1918, respectively, demonstrate a long-standing or revived predominance of collective patronage. Instances of individual patronage for the arts are almost negligible. The prominent individuals that we see in Berlin and that we know to be typical of the *Kaiserreich* were almost completely absent in Dresden until the last decade before World War I.[19]

In view of the relatively unimportant role patronage played for culture and the arts, one is struck by the question, What did patrons support and what was the place of these causes in the Liberal *Weltanschauung* at the turn of the twentieth century? Were there particularly Jewish charitable behaviors?[20] There were two general trends in charitable activity in Dresden. First, the larger foundations, especially, were created with the particular interest and needs of the patron and his class in mind.[21] In the field of education, the tendency to support the patron's own culture was starkly apparent.[22] While only 6 percent of all charity went to elementary schools and similar institutions, higher education received 18 percent of all donations, despite the fact that far fewer children frequented such institutions. The emphasis of this charitable activity was thus on schools and universities which were difficult for lower-class children to gain entrance to. Theoretically, these foundations offered poorer children the opportunity to advance socially and economically through education, though these children had to "pay" with particular industry, conformity, and consistently good behavior. Second, patrons gave priority to charity for social foundations and causes. More than a quarter of all foundations were aimed at supporting the poor in one way or another. Of equal importance was the assistance of the sick, the mentally or physically challenged, and those in need of long-term care. Nearly half of all charitable foundations served these four social groups.

Figure 10.1 clearly shows that only slight differences existed between the levels of participation of Jewish and non-Jewish patrons in charity activities. The minor differences between the two groups in their levels of involvement with social assistance can be explained by the fact that Jewish patrons were involved more in helping the poor, sick, and physically and mentally challenged, while non-Jewish patrons gave more to old age pensions and housing foundations. Overall, however, these minor discrepancies cannot be ascribed to differences in the nature of patronage because of ethnic or religious divisions. It is, nonetheless, particularly interesting that Jewish patrons did not put much emphasis on funding education—traditionally considered the Jewish domain. In fact, funding for education by Jewish citizens was even slightly below the municipal average throughout the period of the *Kaiserreich*.

Overall, it is necessary to judge the charitable actions of Jewish citizens more cautiously. In Dresden, of the 788 foundations created between 1870 and 1914, at the very most thirty-seven—that is, 4.7 percent—were created by Jews. Similarly, while there were 544 patrons during this same period, only twenty-four were Jewish. This percentage (4.4 percent) is decisively above the proportion of Jews living in Dresden (which never exceeded 1 percent). At first glance, these figures seem to support the notion that Jews were disproportionately involved in patronage. However, when one considers the higher prosperity of the Jewish community as a whole, this involve-

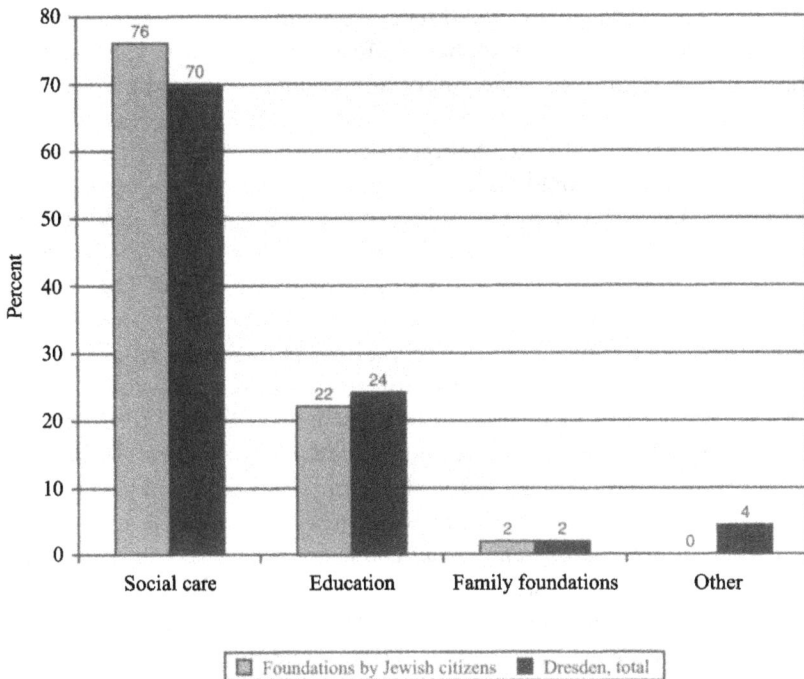

Figure 10.1. Charitable Causes in Dresden, 1870–1914 — General Donations

ment is actually lower than one might expect.[23] Before World War I, Jewish patrons were responsible for providing 911,500 marks out of a total of 35 million marks given to all foundations in Dresden—in other words, 2.6 percent—even less than the percentage of Jews involved in patronage. Evidently, the Jewish bourgeoisie did not have a greater affinity for patronage than the bourgeoisie in general.

With this in mind, it would seem more useful to return to a discussion about the general trends in bourgeois patronage, such as the importance of fundamental elements of political *Bürgerlichkeit* for patronage during this period. Just as Liberalism had the power to unite forces, patronage contributed to the socialization of the various factions within the bourgeoisie, especially in terms of consolidating the ideas of private ownership and education. Patronage fulfilled an integrative and identity-building function for an otherwise heterogeneous social group. The bourgeoisie had abolished traditional modes of inclusion and exclusion, such as birth and social origins, and had tried to assert its leadership in society by using the issues of values, norms, and lifestyles as litmus tests. The ideal of a "Renaissance man" served as the dividing line between the old and new elites. Close contacts between wealthy patrons and representatives of the educated and cultural elites could, in this regard, have a great impact on society. For the patron, such relationships were important to help him make intelligent decisions about how to use his money charitably. Specialists from the *Bildungsbürgertum* (the educated bourgeoisie) knew in which fields and under what conditions one could assure the highest symbolic return on one's "investment." Patronage was thus linked to the negotiation of cultural and aesthetic, as well as social, esteem.[24] Representatives of the *Bildungsbürgertum* enhanced their own social status through this type of cooperation and through the inexhaustible source of cultural capital they provided. Finally, successful businessmen, who felt obliged to be the model of the educated bourgeois, could compensate for deficits in the realization of this ideal of cultural and social prestige in a symbolic as well as literal fashion. Georg Arnhold, a Dresden banker, established an "open house" by holding lecture evenings on natural and social scientific, political, and general topics, in which members of both the *Wirtschaftsbürgertum* (the commercial bourgeoisie) and *Bildungsbürgertum* could come together as equals and profit from one another's strengths. For Arnhold, these evenings were about uniting art, natural and social sciences, economy, and politics and bringing the different bourgeois factions together on a one-to-one basis. Naturally, then, Arnhold's hunger for educational and cultural prestige combined with the latent dependence and obligatory gratitude of the *Bildungsbürger* toward the patrons to form a cement-like bond between the *Bildungs-* and *Wirtschaftsbürgertum*. This relationship can also be likened to a business which ensured an especially effective trade in cultural, social, and economic capital. These transactions brought advantages to both sides and were also actively encouraged by both.

Patronage, thus, functioned as the linchpin which strengthened both the working relationship between the *Bildungs-* and *Wirtschaftsbürgertum* and the cohesion of heterogeneous social groups. Through this cultural practice, the new bourgeoisie self-consciously differentiated itself from the old aristocratic elite. Yet in the process of separating itself from the lower classes, the bourgeoisie obtained an increase in prestige and the ability to influence or dominate society. The new bourgeois elite needed to distinguish itself socially and to firmly define itself, and patronage was centrally important in these endeavors. It realized its goals by fulfilling the fundamental criteria of being wealthy and owning private property and by engaging in integrative cultural practices that generated cultural capital. The formation of a new elite identity did not always mean the delimitation of the bourgeoisie vis-à-vis other social classes or the complete integration of all possible members of the bourgeoisie. Instead, the bourgeoisie always played a game of inclusion and exclusion. Recent research has stressed the contradictory aspects of this game: Patronage—here, in the original sense, the real investment of considerable sums of money for organized causes—created a subsystem within the bourgeoisie which was based on a culture of wealth. According to this research, exceptionally high involvement in patronage was the basis for the emergence of new elites characterized by a specific self-awareness and code of honor. These new elites strengthened the fragmentary nature of the bourgeoisie.[25]

The continual pursuit of social integration can be an important motivation for patronage. Within the administrative boards of various foundations, the criteria of social acknowledgment and aesthetic appraisal were negotiated, social circles were constituted and solidified, and sometimes even marriages were arranged. For the most part, foundation boards were a part of the social network which influenced all elite groups and consisted of the same people who were Liberal dignitaries. Patronage helped to knit this net, to effectively hold it together and to increase its own importance. Most contemporary research does not acknowledge the drive for prestige and social recognition as general motivations for patronage. Elisabeth Kraus, for example, suggests that Rudolf Mosse did not need prestige or social recognition because he had already risen up the social ladder and rejected ennoblement. The latter point, however, only demonstrates Mosse's self-awareness as a bourgeois. One did not gain prestige in the German bourgeoisie by accepting noble titles (which many, including Jewish patrons, rejected) or through quickly earned money; rather, prestige was contingent on demonstrating cultural and social authority.[26] This authority did not, however, arise from a desire for such prestige alone. Instead, as Bourdieu stresses, it required continuous effort in the form of exchanges which led to continually confirmed mutual recognition.[27]

This having been said, another question emerges: Did the socializing pendulum of patronage swing more in the direction of integration or in the direction of distinction and exclusion? The answer is contingent on two factors: the historical conditions, in particular the degree of inner stability and the strength of the new bourgeoisie, and the individually defined social status of the patron. For social climbers, charity and patronage were important strategies that could enable one to become integrated into the "respected" bourgeoisie and find acceptance within it. For those already established and recognized, patronage offered the chance to distinguish oneself from the large number of nouveaux riches. By the end of the nineteenth century, wealth alone was no longer an adequate criterion for acceptance. To have a citywide reputation as a patron or to have accumulated bourgeois honorary titles, such as *Geheimer Kommerzienrat* (commercial privy councillor) or *Konsul,* offered great potential for distinction. These purely honorary, though highly coveted, titles were often conferred on the grounds of past charitable giving. For this reason, patronage and the desire for bourgeois entitlement provided a basis for negotiations between patrons and the municipality. These negotiations are attested to in another aspect of patronage: the issue of bequests and donations made after the patron's death. The proportion of bequests made for charitable purposes by the wealthiest *Wirtschaftsbürger* was the smallest compared to other groups within the bourgeoisie,[28] while a good quarter of the same group held the prestigious title of *Kommerzienrat*.[29] This highlights the importance of social status as a motivating factor.

The preliminary negotiations between potential patrons and distinguished members of the state or municipal governments further illustrate this exchange. Retired entrepreneur Siegfried Schlesinger gave the mayor of Dresden 40,000 marks in 1909 with the expectation that the mayor would decide how the proposed Siegfried-Schlesinger Foundation could best use its money. Although Schlesinger insisted on not being publicly thanked—underscoring his supposed selflessness—he did feel it necessary to write a letter to the mayor two days after the announcement of the plans for the foundation. In this letter, Schlesinger wrote at length about his previous charitable activities. After having agreed on the purpose of the latest foundation—a hospice for soldiers—another letter followed in which Schlesinger outlined his economic successes, introduced his prominent family, and underscored his connections to the city.[30] Bourdieu's suggestion that the transformation of one sort of capital into another is done at a cost and in no way happens on its own is completely confirmed in Schlesinger's letters. The retired businessman combined his many letters with the hope that "this little addition would contribute to the further success of my humble wishes." The question of which humble wish he hoped would be fulfilled is clarified in a letter sent by Mayor Beutler to War Minister von Hausen: "Concerning Schlesinger, I had already considered the recommendation for the title '*Kommerzienrat*' and I will now include him on the list of candidates." Schlesinger had succeeded in converting part of his economic capital into symbolic capital. The symbolic capital which he received from this investment was as inheritable as his material fortune. This struggle for symbolic capital involved very active and strategic family politics.

Patronage can also be explained by the great importance attributed to the bourgeoisie's adoption of symbolic forms and practices since its very beginnings. Being propertied and wealthy did not alone make one a *Bürger*, nor did wealth alone improve one's social standing. If one wanted to distinguish oneself from the parvenus and gain access to the inner circle of the city's powerful and wealthy elite, one had to link one's financial success with a public reputation based on, above all, continual charitable contributions to the community. Desiring economic, social, or symbolic gains without reflecting on social problems was frowned upon, just as angling for economic control without acknowledging the social obligation of wealth was viewed negatively.

It was not, however, just a matter of recognizing the fundamental, cultural, and social aspects of this "game." The successful patron had to be adept at using the appropriate cultural and social codes for a given occasion. Thus, while many patrons had the opportunity to support preexisting causes, they chose instead to establish their own charitable projects, thereby maximizing their symbolic capital. When several sons of the Arnhold family in Dresden inherited a foundation erected by their father in 1911 whose original purpose was to provide fellowships to the academy of applied arts, they chose to use the money to create a new foundation in 1927. Inflation had impoverished the original foundation coffers, but instead of merely donating more money to the existing foundation, the sons created a slightly modified version of the previous foundation which then bore their names.[31] Social giving coincided with the wish of many patrons to have their names inscribed in the city annals for future generations to behold. Charitable giving and patronage were the basis for the bourgeoisie's cultural hegemony and quest to regulate aspects of the municipality; as such, they must be seen as political acts.

Both municipal Liberalism and bourgeois patronage were promoted in such a way as to give them a decisively apolitical aura. As did circles of Liberal dignitaries, patrons attempted to provide a political alternative (though they couched it in apolitical and individualistic rhetoric) to the Social Democrats and their "dangerous" mass politics. Patronage was, in this sense, always linked to concrete, supposedly apolitical, plans which often reflected the serious lack of municipal funds or which initiated reform projects. In the Wilhelmine Empire, such reform projects could be pathbreaking, such as new discussions on hygiene and public health. Karl August Lingner, an entrepreneur and patron, took up this cause. He founded the municipal central office for disinfection and a didactic, scientific, and technical exhibition about hygiene in 1901. Assuming that the municipal administration acted slowly and did not often accept new ideas, many responsible bourgeois sought to preempt the municipal or state bureaucracy or to provide the initial funds for such projects in order to have control over the organizations.

The variety of charitable causes in German cities indicates the extent to which active bourgeois attempted to solve social, sociopolitical, and cultural problems and the extent to which they developed individual solutions and models for reform. The bourgeoisie demonstrated its will and ability to manage the growing problem of urban poverty and—to a large degree through philanthropy—develop a modern system of social assistance. In this context, patrons defined entirely new tasks, such as social housing, and ultimately created new responsibilities for the municipality. Nevertheless, the patrons always acted so that traditional social structures did not entirely erode. They attempted to decrease the negative social consequences of economic modernization without relinquishing their power over society. In this respect, patronage mirrored the political self-confidence (on the national level) of the bourgeois elite, which entrusted itself with the task of solving the new challenges of modernity. In contrast to the national-level political scene, the German bourgeoisie and Liberalism in general no longer appeared weak and fractured between 1900 and 1914; rather, it was thoroughly conscious of its power and its united, flexible, and innovative nature.

There are a surprising number of similarities between Liberalism and patronage. The disposition to participate in patronage was not only—in the narrowly conceived cultural sense—a genuine bourgeois behavior; it was also the expression of political *Bürgerlichkeit*. The bourgeois who were active patrons were less likely to distinguish themselves through political activities. Conversely, those who took political office seldom gained notoriety as a patron. Lawyer Albert Mosse was an active city councilman, but unlike his brothers, he never participated in patronage. But his brothers, like many other important patrons, shied away from direct involvement with a political party or political office during the Wilhelmine Empire.[32] This trend is confirmed in the findings on Dresden, Frankfurt, and Braunschweig. The tendency to opt for either charitable or political participation, however, does not appear to have been true for Nuremberg. According to the research undertaken by Hans-Walter Schmuhl, between 1862 and 1918, a number of political dignitaries, among them twenty Jews, were recognized and respected patrons.[33] However, from about 1900, the tendency to favor either political or charitable activities took hold in Nuremberg, too. Schmuhl interprets this change as a retreat into the private sphere and evidence that a sense of civic responsibility and an orientation toward the common good were fading in the last decade before World War I.[34] But is it not perhaps possible that this situation was, in fact, the result of an effective division of labor in municipal Liberalism? Are patronage and political offices not complementary forms of bourgeois politics in the municipality of the *Kaiserreich*? The example of city councilman Albert Mosse shows that clearly both forms of political influence brought about similar levels of prestige in the bourgeoisie. Despite the fact that Mosse did not participate in patronage and that he was Jewish, he was awarded the highest recognition in Berlin—the freedom of the city. Entrepreneurs who had much money at their disposal and had to invest much of their time furthering their business favored charity, while the *Bildungsbürgertum* mainly favored political activity. In any case, both groups were involved in politics, though they expended much effort in trying to conceal this fact.

In Dresden, there was another indirectly political dimension of patronage: Patrons functioned as the advocates of the new bourgeoisie. Between 1870 and 1914, only 8 percent of all patrons came from the old *Mittelstand*. Six percent belonged to the old elites—noble landowners, officers, and nobles who did not belong to the *Bildungsbürgertum*. Men of private means, who constituted a typically bourgeois group, accounted for 17 percent of all patrons. By contrast, the new entrepreneurs, businessmen, and directors, as well as the *Bildungsbürgertum*—including both noble and nonnoble professors, Gymnasium teachers, and those belonging to the free professions—accounted for more than two-thirds of all patrons in Dresden.[35] While the new bourgeois elites in Dresden controlled this political field, their influence in municipal politics was largely constrained. Members of the old *Mittelstand* dominated the city council for decades. This conservative and anti-Semitic group concentrated on the landlords' association and was able to protect its power base in Dresden against the Liberals and Social Democrats until 1914.[36]

The rather liberal mayors of Dresden, since they were not directly dependent on the city council, came together with those bourgeois who were active in patronage. Thus, primarily culturally defined involvement formed a second power base and a type of liberal counterpublic sphere.[37] The liberal bourgeoisie and the municipal ruling elite realized their vision of the municipality through the creation of a modern municipal welfare program. The activities of the latter can be seen in the attempt to erect an endowed university (which did not come to fruition because of the outbreak of World War I).[38] After the turn of the twentieth century, there was also a perceptible increase in the amount of money given to public institutions which operated according to patrons' wishes.[39] The patrons allowed municipal civil servants a large degree of autonomy in managing the foundations, yet they wielded influence on the municipal administration to the point that they could have even forced the creation, under certain circumstances, of a modern social welfare system. In any case, to be able to reform the municipal administration, one had to confront the Conservative and anti-Semitic city council. To be sure, if observations about Dresden were compared to the development of Braunschweig, Munich, Nuremberg, or Frankfurt am Main, differences would be apparent. However, it still seems clear that patronage fulfilled a complementary political function.

It must now be obvious that patronage in the *Kaiserreich* was more than a cultural bourgeois behavioral pattern. Charity and patronage were, to a large extent, expressions of political *Bürgerlichkeit,* which existed between the public and private spheres. The involvement of patrons always oscillated between these two poles—individualism and the bonding of social groups or classes. Patrons occupied the center of political *Bürgerlichkeit*. As a political and cultural act and as a bourgeois habit, patronage is demonstrably not a special Jewish behavior but is an integral part of a bourgeois-liberal concept of power and control. Jewish citizens did not avoid engaging in patronage, but they did not assign it more meaning or importance than did non-Jewish bourgeois.

THE SWEET SMELL OF SUCCESS?

The economic and symbolic relevance of charity and patronage is, above all, political. In all cities, many social climbers participated in patronage. Karl August Lingner, Max and Georg Arnhold, Siegfried Schlesinger, or Georg Wilhelm Arnstaedt, though they were not originally from Dresden, had each made his fortune there.[40] They wanted to give back to the community that had made their fortunes possible. Above all, they had to cleanse themselves of the "stink" of new money and make themselves acceptable to society. A patron would be considered worthy and integrated once the state or municipality accepted his contribution. That stamp of approval would mean that the donor was a "good businessman" and an agent for cultural ideas and ethical progress, not merely one of those dirty, greedy, typical capitalists. The goal of a *Wirtschaftsbürger* was not only to make profits through careful management but also to spread civilization, culture, and humanity.[41] Jewish and non-Jewish citizens wanted a symbolic expression of their moral probity. For example, in Dresden, Bienert—a social climber of an earlier generation—and Karl August Lingner—the ambitious and wealthy "Mouthwash-King"[42]—both took similar actions to those of the Jewish "newcomer," Nathan Eckstein, who became one of the wealthiest men in the city thanks to his cigarette factory. The same can be said for the Arnhold brothers, who originally came from Dessau but founded their bank in Dresden in 1864. This bank, despite a small amount of starting capital, became one of the most important private banks in Germany.[43]

Nevertheless, latent anti-Semitism could have played a role in their charitable activities. At the very least, it is hard to imagine that Jewish bankers were not somehow affected—even when they were not personally attacked—by the press, which presented them as greedy and uncultivated, making the confrontation less about aesthetic or pecuniary values and more about ethnicity. It was obvious that Jewish patrons attempted to convince the public otherwise through zealous accumulation of cultural capital. Even a banker, as Georg Arnhold stressed, always had to work against the impression that "he [the banker] was a man who was interested in nothing more than money. And if the bank were owned by Jews, then one is from the very start treated with hostility by many circles. So please," he reminded the management of his bank, "those of you who know how hard we work and that we surpass all others in providing for the common good, please preserve the honor of this House."[44] A good reputation, renown, and honor were indispensable for entrepreneurs who were the most dependent members of the *Bürgertum* on the regional market. This group included private bankers, industrialists, lawyers, and doctors. As a rule, Jews were overrepresented in precisely these professions. About 15 percent of all lawyers, notaries, and patent lawyers in the *Kaiserreich* were Jewish. In 1912, 6 percent of all doctors were Jewish and over 8 percent were scholars and journalists.[45] For historical reasons, banking was predominantly a Jewish affair. In Dresden, for example, five of the six most important private banking houses were owned by Jewish citizens between 1871 and 1933.[46]

Actually, though, the analysis of the nature of patronage in Dresden shows that the majority of Jewish patrons were involved in upper management and banking. Almost half of all foundations erected by Jews were founded and financed by managers and, more often, bankers. Symbolic capital was especially important for members of these professions, since it could indirectly (and for this reason, very effectively) help increase the individual's material capital. Moreover, patrons such as the Arnholds were farsighted, calculating, and innovative entrepreneurs; they recognized that patronage could serve the reputation of their companies. A private bank which could afford to undertake social projects for the common good gained a reputation among potential customers as being "healthy" and trustworthy.[47] In this way, an increase in symbolic capital could cause an increase in economic capital. Private banks, which competed with shareholding banks, were more dependent on a network of personal cooperation and connections which had to be constantly nurtured. Part of this nurturing consisted of convincing the potential customers that the institution was respectable and trustworthy. Although Aby Warburg was dedicated to intellectual pursuits and not banking, he was convinced that his Hamburg institute could and should provide the family bank with legitimacy.[48] One cannot overlook the fact that over time certain elements of self-representation were normalized and internalized and were no longer staged. Nonetheless, these foundations were not an unnecessary luxury. They were useful —as Bourdieu suggests—in constantly transforming and appropriating different forms of capital.

In the workplace, acts of patronage could exert a similarly important influence. Generally, paternalistic attitudes mixed with efforts to realize a modern social partnership dominated by the employer and characterized by anti-trade-unionist sentiment. In 1901, Max Arnhold founded a pension association (*Pensionsverein*) which provided care for the old and infirm as well as life insurance for the bank's management. This group had to pay 5 percent of the cost for this insurance before 1908 and 2 percent thereafter.[49] Since the profits of the bank were dependent on the success of certain industrial companies, the Arnholds suggested to these business partners that it was in their best interests to adopt a similar pension system. In the bank alone, the pension association proved to be an effective means of binding the management to "their own house" on a long-term basis and guaranteeing their loyalty. Obviously, the bank owners implemented a fundamental repertory of sociocultural practices, which was considered the rulebook among the bourgeoisie for social interaction. "Gifts" such as the creation of a pension association and, later, vacation spots or bonus pay, generated very subtle relationships of control and dependence.[50] However, for some prospective recipients of this aid, the sacrifices were too much—in accepting such aid, the recipient also acknowledged the fact that he would never be able to repay the aid and thus put himself into a position of dependency and solidified his adherence to a lower class. While these gifts created social distinctions, they also spawned a sense of obligation to show one's gratitude. The bank owners hoped that this gratitude would manifest itself in the management's rejection of trade unions and involvement in the Social Democratic movement.[51] The logic of patronage, though, worked in more than one direction. The patrons gave with the expectation that their efforts would be rewarded from "above" in the form of bourgeois titles such as *Kommerzienrat* or such honors as the freedom of the city.

In the end, patronage must be seen as a general bourgeois phenomenon. There was no difference between Jewish and non-Jewish patrons in terms of numbers or the charitable causes patrons chose. Moreover, the motives for engaging in patronage were primarily *bürgerlich*. The majority of Dresden Jews did not become patrons because of their adherence to a specific religious community or distinctive ethnicity; rather, they did so because of social, political, and cultural interests they shared with the entire bourgeoisie. Nearly all Jewish patrons belonged to the *Wirtschaftsbürgertum*, of which most were bankers. This latter group, especially, was concentrated geographically in the large banking centers of Berlin and Frankfurt am Main. However, this group was not entirely representative of Jewish patronage. The exceptional charitable patronage of Jewish citizens in both cities could have grown out of this constellation; that is, out of the very specific professional and social structure of the Jewish communities.

Jews founded nearly one-quarter of foundations in Frankfurt around 1914. This is a remarkably high number given the fact that Jewish citizens accounted for only 10 percent of the overall population of the city. Yet these numbers are perhaps less remarkable when one realizes that 35 percent of all taxes were paid by Jewish citizens. Similar results can be seen in

Munich, where Jewish citizens accounted for 15 percent of the patrons of the Deutsche Museum. This number was eight times the percentage of Jews living in Munich but was only marginally higher than the percentage of entrepreneurs who were Jewish.[52] And in Berlin, where 38 percent of all money donated to foundations or charitable causes came from Jewish citizens, only 4 percent of all Berliners were registered as Jewish. Nevertheless, if one were to look at the 111 Berlin enterprises which were valued at 6 million marks or higher, more than 60 percent were owned by Jews.[53] Religious traditions and the ever-increasing importance of anti-Semitism were not entirely without influence over the cultural practice of patronage among Jews. However, and more important, Jewish participation in patronage and other typically bourgeois behaviors exceeded their proportion of the overall municipal population. Clearly, one can hardly speak of a deficit of *Bürgerlichkeit* in the German municipalities before 1914.

NOTES

A more extensive version of this chapter was published in *Jahrbuch zur Liberalismus-Forschung* 13 (2001). I am very grateful to Sarah Wobick for translating this chapter. I would also like to thank Thomas Adam for his editing help.

1. Elisabeth Kraus, "Jüdisches Mäzenatentum im Kaiserreich: Befunde—Motive—Hypothesen," in *Bürgerkultur und Mäzenatentum im 19. Jahrhundert*, ed. Jürgen Kocka and Manuel Frey (Zwickau: Fannei & Walz Verlag, 1998), 40; Ralf Roth, "Der Toten Nachruhm: Aspekte des Mäzenatentums in Frankfurt am Main, 1750–1914," in Kocka and Frey, *Bürgerkultur und Mäzenatentum*, 99–127; Gerhard Schiebeler, *Jüdische Stiftungen in Frankfurt am Main* (Frankfurt am Main: Kramer, 1988).

2. Peter Paret, "Jüdische Kunstsammler, Stifter und Kunsthändler," in *Sammler, Stifter und Museen*, ed. Ekkehard Mai and Pater Paret (Cologne, Weimar, and Vienna: Böhlau, 1993), 173–185; Elisabeth Kraus, "Jüdische Stiftungstätigkeit: Das Beispiel der Familie Mosse in Berlin," *Zeitschrift für Geschichtswissenschaft* 45 (1997): 101–121; Michael S. Cullen, "Juden als Sammler und Mäzene," in *Juden als Träger bürgerlicher Kultur in Deutschland*, ed. Julius H. Schoeps (Stuttgart: Burg Verlag, 1989), 123–148; Derek Penslar, "Philanthropy, the 'Social Question' and Jewish Identity in Imperial Germany," *Leo Baeck Institute Year Book* 38 (1993): 51–73; Cella-Margaretha Girardet, *Jüdische Mäzene für die preußischen Museen zu Berlin* (Egelsbach: Hänsel-Hohenhausen, 1997); Georg Heuberger, "Jüdisches Mäzenatentum—von der religiösen Pflicht zum Faktor gesellschaftlicher Anerkennung," in *Stadt und Mäzenatentum*, ed. Bernhard Kirchgässner and Hans-Peter Becht (Sigmaringen: Jan Thorbecke Verlag, 1997), 65–74.

3. For a very balanced interpretation, see Manuel Frey, *Macht und Moral des Schenkens: Staat und bürgerliche Mäzene vom späten 18. Jahrhundert bis zur Gegenwart Jahrhundert* (Zwickau: Fannei & Walz Verlag, 1999), 97ff.

4. Manfred Hettling, *Politische Bürgerlichkeit: Der Bürger zwischen Individualität und Vergesellschaftung in Deutschland und der Schweiz von 1860 bis 1918* (Göttingen: Vandenhoeck und Ruprecht, 1999), 37–54; Till van Rahden, *Juden und andere Breslauer: Die Beziehungen zwischen Juden, Protestanten und Katholiken in einer deutschen Großstadt, 1860 bis 1925* (Göttingen: Vandenhoeck und Ruprecht, 2000), 52–94.

5. To be precise, 10.7 percent of all Jews in Dresden belonged to the upper class, while 42.9 percent belonged to the upper middle class and 42.9 percent belonged to the lower middle class. Wählerverzeichnisse der Israelitischen Religionsgemeinde Dresden, in GA Gemeinde Dresden 75 A Dr. 1 no. 20, Centrum Judaicum Berlin. This statistical analysis is based on Reinhard Schüren, *Soziale Mobilität* (St. Katharinen: Scripta-Mercaturae-Verlag, 1989). Because the information is derived from voting lists, women are not included.

6. Schüren, *Soziale Mobilität*, 144ff.; Hans-Ulrich Wehler, *Deutsche Gesellschaftsgeschichte*, vol. 3, *Von der "Deutschen Doppelrevolution" bis zum Beginn des Ersten Weltkrieges, 1849–1914* (Munich: Beck, 1995), 763–772.

7. Avraham Barkai, *Jüdische Minderheit und Industrialisierung: Demographie, Berufe und Einkommen der Juden in Westdeutschland, 1850–1914* (Tübingen: Mohr, 1988); Michael Brenner, Stefi Jersch-Wenzel, and Michael A. Meyer, eds., *Deutsch-jüdische Geschichte in der Neuzeit*, vol. 2, *Emanzipation und Akkulturation, 1780–1871* (Munich: Beck, 1996), 57–95, 309–315; Werner E. Mosse, *The German-Jewish Economic Elite, 1820–1935: A Socio-Cultural Profile* (Oxford: Clarendon Press, 1989).

8. James Retallack defines *Bürgerlichkeit* as "the extent to which middle-class values and interests altered the texture of nineteenth-century European society." *Germany in the Age of Kaiser Wilhelm* (London: MacMillan Press, 1996), 99.

9. Jürgen Kocka, "Bürger als Mäzene: Ein historisches Forschungsproblem," in *Mäzenatisches Handeln: Studien zur Kultur des Bürgersinns in der Gesellschaft*, ed. Thomas W. Gaethgens and Martin Schieder (Zwickau: Fannei & Walz, 1998), 34.

10. For important local studies, see Kocka and Frey, *Bürgerkultur und Mäzenatentum*.

11. Manfred Hettling, "Die persönliche Selbständigkeit: Der archimedische Punkt bürgerlicher Lebensführung," in *Der bürgerliche Wertehimmel*, ed. Manfred Hettling and Stefan-Ludwig Hoffmann (Göttingen: Vandenhoeck und Ruprecht, 2000), 57–78.

12. For case studies on Breslau, Munich, Frankfurt am Main, Nuremberg, and Braunschweig, see Hettling, *Politische Bürgerlichkeit*; Rahden, *Juden und andere Breslauer*, 300ff.; Ralf Roth, *Stadt und Bürgertum in Frankfurt am Main: Ein besonderer Weg von der ständischen zur modernen Bürgergesellschaft, 1760–1914* (Munich: Oldenbourg, 1996), 515ff.; Hans-Walter Schmuhl, *Die Herren der Stadt: Bürgerliche Eliten und städtische Selbstverwaltung in Nürnberg und Braunschweig vom 18. Jahrhundert bis 1918* (Gießen: Focus-Verlag, 1998), 236–252, 469–478; Peter Pulzer, *Jews and the German State: The Political History of a Minority, 1848–1933* (Oxford: Blackwell, 1992).

13. Hans-Walther Schmuhl, "Mäzenatisches Handeln städtischer Führungsgruppen in Nürnberg und Braunschweig im 19. Jahrhundert," in Kocka and Frey, *Bürgerkultur und Mäzenatentum*, 54–80.

14. On a national level, the Arnholds participated in the German Peace Society, the Esperanto movement, the German Colonial Society, and the Kaiser Wilhelm Society.

15. Dieter Hein, "Bürgerliches Mäzenatentum im 19. Jahrhundert: Überlegungen am Beispiel der Kunst- und Künstlerförderung in Karlsruhe und Mannheim," in Kocka and Frey, *Bürgerkultur und Mäzenatentum*, 84–99.

16. Ibid.

17. For the concept of patronage as a method of social control, see Michael Werner, "Stiftungen in Dresden zwischen Reichsgründung und Erstem Weltkrieg" (M.A. thesis, Humboldt University Berlin, 2000), 79; Thomas Adam, "Meyersche Stiftung—'Es hat keinerlei Unternehmergewinn zu erfolgen,'" in *Leipziger Kalender* 1997, 135–154.

18. One of the few exceptions is the Henriette Foundation (Henriettenstift), founded by Wilhelm Schie for the purpose of helping poor Jews in old age. See GA Gemeinde Dresden 75 A Dr. 1 no. 23, Centrum Judaicum Berlin. See also Anke Kalkbrenner, *Das Henriettenstift: Zwischen Asylheim und Alten-Damenstift* (Dresden: Technische Universität, Fak. Erziehungswissenschaften, Institut für Sozialpädagogik, 1999).

19. Frey, *Macht und Moral,* 120.

20. It has not always been easy to classify charitable causes; for this reason I have included the same foundation in several categories.

21. Noble patrons erected family foundations and foundations for their own class much more often than the bourgeoisie did. See Werner, *Stiftungen in Dresden,* 63.

22. See Thorstein Veblen, *Theorie der feinen Leute: Eine ökonomische Untersuchung der Institutionen* (Frankfurt am Main: Fischer, 1993).

23. For Saxony, see Dolores Augustine, *Patricians and Parvenus: Wealth and High Society in Wilhelmine Germany* (Oxford: Berg, 1994), 350.

24. See Kocka, "Bürger als Mäzene," 30–38.

25. Roth, *Stadt und Bürgertum,* 595–600; Wolfgang J. Mommsen, "Kultur als Instrument der Legitimation bürgerlicher Hegemonie im Nationalstaat," in *"Der Deutschen Kunst . . ." Nationalgalerie und nationale Identität, 1876–1998,* ed. Claudia Rückert and Sven Kuhrau (Amsterdam and Dresden: Verlag der Kunst, 1998), 15–30.

26. Eduard Arnhold, James Simon, Carl Fürstenberg, and Hugo Stinnes rejected ennoblement. See Frey, *Macht und Moral,* 78.

27. Pierre Bourdieu, *Sozialer Raum und 'Klassen': Leçon sur la leçon* (Frankfurt am Main: Suhrkamp, 1985), 193. With Bourdieu's ideas in mind, the social structure of the bourgeoisie can be understood to be continually changing.

28. This statement is based on the databases of Michael Werner, who was unable to classify 32.2 percent of the foundations. Of those he could classify, 31.6 percent were erected during the patron's lifetime and 36.2 percent were created after the death of the patron.

29. Werner was able to show that 27 of 116 patrons who belonged to the *Wirtschaftsbürgertum* held bourgeois titles. For a discussion on titles in general, see Augustine, *Patricians and Parvenus,* 35–48.

30. Ratsarchiv B XI 203, Bl. 62–78, Stadtarchiv Dresden.

31. MdI no. 12851, MfVB no. 19425, Hauptstaatsarchiv Dresden.

32. Elisabeth Kraus, *Die Familie Mosse: Deutsche-jüdisches Bürgertum im 19. und 20. Jahrhundert* (Munich: Beck, 1999).

33. This was true for six of the twenty Jewish dignitaries. See Schmuhl, "Mäzenatisches Handeln," 74ff.

34. Ibid.

35. See Werner, *Stiftungen in Dresden,* 125.

36. See Karl Heinrich Pohl, "Power in the City: Liberalism and Local Politics in Dresden and Munich," in *Saxony in German History: Culture, Society, and Politics, 1830–1933,* ed. James Retallack (Ann Arbor: University of Michigan Press, 2000), 297ff.

37. Gustav Otto Beutler, *Die sozialen Aufgaben der deutschen Städte: Zwei Vorträge* (Leipzig: Duncker & Humblot, 1903).

38. Between 1912 and 1914, there was intensive discussion between leading businessmen and patrons, on the one hand, and Mayor Beutler, on the other. The first tangible accomplishment was the donation of the land for the future university by Theodor and Erwin Bienert. Ratsarchiv B VII a 208, Stadtarchiv Dresden; Werner, *Stiftungen in Dresden,* 53.

39. See Werner, *Stiftungen in Dresden,* 52.

40. Interestingly, the three important art collectors of Dresden were not originally from that city. See Heike Biedermann, "Aufbruch zur Moderne—Die Sammlungen Oscar Schmitz, Adolf Rothermundt und Ida Bienert," *Dresdner Hefte* 51 (1997): 30–38.

41. See Eduard Arnhold, *Ein Gedenkbuch* (Berlin: Privatdruck, 1928), 9.

42. Walter A. Büchi, "Schlossherr ohne Adelstitel—Lingner, die Exzellenz," in *In aller Munde: Einhundert Jahre Odol,* ed. Martin Roth, Manfred Scheske, and Hans-Christian Täubrich (Dresden: Deutsches Hygiene Museum, 1993), 72–83; Susanne Roessinger,

"Karl August Lingner—Odol-König, Mäzen, Museumsgründer," *Dresdner Hefte* 51 (1997): 47–54.

43. For more on Eckstein, see NLP 123 (Eckstein), Hauptstaatsarchiv Dresden MfVB no. 19590, Central Archives for the History of the Jewish People, Jerusalem. For more information on the Arnhold family, see Simone Lässig, "Nationalsozialistische 'Judenpolitik' und jüdische Selbstbehauptung vor dem Novemberpogrom: Das Beispiel der Dresdner Bankiersfamilie Arnhold," in *Dresden unterm Hakenkreuz,* ed. Reiner Pommerin (Weimar, Cologne, and Vienna: Böhlau, 1998), 129–192.

44. Georg Arnhold, *50jähriges Betriebsjubiläum 31. März 1925* (Dresden, 1925). For the social character of Jewish businessmen, see Hans Dieter Hellige, "Jüdische Unternehmer zwischen wirtschaftsliberalem Laissez-faire, sozialliberalem Emanzipationsdenken und industriekonservativer Sammlungsbewegung," in *Das deutsche Judentum und der Liberalismus: Dokumentation eines internationalen Seminars der Friedrich-Naumann-Stiftung in Zusammenarbeit mit dem Leo Baeck Institut* (St. Augustin: COMDOK Verlagsabteilung, 1986), 142–171.

45. Jakob Segall, *Die beruflichen und sozialen Verhältnisse der Juden in Deutschland* (Berlin: Schildberger, 1912), 26–74.

46. Simone Lässig, "Jüdische Privatbanken in Dresden," *Dresener Hefte* 61 (2000): 85–98. Alfred Marcus suggests that about 57 percent of all German private banks were owned by Jewish citizens in 1923. Alfred Marcus, *Die wirtschaftliche Krise des deutschen Juden: Eine soziologische Untersuchung* (Berlin: Stilke, 1931), 47.

47. Simone Lässig, "Juden und Mäzenatentum in Deutschland: Religiöses Ethos, kompensierendes Minderheitsverhalten oder genuine Bürgerlichkeit?" *Zeitschrift für Geschichtswissenschaft* 46 (1998): 211–236.

48. Ulrich Raulff, "Von der Privatbibliothek des gelehrten zum Forschungsinstitut: Aby Warburg, Ernst Cassirer und die neue Kulturwissenschaft," *Geschichte und Gesellschaft* 23 (1997): 36. For a further investigation into the symbolic dimension of patronage, see Werner Weisbach, *Und alles ist zerstoben: Erinnerungen aus der Jahrhundertwende* (Vienna, Leipzig, and Zurich: Reichner, 1937), 96.

49. MdI no. 13267–70, Altbankbestände Dresden, Bankhaus Arnhold no. 902, 228–229, 1827, Hauptstaatsarchiv Dresden.

50. Helmuth Berking, *Schenken: Zur Anthropologie des Gebens* (Frankfurt am Main and New York: Campus Verlag, 1996), 10. See also Manuel Frey and Tilmann von Stockhausen, "Potlatsch in Preußen? Schenkriten an der Berliner Gemäldegalerie im 19. Jahrhundert," in Kocka and Frey, *Bürgerkultur und Mäzenatentum,* 18–37; and Philipp Sarasin, "Stiften und Schenken in Basel im 19. und 20. Jahrhundert: Überlegungen zur Erforschung des bürgerlichen Mäzenatentums," in Kocka and Frey, *Bürgerkultur und Mäzenatentum,* 192–211.

51. Pierre Bourdieu, *Sozialer Sinn: Kritik der theoretischen Vernunft* (Frankfurt am Main: Suhrkamp, 1987), 229.

52. Gerhard Neumeier, "Bürgerliches Mäzenatentum in München vor dem Ersten Weltkrieg—Das Beispiel des Deutschen Museums," in Kocka and Frey, *Bürgerkultur und Mäzenatentum,* 144–163.

53. Statistics found in Frey, *Macht und Moral,* 99. According to Elisabeth Kraus, a quarter of all Berlin foundations were administered by the Jewish community. See Kraus, *Familie Mosse,* 153; and Kraus, "Jüdisches Mäzenatentum," 40.

CONTRIBUTORS

THOMAS ADAM is Assistant Professor of German and Transatlantic European History at the University of Texas at Arlington. He received his D.Phil. from the University of Leipzig in 1998. In 1999 he was awarded a Feodor Lynen Research Fellowship for a two-year term at the University of Toronto. His publications include *Zwischen Markt und Staat: Stifter und Stiftungen im transatlantischen Vergleich* (with James Retallack, 2001); *Arbeitermilieu und Arbeiterbewegung in Leipzig 1871–1933* (1999); "A Rich Man's Guide to Social Climbing: Philanthropy as a Bourgeois Behavioral Pattern in Nineteenth-Century New York" in *The Journal of Arts Management, Law and Society* (2002); and "Transatlantic Trading: The Transfer of Philanthropic Models between European and North American Cities during the Nineteenth and Early Twentieth Centuries" in *Journal of Urban History* (2002). He is currently writing a comparative cultural study of philanthropy as a bourgeois behavioral pattern in German and North American cities during the nineteenth century.

MARIA BENJAMIN BAADER is a postdoctoral fellow of the American Academy for Jewish Research at the University of Toronto. Her Columbia University doctoral dissertation, which is under revision for publication, is entitled "Inventing Bourgeois Judaism: Jewish Culture, Gender, and Religion in Germany, 1800–1870."

KARSTEN BORGMANN is a doctoral candidate at the Humboldt-University in Berlin as well as a full-time editor for the academic online network H-Soz-u-Kult. He did extensive research on the history of cultural institutions in Berlin and the United States and received support from the research group "Bürgerliche Gesellschaft, Wertewandel, Mäzenatentum" at the Freie Universität Berlin. He has been a visiting fellow at Johns Hopkins University and the German Historical Institute, Washington, D.C.

TOBIAS BRINKMANN is a Research Fellow at the Simon-Dubnow Institute for Jewish History and Culture, Leipzig, and teaches in the American Studies and History Departments at the University of Leipzig. He received his M.A. from Indiana University (1992) and Ph.D. from Technical University Berlin (2000). He is the author of *Von der Gemeinde zu "Community": Jüdische Einwanderer in Chicago 1840–1900* (2002); "From Inclusion to

Exclusion: The Independent Order B'nai B'rith in Chicago, 1857–1881" in *Simon-Dubnow Institut Yearbook* (2002); and "Charity on Parade—Chicago's Jews and the Construction of Ethnic and Civic 'Gemeinschaft' in the 1860s" in *Celebrating Ethnicity and Nation: American Festive Culture from the Revolution to the Early Twentieth Century*, edited by Jürgen Heideking and Geneviève Fabre (2001). He is currently working on a book on migrants in Berlin during the 1920s.

BRETT FAIRBAIRN is Professor of History at the University of Saskatchewan, Canada, and Director of the Centre for the Study of Co-operatives. He teaches, does research, and is involved in community extension education on the history of cooperatives, community development, democratic participation, and related subjects. He is also a specialist in the political and social history of modern Germany. Fairbairn did his graduate work in England and has a D.Phil. from the University of Oxford. He has twice lived in Germany, including in 1997–1998 on an Alexander von Humboldt Foundation Research Fellowship at the Freie Universität Berlin. Currently, he is principal investigator for a grant from the Social Sciences and Humanities Research Council of Canada to investigate cooperative membership and social cohesion. He has more than seventy publications, including *Canadian Co-operatives in the Year 2000: Memory, Mutual Aid, and the Millennium* (2000) and *Democracy in the Undemocratic State: The German Reichstag Elections of 1898 and 1903* (1997).

ECKHARDT FUCHS is Assistant Professor in the Department of Education at the University of Mannheim. His main field of research is modern American and European intellectual history. Currently, he is working on the history of scientific internationalism. Among many publications in these fields, he is author of *Across Cultural Borders: Historiography in Global Perspective* (which he edited with Benedikt Stuchtey, 2002); *Weltausstellungen im 19. Jahrhundert* (1999); *Macht und Geist: Intellektuelle in der Zwischenkriegszeit* (with Wolfgang Bialas, 1995); *Geschichtswissenschaft neben dem Historismus* (with Steffen Sammler, 1995); *Henry Thomas Buckle: Geschichtsschreibung und Positivisms in England und Deutschland* (1994); and *"J'accuse": Zur Affäre Dreyfus in Frankreich* (with Günther Fuchs, 1994).

DAVID C. HAMMACK is Hiram C. Haydn Professor of History at Case Western Reserve University, where he is also a member of the Faculty Council of the Mandel Center for Nonprofit Organizations. He has been a Resident Fellow at the Russell Sage Foundation, a Guggenheim Fellow, and a Fellow of Yale University's Program on Non-Profit Organizations. His publications include *Power and Society: Greater New York at the Turn of the Century* (1982), *Making the Nonprofit Sector in the United States: A Reader* (which he edited, 1998), and many other books and articles.

DIETER HOFFMANN is a research scholar at the Max Planck Institute for the History of Science and a Privatdozent at Humboldt University in Berlin. He writes biographies and researches institutions in the history of modern medicine and the history of physics in Germany during the nineteenth and twentieth centuries. Since 1989, he has increasingly dealt with the history of science and technology in the German Democratic Republic. Among numerous publications on these topics, he is author of *Studien und Dokumente zum Leben von Ernst Mach* (1991); *Operation Epsilon. Die Farm-Hall Protokolle oder die Angst der Allierten vor der deutschen Atombombe* (1995); *Science under Socialisms* (1997); and *Wer war wer in der DDR. Ein biographisches Lexikon* (2000).

SIMONE LÄSSIG received her Ph.D. in 1990. From 1993 to 1998 she taught at the University of Dresden, and from 1999 to 2002 she held fellowships of the Deutsche Forschungsgemeinschaft and the Saxon Ministry of Science and Culture. Currently, she is a research fellow at the German Historical Institute in Washington, D.C. She is the author of *Wahlrechtskampf und Wahlreformen in Sachsen 1895–1909* (1996), which was awarded the Horst-Springer-Preis of the Friedrich Ebert Foundation; *Reichstagswahlen im Königreich Sachsen* (1998); and the forthcoming *Fundamente eines prekären Erfolgs. Die Verbürgerlichung der deutschen Juden im Zeitalter der Emanzipation.* She has also edited three volumes and published a number of articles and essays in collections and journals. Her research interests include German-Jewish history, the history of patronage and philanthropy, and the German migration into the United States and several other countries during the twentieth century. She is currently preparing a five-generation biographical study on the Dresden banking family Arnhold.

MARGARET ELEANOR MENNINGER is Assistant Professor of History at Southwest Texas State University and received her Ph.D. in History in 1998 from Harvard University. Menninger has presented papers on cultural philanthropy at conferences in the United States, Canada, Germany, and Great Britain and is currently completing a manuscript on cultural philanthropy and civic identity in nineteenth-century Saxony.

SUSANNAH MORRIS holds a lectureship in social policy at the London School of Economics. She completed her doctorate in history at the University of Oxford, where she subsequently held a Prize Research Fellowship at Nuffield College. Her research interests and publications concern the historical study of the nonprofit sector, in particular the relationship between nonprofit and for-profit providers of social welfare services and the use of historical experience in nonprofit-sector research and theory.

INDEX

www.ingramcontent.com/pod-product-compliance
Lightning Source LLC
Chambersburg PA
CBHW050228270326
41914CB00003BA/612